JN014903

人を着る

というこ
と

小野原教子

晃洋書房

はじめに

本書『人を着るということ Mind That Clothes the Body』は八本の日本語で書かれた論文と五本の英語で書かれた論文で構成されている。前著『闘う衣服』（水声社、二〇一一年）において、「人はなぜ服を着るのか」という根源的な問いと「人間は衣服を着る動物である」という仮説を、様々な具体的事例を分析しながら展開した。引き続き同じこの深遠なる問いに向かうが「（人間は）人（という衣服）を着ている（動物なのではないか）」という考え方が本書全体に流れ漂っている。パジャマのままで外へ出て行きたい子ども、長い和服の歴史のあと洋服を着用するようになった日本人、嗣いでいく仏法そのものである宗教的衣装、こころとからだについて、人という生き物と服の関係について、常に見えてくる葛藤・調和を文化としてとらまえながら、時間をかけて取り組んできた軌跡になっている。

近年世界へ日本文化を発信する政策（「クールジャパン」運動）とその是非についての言説が見られる。本書では英文の研究論文の形で応答してみたい。伝統文化としてのキモノ、大衆文化としてのゴシックロリータやマンガ、海外での禅仏教──いずれも国や時代を超えて相互的に影響を受け合いながら変化を続けてきた。衰退や発展とともに、異種のものが混交し新奇の発明になることもある。大きな音を立てるものもあれば、静かであっても動いているものもある。国際的な見地から英語で発表した研究を中心にあらたに英訳したものも含めて所収した。レコードの裏面のように裏表紙から独立して読むことができる。そもそも全体として順番に関わりなく各章を自由に読んでいただける書物として著した。

読者の方々が手に取られて一本でも興味・関心を持ち、本書が知的好奇心の広がっていくきっかけになれば筆者として幸いであり、ゆっくり地味に続けてきた学問の成果が報われ、生まれ変わる有り難い瞬間になる。

表紙は、のむらみちこさんの作品「詩人のための夏服」(二〇一二年、神戸ファッション美術館二階ロビー展示)で、筆者の指導教官だった松島征先生(京都大学名誉教授、二〇一一年六月没)の蔵書のアルチュール・ランボウの詩集で制作されている「本の服」。筆者の母が洋裁学校時代にデザインしたパターンで仕立てられ、一冊の本が材料で、一文ずつが糸のようになり織り上げられ一枚の衣装になった。詩やマンガは付録で、拙詩「真夏の星座」(『gui85』Vol. 30 二〇〇八年)の英訳は北園克衛研究者でアメリカ在住の詩人ジョン・ソルト氏によるもので未発表、マンガ「きぼうまめ」は森元暢之氏の作品(『アックス』Vol. 33 青林工藝舎、二〇〇三年)で未発表の仏訳は日本と並んで独特の漫画(バンデシネ)文化の歴史の長い国フランス在住の漫画家バンジャマ・アリオ氏が筆者の英訳を通じて独自に担当した。裏表紙のイラスト 'Kimonologue' (2013) は、イギリス在住の漫画家ポール・アシュリー・ブラウン氏による。

各章の初出情報(一部改題・すべて改稿)

序　論　「服は「言葉」でできている」(パジャマで外に行ってみると)『母の友』福音館書店、二〇一五年)

第一章　「闘う身体：人を着ているとは言えないだろうか」(『Dresstudy』Vol. 16、京都服飾文化研究財団、二〇一二年)

「〈人を〉着る〈という〉こと」(日本記号学会編『叢書セミオトポス9　着ること／脱ぐことの記号論』新曜社、二〇一四年)

第二章　「北園克衛とファッション」(未発表、関連論文「一九二九(昭和四)年──言葉と衣服のモダニズム」『Clothing Japan』第1号特集：日本の洋装化一四〇周年 Clothing Japan 編集室、二〇一二年)

第三章　「身支度について──林芙美子『女家族』を読む」(『八事』第二四号、中京大学、二〇〇八年)

第四章　「現代イギリスファッションにおけるキモノ文化受容について」(『デザイン史学』第一五号、デザイン史学研究会、二〇一七年)

第五章「袈裟とファッション」（日本記号学会編『叢書セミオトポス9　着ること／脱ぐことの記号論』新曜社、二〇一四年）

第六章「智慧としてのファッション――こころは服を着るからだ」（『服の記憶――わたしの服は誰のもの？』BNN新社、二〇一四年）

結論にかえて「我着る、ゆえに我あり」（書き下ろし）

英語の論文については英語パートの冒頭に同様に記す。

人を着るということ

Mind That Clothes the Body

Contents

Preface for English Part

Cover : Paul Ashley Brown 'Kimonologue'

着ることと脱ぐことの間——パジャマのままで走ってきたの

人を着ているとき、裸は脱がれている。裸を脱ぐ、とは、人は体を脱げないのだから、表現としておかしい。裸を着る、の方が比喩的にもイメージができるかもしれない。わたしたちは社会的動物である。「社会的動物」とはアリストテレスにならっているが、わたしたちは「衣服を着る動物」であると言えないだろうか。

人であることの条件は、裸であることを脱することで、そのような意味で使ってみよう。子どもは社会で裸のままでもいい、その裸を脱ぎ、パジャマも脱いで、しかるべき服に着替えて保育園や幼稚園へ通うようになると、人の仲間入りをする。つまり、人を着て、社会へ出て行くようになる。

本章は、「子どもにかかわるすべての人」を読者に持つ雑誌から受けたインタビューのまとめを改稿した。「パジャマで外に行ってはいけないの」と子どもに聞かれたとき、どう説明すればいいのか。ファッション研究者として話したが、それはファッション論の重要な問題を孕んでおり、本書の導入に相応しいと考える。

服と言葉——

パジャマで園に行きたいと駄々をこねられた。それならば、「行ってみたら？」と言ってみよう。そしてその理由を一緒に考えてみよう。

まず「人はなぜ衣服を着るのか」という問いを立てててみる。真っ先に思いつく答は、「自然環境から身を

守るため」。つまり、寒さを防ぐため、強い陽射しを避けるために服を着る。真冬であれば、パジャマで外に出るのは寒い。風邪をひいてしまうかもしれない。季節や時期によっては、大丈夫だろう。

また、服を着る理由の一つに「差恥心から」ということもある。聖書では、アダムとイヴは「知恵の木実」を食べ、裸でいることを恥ずかしく思った。パジャマを着ていれば、裸ではない。

こう考えてみると、パジャマで外に行ってはいけない理由はないような気もする。そういえば万有引力を発見した天才アイザック・ニュートンもパジャマで大学の授業をしたそうだ。この伝説は「彼は変わった人だった」ということを伝えるためのもので、考え事に没頭する癖があり、懐中時計を卵と間違えてゆでた、など様々な逸話も残っている。

機能面から考えれば、パジャマで外に出てもおかしくない、けれども「それは変だ」と思うことは自然である。なぜなのか。

服は「自然環境から身を守る」以外に、別の役割を持っているからだ。服が「周囲の人へのメッセージ」でもあるからだ。綿や毛のような目に見えて手で触れられる物質である素材でできていると同時に、服は目に見えず手で触れられない「言葉」でできている。それゆえに、あらゆる服は「読み解く」ことができる。

服についてさらに考えてみると、言葉についても考えてみよう。人は言葉を用いて、他人とコミュニケーションをする。意思や情報を伝える。言葉の使い方には各言語ごとにルールがある。文法というルールを守らないと、思っていることがうまく相手に伝わらない。「他人が知らない自分だけの言葉」を使いたい場合、他人と意思疎通をはかるのは難しい。ふつう相手には「わからない」からだ。

また文法ほど強固ではない、あいまいなルールもある。たとえばある語彙をどんな状況で使うか。あいさつの言葉「やあ」と「こんにちは」は基本的に同じ意味でも、相手によって使いわける必要がある。友人には用いても、目上の人には相応しくない表現もあり、逆もあり得る。また場所によって異なるルールもあり、たとえば関西では「ありがとう」という意味で、「おおきに」という表現もある。関東では言わない。だれ

が決めているのか。

人間の集まりである「社会」が決めている。ある社会、あるグループに属する人間の意識が集まって、ルールが生まれる。それは法律のように明文化されていないことも多く、どこかふわっとしている。しかし、人は敏感に自分が属する「社会のルール」を感じとって、言葉を用いている。

服と社会──

さて、服の話に戻ろう。動物の中で、人間だけがすることのいくつかが、言葉を用いたり、服を着ることだろう。犬や猫などが服を着ていることもあるが、それは果たして着ているといえるだろうか。着せられていることがほとんどに違いない。つまり自発的ではない。服もまた、自分が属する社会とそのルールに深い関係がある。

ここでパジャマという服の言葉を「読み解く」試みをしてみよう。「家で寝るときに着る」という社会のルールが書き込まれているに違いない。そのルールを信じる人は、パジャマを家の外で着ている人を見ると「おかしい」と感じる。「ニュートンのパジャマ」はどうだろう。学生たちに「私は社会のルールに無頓着です」というメッセージを発信したかったのかもしれない。ニュートンがパジャマを着て授業したのは「うっかり」だったのか「わざと」だったのかは謎のままだ。

おそらく、まだこうした「社会のルール」、言い換えれば「大人のルール」の存在を知らない。だとすれば、パジャマの着がえを拒否するのはむしろ当然とも言える。小さい子どもは、あいさつやごはんの食べ方などの「マナー」を教えようとすると、嫌がって反抗することも多い。マナーもまた社会＝大人のルールに基づくものである。ときに抵抗という子どもの反応には、理屈が通っていることもあるかもしれない。様々に絡まり合って発せられた子どもの感情はストレートで本来の正しいあり方が見え隠れしている可能性もありそうだ。

パジャマで園に行きたいと言った子どもはどうだろう。

やがて成長すると、社会の中で生きていかねばならないから、やはり大人は子どもに「社会のルール」を伝えていく必要がある。

にもかかわらず、なぜ冒頭で、パジャマで「行ってみたら？」と言ったのか。振り出しに戻ってみよう。それは子どもならではの「貴重な機会」でもあるからだ。もう少し大きくなれば、たとえば女の子は「ピンクの服がいい！」など、服にこだわりが出てくるに違いない。そのとき、属する社会のルールの存在を敏感に感じ始めていると言えるかもしれない。

「女の子はピンクや赤などの暖色系、男の子は青など寒色系の色を好む」というイメージがある。このイメージは日本だけでなく、世界中に広がっている。イギリスはロンドンで、二歳の男の子にピンク色の服を着せていた母親が、通りすがりの年配の英国人女性に、「男の子にそんな色の服を着せてはいけない」と言われたという話を聞いたことがある。

好みの色が違うのは人の生まれつきの嗜好によるのだろうか。その可能性がゼロだとは言い切れないが、後天的な要素、社会の影響も強いと考えられる。第一次大戦以前の英米社会では、ピンクは強く情熱的な「赤」のヴァリエーションとして男子の色であり、ブルーは聖母マリアの「青」の貞淑なイメージや繊細な色として女子に推奨されていた。つまり百年前、男女の色は逆だったことがある。

ところが、次第にピンクは「女性らしい色」と考えられるようになっていく。なぜだろう。様々な説があり定まらないが、商業主義的な戦略のもとにそのイメージが広がり始めたのが、第二次大戦後だと言われている。つまりここ半世紀ほどのことなのだ。

ところで、英語では新生児の赤ちゃんのことを代名詞でうけるとき「he（彼）」でも「she（彼女）」でもなく「it」を使う。男女の別はない。しかし、今は英語圏でも生まれた直後から男女で服の色を分ける傾向がある。こうした発想はなぜ生まれてきたのか。やはり早いうちから大人のルールが応用されているからだろう。

古今東西、いろいろな文化のファッションを見渡して、男女ともに同じ衣装を着用していた文化は、おそらく存在しない。男と女。それぞれの肉体にはもちろん生物学的な違いはあっても、その違いは服を着る上では、実はそれほど大きなものではない。にもかかわらず、なぜ、男女の服の形や色は違うのか。やはりそこには「分けたい」という思いや願いがあるからだ。「体が違うから、異なる服を着る」のではなくて、「異なる服を着ることで、男と女は違うのだということをより強く意識したい」。そうした心理が人間の中にあるからだ。

服とわたし──

　いうまでもなく、人が服によって示したいと思っているのは男女の違いだけではない。たとえば「階級意識」が日本より強く残るイギリスでは、それぞれの階級で着用する衣服の傾向が違う。

　ただし労働者階級の人が上流階級の人の格好をしたいと思って着用しているかといえば、それは違う。出世したいと願っている人はいるかもしれないが、自分が暮らす社会、育ってきた環境、つまり「わたしらしい服」を着たいと思っているのではないだろうか。

　たとえば、フランスの思想家ロラン・バルトはこんなことを言っている。「衣服とは『わたしは誰か』という重大な主題との『たわむれ』である[*1]」と。

　服を着る、あるいは服を選ぶ、ということは、「自分らしさ」について考えることにつながる。アイデンティティの表現とも。服は『周囲の人へのメッセージ』を示すだけなく、「わたしはこういう人間です」という意味を持つと既に述べたが、そのメッセージは『社会のルール』との『距離感』を表明することにもつながる。性別や階級について取り上げたが、他に職業・宗教・学校など様々な共同体に属するアイデンティティをわたしたちは生きている。

　小さな女の子はきっと「わたしは男の子じゃない、女の子なの」と、自分を女の子という存在として自覚

したばかりかもしれない。それは「どうやら女の子はピンク色を着るらしい」ことを同時に感じとったのだ。ピンクの服に強いこだわりを見せるのは、無意識のうちに、「ルールがわかっている」というメッセージを発信したいからなのかもしれない。

服と自由──

「服がわたしを表現する」のであれば、人はだれしも好きな服を着るべきだろう。それが「自由」ということだ。ピンクの服が着たいなら着たらいい。しかし、好きな服を着ることで、だれかの気持を傷つける場合があることを、子どもは想像しているだろうか。

たとえば、形や色づかいが奇抜だったり、不道徳的とされるマークがあしらってあったり、社会のルールからあえて外れた服というものも存在する。いわゆる「不良のファッション」である。

筆者は十代の頃に「パンク」と呼ばれるイギリスの「不良ファッション」に強く惹かれていた。実際に穴の空いたズボンや、鋲のついた服を身につけていたこともあった。その背景には、当時、自分が属する社会、学校への反発心があったように思う。そんなパンクファッションを身につけたとき気持は満足して、「本当の自分になった」とさえ感じたけれど、親の方はきっと心配していたことだろう。

自分の子どもでなくても、他人の奇抜な服装を見るとき、人は「不快」あるいは「不安」な気持になることがある。おそらく、信じている社会のルール、言い換えれば人生の価値観に揺さぶりをかけられるからだろう。自分を否定されたような気持になることもあるかもしれない。

服が他人の気持を動かすことがあるということを、子どもも次第に意識したり想像できたりするようになる。服は自分だけのために着るものではないのだから、「だれか」のことも自然に考えて着ているのだ。

他人のために服を着るという発想は、日本には古来からある。たとえば、僧侶が絽（ろ）や紗（しゃ）と言われる、夏に

透ける素材の着物を着るが、本人は実はたいして涼しくはない。見ている人の目を涼ませるためでもある。

また、人が毎朝、毎晩のように着がえるのも、衛生面のことから、周囲の人たちが不快な気持ちにならないように、という配慮もある。

「他人のことも考えるべき」という考えと、先に述べた「好きな服を自由に着るべき」は矛盾するようにも見える。けれども、この悩ましさは、ファッションの重要な要素を含んでいる。相反する両者のバランスをとろうと試みるところに、「おしゃれ」＝ファッショナブル、が生まれるのだ。

さて、話を戻そう。子どもがパジャマで外出したい理由は、単純に自分が楽だから。園に行ってみたら、なにが起きるだろう。友達はなんて言うだろうか。先生はどう思うだろうか。連れていったお母さんはどんな顔をしているだろう。きっといろいろな反応を体験できる貴重な機会になるはずだ。「服ってなんだろう」と親子で考える良いきっかけとなるに違いない。冒頭で「行ってみたら？」と提案をした理由である。

服とファッション――

パジャマから服を着ることについて考えてきた。「衣服が自分らしさの表明」などと聞くと、今着ている服でいいのかとふと立ち止まりたくなる。「好きな服」を着ているなら、大丈夫だと信じたい。あまりこだわらないで、自分らしい服で過ごしたいものだ。

「好きな服と似合う服は違う」という考えもある。「好きな服はいずれ似合ってくる」と考えている。「似合う」とは、自分あるいは周囲の人が見ても「しっくりくる」、ということ。長いこと着ていれば、いずれ見慣れてもくるもの。自分らしい服とはどんな服だろう？　という疑問が湧いたなら、「トドラー・スタイリング」という興味深い試みを紹介したい。

トドラーは英語で幼い子どものことである。アメリカでファッション関係の仕事をしている女性が、三歳の息子に自分の服を自由に選ばせて、一週間ほど子どもの選んだ服装を身にまとい、その写真をインターネ

ット上で発表している。ぎょっとするような服の組み合わせになることもあったようだが、同じことを始め
る人が増えたとか。トドラー・スタイリングは、子どもの力を借りて一度「今の自分」の枠組みをこわす、新
おもしろい試みでもある。親が子どもの衣装を決めることはあっても、子どもの視点を取り入れる発想は新
鮮である。また、この試みを始めた女性が「子どもが選んだ服を着たその日一日、笑顔でいられた」とも書
いている。単に我が子が選んだ「変な服」を身にまとう自分がおかしかったのかもしれない。たとえそうで
あったとしても、この言葉にはファッションの神髄が現れている。おしゃれの醍醐味は、まずは服を「楽し
むこと」である。「わたしは誰か」という問いと戯れる。

日本人の多くは幼稚園、あるいは中学、高校で制服を着用する。制服には制服の良さがある。たとえば家
庭の経済状況によらず皆同じ服を着るため「平等」であると言えるし、また、憧れの学校に合格して着る制
服ならば、着ることのよろこびも感じるに違いない。また、制服であっても、「自由」を表明することは可
能だ。ロラン・バルトはモードにとって「細部（ディテール）」が重要であると述べた。[*2] ほんの小さなことで
全体の印象ががらりと変わるのがファッションのおもしろさだ。制服という厳重な規則や制限のなかで、た
とえばスカートやズボンの丈がほんの数センチ違うだけで他人から見たイメージは変わってくる。また服で
なくても、通学カバンや小物の存在も大きい。幼稚園バッグに母親がつけてくれる小さな刺繍、それが子
どもに大きな安心感を与えることもある。ただ、組織のルールを作る側からすれば、そんな小さな違いなど
認めたくない場合もある。そのときいっそう、「自由」が大切であると実感するのだ。ファッションという
遊びを享受しながら、服という言葉の社会性を理解し自由に表現をしていきたいものだ。

注
* 1　Barthes, Roland, *Système de la mode*, Seuil, 1967, p. 260.（佐藤信夫訳『モードの体系』みすず書房、一九七二年、三五四頁）。
* 2　*Ibid.*, pp. 246–247.（佐藤同書、三三六頁）。

人を着ているとは言えないだろうか

本章では、本書のタイトルでもある「人を着る」ということについて引き続き考えよう。人間はまぎれもなく動物だが、衣服を着る動物である。衣服を着る理由にあげられる「身体保護」や「身体装飾」は、他の動物にもみられるから、共有している要素である。「差恥心」は、人間に特徴的な要素だと言われる。社会が発展すると、衣服そのものがフェティッシュ化して衣服が登場し、狭義のファッション＝流行現象が生まれる。さらに高次に進むと衣服の記号としての衣服が登場し、狭義のファッション＝流行現象が生まれる。さらに高次に進むと衣服そのものがフェティッシュ化して、記号性が一人歩きしたり、形骸化してコスプレのような遊戯も登場する。人間が他の動物と一線を画すとすれば、それは人間の精神活動のなせる技であり、その技を技として理解するのもまた人間自身である。

人はなぜ服を着るのだろう。この根源的にして深遠な問いを考えるとき、動物と人間の境はどこにあるのかという問いに直面することになる。

本章では、まず最近のヨーロッパの作家たちの作品を紹介しながら、服とからだの問題に迫ってみたい。作品上とはいえ、動物と人間の境を行き来することで、懐かしいような、逸脱したような、そんな感覚の体験を共有することで、衣服を着ることについての問題の枠組みを提供してみよう。

次に、こころの問題も併わせて、さらに考察を進める。他動物あるいは生き物と人間を分かつのはわたしたちが服を着ることにあるのではないか、という考えを下敷きにして企画した「〈人を〉着る（という）こと」とい

うトークセッションの成果をまとめる形で展開を試みたい。

1　闘う身体

不安なからだ

まずスウェーデンの女性作家サラ・クレップ（Sarah Kläpp）のコミック作品の紹介から始めたい。『閉ざされた部屋 *The Shut Room*』（2010）と題された八頁の作品は「どこからどこまでがわたしたちの体なのか」、そして服の在り処を問わずにはいられない。奇妙なユーモアに貫かれていて、台詞がないのも特徴で、コミックと呼んでいいのかも疑問である。

ガスマスクが壁に掛けられた部屋の歪んだ描写。指、コルセット、足、脚、ドロワーズ（ズボン型の下着）──人のからだの細部へと視線は動いて、「身体」がクローズアップされていく。その動作は脱いでいるのか着ているのか、描かれているのは体なのか服なのか。その答えは判然としない。眺めるもの／読むものを「不安」にさせる。ロラン・バルトは、『モードの体系』についてのインタビューの中で、「記号はそもそも言語から完全に独立できるものなのか」と問われた際、言葉のない映像が持つ意味の多義性を「不安（anxiety）」と説明している[*1]。

いわば意味を奪われた体は行き先が定まらないまま、モノクロ・ページの上でうつろにたゆたう。無声の記号。

人がベッドの上で抱き合っている（図1）。二人の人＝絡まり合う四本の脚、濃い体毛を持つ二本の脚、つるんとした真っ白な脚、対照的に描かれる。男性的な下半身から延びた継ぎ目のない上半身は、女性の裸かと思いきや、人のからだという衣装であった。仕事を終えた後の着ぐるみのように、体はやがて脱ぎ捨てられ、気だるくハンガーに吊るされるモノとなる（図2）。

抱きしめていたのは誰なのか。抱きしめ合っていたのではなかったか。情

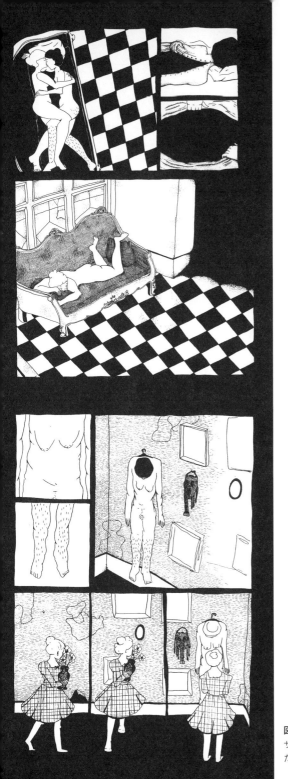

事の後、壁に掛けられた「からだ」に向かい、ふと手を伸ばしてみる。あなたなのか、わたしなのか。あなたの体なのか、わたしの体なのか。どちらの服なのか。身に着けるときわたしは一人である。目の前にぶらさがる体を身に着けて、バックボタン、ガーターベルト、ガスマスクを装着してドレスアップが完了する。彼女〈彼?〉は一人であり、裸体は衣装だった。男を着るか、女を着るか、部屋の外ではなく中にいても、裸の〈わたし〉は、まだ裸ではない。服を着るように、体を着ているのだ。サラの作品は、着ることと脱ぐことが日々繰り返され、止むことのない孤独な一個の身体の闘いを、言葉を介さずに物語っている。

さて、不安な体を残したまま、先へ進もう。次に紹介するのは、イギリス人のファッションイラストレーター、ルイーズ・ハリソン (Louise Harrison) の『悪態をつく、らしからぬ動物 Inappropriate Animal with Bad

図1（上），図2（下）
サラ・クレップのコミック作品『閉ざされた部屋』からの一場面

図3（右），図4（左）
ルィーズ・ハリソン《悪態をつく，らしからぬ動物》

Behaviour』（2011）と題されたシリーズ作品。動物たちは、人間離れならぬ動物離れした抜群のプロポーションを持ち、魅力的でファッショナブルである。人間を誇張的に表現しているレトリックやアレゴリーなどと単純に処理するわけにはいかない。銃を持ち煙草をくわえ、時計を身につけて魅惑的な脚線美を持つウサギ（らしき動物）は、ドット柄のドレスとタイツ、白黒のコンビのショートブーツと真っ赤なアームグローブを身につけ、活動的でドレスアップされたファッションである（図3）。動物のウサギを思い出せば、耳は短めである。くびれたウェストも手伝って、女性的な表現で描かれた「体」である。人間よりも人間離れしたスーパーボディを持つ動物たちは、決してここでは飼いならされない。真っ赤なタイツにグリーンのピンヒールの出で立ちの馬は、挑発的なポーズである。全身網タイツのゴリラは、焔をかかげな
がら吠えている。人間的バランスを獲得した長身のキリンは、一戦を交えた後なのか、血糊のついた剣を手に一服ふかしている（図4）。

人＝服を着る動物

ジャック・デリダは著書『我動物なる故に我あり *The Animal That Therefore I Am*』で、「動物は裸だから、裸

になるということがあり得ない、人間という例外をのぞいて、原則として動物は服を着るという発想を持ち得な

*2

い」と述べて、人が服を着る動物であることの妥当性に迫っている。衣服は、「人として適切な (proper) こと」

＝（人の）所有物 (property)」だと定義する。ルィーズが描く動物たちに視線を戻せば、ウサギという動物が持ち合わせて

的な丸い尻尾はアクセサリー・ファーのような装飾的な役割を担っているし、キリンという動物が持ち得た特徴

いるカラダの色柄は美しいデザインの一枚の衣装を纏っているように見える。人と違って、動物は裸になるとい

うことがない。言い直せば、自発的に着ることがないので、あえて脱ぐという行為はない。ルィーズの作品の動

物たちは、人のようにデフォルメされている。そして、人に支配されていない＝飼いならされないという、他者

（人間）との関係を、衣装やファッションを通して表現しているのではないか。

ハンガリーとスウェーデンの研究者によって、シマウマのストライプであるゼブラ柄について興味深い実験が

行われた。この絶妙ともいえるデザインは、動物学的進化の過程では合理性を持っていることが、実験結果によ

って明らかになった。その方法は、黒と茶色のストライプや、ドット柄や単色などのヴァリエーションを、シマ

ウマのカラダに人工的に施すことによって試みられた。白と茶の間隔の狭いストライプは、白い部分が光を反射

することにより、シマウマの天敵である吸血性の昆虫を寄せつけなかった。動物の持つ文様は人間のファッショ

ンにもよく取り入れられる。人気柄だと言えるこのゼブラ柄は、シマウマにとっては他種の生物＝（天敵である）

昆虫には魅力的なデザインどころか、種の生存のための理にかなった生物学的進化の結果なのだ。

デリダは前掲書において、'I, the Animal'と定冠詞と単数形の大文字で表現することによって、人間は他の

あらゆる生き物とは隔絶している「動物」であること（という考え）を主張する。また、これは文法的には動物一

般を意味する用法でもあるが、私という「自己」を意識する言葉とともに用いることができ、'we, the animals'

*4

という言葉で表現される意味との差異を喚起させる。動物は〈わたし〉を意識しない、「わたし」とは言わない

のだ。

ファッションは、「人と違っていたい」「人と同じでありたい」という二つの相反する欲求が拮抗する〈わた

し）の表現の上に生まれる。[*5]「人は（だけが）衣服を着る動物である」というテーゼが潜んでいる。シマウマのストライプは「（他の動物と区別して）同種の仲間にアピールするための文様であり、個あるいは私として突出するためのデザインや衣装ではない。

いのちと服

飼いならされない＝人間化した動物、と、衣装が投げかけてくる問いをいったん傍らに置いておこう。次の作家は、ダヴィッド・リシャール（David Richard）というフランス人のコミック作家。『パンツの中のインクの汚れた嗜好 Un Sale gout d'encre dans la culotte』（2012）と題されたドローイング集には、「倒錯した身体」と呼べるような身体表現が執拗に繰り返されている。

はにかんだような可愛らしい女の子、獣のように毛で覆われて獰猛な二本の足を持っている（図5）。同じような動物的下半身と人間的上半身のモチーフを使ったイラストでは、臍出しルックの女の子が読者に向けて自分を'Sexy?'と問う。

動物と人間を分かつところはどこにあるのか。たとえば人間が毛皮のコートを防寒に着用するように、動物は毛に覆われているといえるだろうか。獣毛は温度調節を担っている。メスへの求愛行動が主たる目的で、オスの方がメスのからだよりも美しい色彩や柄を持っている事例が多く見られることが、特徴的なダンス行為と共によく知られている。流行のファッションを身につけて、体を着飾り、脱毛し、顔に化粧を施す人間の装飾行為に相当すると言えるだろう。人の美容や装飾行為は、恥じらいから性器などを隠す「羞恥心」とも関連している。着ることで隠しているが、隠すことで顕われることもあり、表現として魅せられることもある。

人間以外の動物も、からだを隠したり顕したり、「着る」という表現で説明できることもあるかもしれないが、「脱ぐ」という行為を能動的に行うことはない。毛を剃ったり、ハサミでカットしたり、身体加工を施すことも

ない。ダヴィッドが描く女の子の髪は、放っておけば永遠に伸び続ける植物の蔓のようである（図6）。仏教的な「いのち」の平等をここで取り入れるならば、この作品集のなかでは、人も動物も植物もみな同じ生き物として並列に描かれている。そして一個のからだ／いのちに別の種が混成しているかのようだ。人間は他の生物、動物や植物とどこがどう違っているのだろうか？

デリダは、「獣と主権者 Le bête et le souverain」と題された講演の中で、アリストテレスの唱えた「社会的動物」という概念を敷衍して、「政治的存在」としての人間の問題を、bête というフランス語独特の単語によって展開している（この言葉は、「獣」の意味を持つ名詞としてだけでなく、英語にはない「愚かさ」という形容詞としても使われる）。La という女性名詞に付く定冠詞をともなった「獣」と、le という男性名詞に付く定冠詞をともなった「主権者」との間にあるのが、法のもと政治的社会に生きている生来の「人間」であり、獣と主権者は極の位置にありながら似通った性質を持つ存在でもある。この二つは、法外の、あるいは法からは遠く離れた非政治的存在だというスキームを提示する。ダヴィッドの描く少女を再び思い出せば、髪はいつまでも伸び続け、やがて地面と繋がり一つになっていくことが容易に想像できる。ヒエラルキーのない社会にはタブーや法的規制もないが、ハサミを入れて軽快さをデザインしたり、流行という刹那的な時間を
[*6]

図5（上），図6（下）
ダヴィッド・リシャール《パンツの中のインクの汚れた嗜好》シリーズ

享受するファッション性は存在しない。「色っぽい?」と問われて、なんと答えるべきか。動物としてのわたしか、人間としてのわたしか、女か、男か、どのような立場の〈わたし〉で反応しよう? 動物としてのわたしたちは動物である。けれども他の動物とは違っているということを「人は服を着る動物」として説明できないか再び考えてみたい。

本章の最後のコミック作家は、ドイツ人のアイシャ・フランツ (Aisha Franz) で、一匹の犬が繰り広げるハードボイルドタッチのシリーズ作品がある。主人公が動物で、人間社会に入りこんで活躍するストーリーは、ドイツや日本に限らず世界共通であり、フィクションの古典的手法ともいえるが、紹介する『ブリジット Brigitte #2』(2011) は、時として深くて重いテーマが展開されるヒューマンドラマである。なぜブリジットは動物でなければならないのか。あらためて作者に尋ねてみたくなる。ブリジットが不妊手術を嫌々受けさせられる回想シーンから本編は始まる。「真珠商人 The Pearl Merchant」と題された二つ目の挿話より——舞台は病院のベッドから常夏の島ハワイへ移り、スピード感のある復讐劇が繰り広げられる。ブリジットは、ワンピースに帽子とウィッグを身につけ、口紅と睫毛が印象的な濃い化粧を施し、妊婦になりすましてハワイへ入国する。偽造パスポートの名前は、実在のアメリカ人変装アーティストと同名の "シンディ・シャーマン Cindy Sherman" である。読者はそのユーモアに気づくだろう。

タクシーから降りると、「もうこんな格好やってられないわ」と腹部に詰めたクッションをおもむろにはぎ取り、ウィッグを大胆に脱ぎすてる (図7)。ハワイ島では、ここでしか採取できないという幻の黒真珠マルガリータをめぐって、闇取引が行われている。人間を好きにならない薬を飲み、全身黒タイツを着用し、身を隠す。とうとう復讐相手であるイワンを見つけ、銃口を向けて発砲のタイミングを狙うべく、イワンの妻で現地ハワイアン女性のお腹に思わず目をやるのだった。妻は妊娠している。ブリジットにとってはもはや叶わぬ夢となったが、自分の妊婦姿を想像せずにはおられない。そして、銃を置く。そのときタイツでは隠しきれなかった尻尾で滑り、床へと転げ落ちてしまう (図8)。復讐には失敗したが、「人道」的には失敗しなかったブリジット。

4.Okay, enough - go back to your room or take a bath or so...

1.You can stop here! 2.Are you sure, Ma'am! 3.And how! 5.How I hate this disguise!

図7（右），図8（左）

アイシャ・フランツのコミック作品『ブリジット #2』からの一場面

人という衣装

　デリダは前掲書で、一七世紀の詩人ラ・フォンテーヌの「最強者の理由が最善のものとなる」（「寓話」より）という言葉をたびたび引用する。「主権者がそれを正しいというとき、否応なく力によってそれが勝利となる」ことはフランス人なら誰もが学校で習い知っている教訓であるという。悲しい運命を生きる犬ブリジットは、人間によって否応なく生殖能力を奪われ、目的のために服を着て人間に変装し、そして服を脱ぎ、また身を隠す。この動物＝犬は、人という動物を身に着けることが生きる術なのだ。デリダは政治的存在からかけ離れた人間に「愚かさ」を見いだし、またそれは「生来的」だと付け加える。この形容詞は人間以外の動物には使われることはない*7。

　人間にとって（人間以外の）動物は、科学実験の材料となったり、支配下におかれ労働させられたり、家畜として食べられることもある。人と動物の間には非対称性が存在する。通りを歩

けば、人間の子供服のように酒落た装いの愛玩動物が、飼い主と散歩している光景は珍しくない。動物は家族の一員、つまり人間化している現実もいなめない。だがそれは幸福で平等な関係とも言い切れない。犬は自分自身で服を選び、「おしゃれ」したいという意思のもとに、人に変身しているとは考えにくい。

わたしたちは「人を着ている」とは言えないだろうか。人を身に着けて生きる運命を背負うアイシャの描く犬、半身動物半身人間の生き物を描き続けるダヴィッド、人間離れした身体を持つルィーズのファッショナブルでセクシーな動物たち、そして人という体を脱いで壁に掛けてまた手を伸ばして人を着たり脱いだりする日常の闘いを描くサラの服（その「人」は女か男かも不明）……。自らのなかの動物性をもてあまし、身の置き場がなく戸惑い、不安な現実に浮遊している体を突きつけられているのではないか。

闘う身体を著（き）る

美術史を遡ってヌードと裸体の問題に取り組んだ著書『物の見方 *Ways of Seeing*』（1972）で知られるジョン・バージャーのエッセイ「猿の劇場 Ape Theatre」[*8]と、ホモセクシャルの罪で投獄された小説家オスカー・ワイルドが出所してすぐ友人に書いた手紙を紹介しておきたい。[*9]

バージャーは、子どもの頃から動物園に行くのが楽しみで、とりわけオランウータンやチンパンジーなど類人猿を見るのが好きだった。劇場で芝居を見ているような感覚もおぼえるが、果たして、猿たちにとっては、バージャーら人間が観衆なのではないかと問う。バージャーは、進化論の過程を紐解くような発見を動物園で見いだす。生まれるということは分かたれるということであり、その信じがたく受け入れがたい別離を受け入れるとき、想像力が生まれる。オランウータンが赤ちゃんの頭を自分の胸に強く押し付けた。バージャーは、その動物から人間という動物を見た気がした。想像力は分かたれたものを自分の胸に懸命に結びつけようとするのだ。

ワイルドは、一九世紀ロンドンの上流社会を風刺的に描いた喜劇『理想の結婚 *An Ideal Husband*』（1989）の中で、「ファッションは着る人を物語ります、また他の人の着ているものがファッショナブルではないというこ

とも示すのです」*10と、自らのファッション論を登場人物に語らせる。ファッションは一時的に絶対的な価値しかもたない、時と場所によって変化する、着る者にとっての「現在」を映し出す鏡のような現象である。この小説を出版した人物スミザーズ（Smithers）を、ワイルドは手紙の中で描写している。人物像よりも彼の風貌をこと細かに説明しているのが興味深い。「大きな麦わら帽をかぶり、青いタイは繊細な感じでダイヤモンド・ブローチで留めているが、そのブローチは濁った水かワインのような色だ。きれいに髭を剃った顔は祭壇に仕える牧師のようだが、血色が悪く彼が仕えている神とは文学なのである。その悩みは作品そのものではなく、出版社を探す詩人たちが理由になっている」。性格描写はといえば「彼と一緒に居ることは喜びであり、とても親切な男だ」の一行。

同じ頃、ワイルドが女流小説家エイダ・リヴァーソン（Ada Leverson）に宛てて手紙を書いている。二年間にわたる闇のような獄中生活の最中、彼女の素晴らしさを思い出さない日はなかったこと、出所後すぐに再会ができた喜びを詩のように綴っている。エイダの美しさは月を見守るスフィンクスのようだと讃え、その名でもって呼びかける。「美しいものはいつだって美しい」——その一行とともに。神話のなかのスフィンクスは、からだはどっしりとしたライオンのそれであり、鳥の翼を持ち、女性の顔をしているけれども、エジプトでは男性として知られている。

人として作られている〈わたし〉は、作っている人へ還ろうとする。もてあます動物性を内に抱え、〈わたし〉を識ろうと身体は葛藤する。闘いの中で絶対矛盾的自己同一を著ること（き）ができた時、わたしたちは〈わたし〉という存在のなかに、真なるものや美なるものを発見することができるのではないか。人は動物である。分けるのは人であり、本来いのちに境はないのだ。

2　（人を）着る（という）こと

からだはどこかで言葉に触れている、でもいったいからだは言葉を求めているのでしょうか、それとも言葉から逃れようとしているのでしょうか。

——谷川俊太郎「質問集続」[*11]

こころをのぞく

どんな衣服を着ていたとしても、自ずと何らかの意味を服は放っている。たとえ服を脱いで裸になっても、むしろその裸体には過剰な意味が発動する。

わたしたちは、〈わたし〉の「からだ」から出ていくことができないとして、「こころ」の方はどうだろうか。いうまでもなく、からだとこころを切り離すことはできない。それは「人」である、ということでもある。そのような問いを掲げながら、引き続き「人を着るということ」について、展開したい。

他動物あるいは生き物と人間を分かつのはわたしたちが服を着ることにあるのではないか、という考えを下敷きにして、「（人を）着る（という）こと」と題したトークセッションを企画したことがある。つまり、「着る」という行為には、おのずと人という衣服をわたしたちは着ているのではないか、という仮説を立てた。

講演者は三人で、曹洞宗僧侶である幣道紀老師・音楽家の塩見允枝子氏、フランス文学シチュアシオニスト研究者の木下誠氏。それぞれ「袈裟を着る」「音を着る」「都市を着る」というテーマで講演を依頼、共通している

キーワードは「着る」ということだけであり、互いに隔たったように映るかもしれない。共通項である「着るという行為」から、それぞれを繋ぎ合わせてもらうべく、三分野いずれにも明るい鈴木創士氏にコーディネートを依頼した。その全体のセッションを解題する形で、以下本節ではこころの問題を合わせて、さらに考察を進めて

行く。

重奏するこころ

　からだを媒介に衣服を着るイメージはしやすいが、人について考えるとき、同時にこころの問題も併わせて見ていかねばならない。袈裟はこの点で最適の出発点になると考えた。古代インドの僧世親（ヴァスバンドゥ）の著した成唯識論の一節に、「是諸識転変　分別所分別　由此彼皆無　故一切唯識」とある。[*12] これは幣老師も講演で触れていた玄奘三蔵（六〇二─六六四）による新訳からの引用だが、玄奘は仏典を漢訳し、中国より日本にもたらした。日本人が成唯識論に出会うのは、この韻を踏む漢詩の形で読むことが一般的である。[*13] この一節が述べているのは次のような考えである。わたしたちは通常、主観と客観によって現実の認識は成立すると思っているが、その認識はなんら実体があるものではなく、すべてはこころのはたらきにすぎない。あるいは、自分自身を認識する場合でも同様のことが言える。その場合でも、わたしたちは自己をいったん外に投げ出して対象化している。[*14]

　つまり、分別するもの〈見分〉と分別されるもの〈相分〉という二つの領域に分けられた認識は、あくまでこころ〈自証分〉の転変や変化に拠っている「虚妄」「影像」にすぎない。そしてそのこころとは、いわゆる五感の「前五識」、知・情・意である「第六意識」、個の意識下にある「第七末那識」、過去から未来へ繋がる命が備える水のような深層無意識＝「第八阿頼耶識」から成っている、と。つまり、こころは多数のレベルで折り重なっていて、それぞれ重奏／重層しながらつねに揺れているのではないか。こころをこのように捉えることは、「虚妄」や「影像」、あるいは〈わたし〉への執着から解かれた〈己〉の、つまり、本来のありかたの〈わたし〉を見出そうとすることにつながるだろう。

　振り返ってみれば、これまでのファッションや衣服をめぐる実践的問いは、あまりにもこのような〈わたし〉の方に執着していたのかもしれない。さまざまなメディアが喧伝する、誰かや何かが決めた「新しい」スタイル（色、素材、構造）＝ファッションを装いたいという煩悩のために、わたしたちは〈わたし〉自身をめぐるしく消

費してきた。これに対して、「袈裟」は、二五〇〇年以上ものあいだ、その意匠と構造が伝承され続けている。[*15]

執着される〈わたし〉から離れて、衣服を分解した布や織物、さらには繊維や糸に意識が向う。そして、身に着ける衣服は、自らの手で丁寧に縫い、纏われる。衣服を製作していると同時に、ある思想や態度＝仏教の法を正しく相伝していることである。能動的に〈人〉を〈着る〉行為がここにある。〈わたし〉を脱ぐべく「袈裟」は、

「人はなぜ衣服を着るのか」という問いに、一条の光を照らしてくれる。

音を着る

次に、「（人を）着る（という）こと」を、「音を着る」というキーワードで考える。塩見氏によれば、「音を着る」ということは「音を切る」ということだと言う。つまり、それは音を意識的に聴くということ。音を着る＝切ることは〈わたし〉のありかたとも深く結びついている。楽器という道具を媒体にして、人間は音楽を演奏する。音を分別し選取し表現する。その音楽を演奏するという行為は、衣服を着用するという行為にも似ている。音を「着る」ということと〈わたしたち〉のつながりが、ときどき同じように、からだだけでなくこころも存在している。

また、自然のなかで耳を澄ますといろいろな音が聞こえてくると塩見氏は言う。目を閉じて音に意識を向けていくと、自分と音が一体化していくような体験をする。このように「音を着る」とき、〈わたし〉はいったいどこにあるのか。それとも〈わたし〉を忘れているのだろうか。〈わたし〉のありかたが拡大し、延長しているのだろうか。むしろその際、本来のありかたの〈わたし〉、あるいは〈わたしたち〉に目覚めるような、なおかつ自然のなかですべてと溶け合っているような、いのちの輝く瞬間が生じているのかもしれない。塩見氏が講演の中で行った小さなワークショップでは、聴衆全員が好きなタイミングで好きな音を発した。ばらばらな音として鳴り響き、溶け合いの瞬間を表現する美しい実験と塩見氏の指揮のもとに、偶発的な一つの不協和音作品として鳴り響き、手を鳴らした。音を「着る」ということと〈わたしたち〉のつながりが、ここでは実践を通じて共有されているのではないか。

都市を着る

最後に、木下氏によるドゥボールの映像を中心とした作品紹介や解説から、とりわけ「都市を着る」という観点を抽出してみたい。シチュアシオニスト（状況主義者）であるギー・ドゥボールは、「芸術活動の理念」を、一個人の〈わたし〉が生み出す芸術作品の制作としてではなく、〈わたしたち〉が共有する「状況」を「構築」することだと考えていた。どのような「状況」で、どのように「構築」するのか。ドゥボールは両大戦期に、パリ市の統一的都市計画に抵抗するべく、自分たちの生き生きとした情動に沿った「心理地理学的地図」を作成しているが、その街並みにしたがってただ街を歩くだけではない。それは、静態的な紙のうえに書かれたイメージかもしれないが、その街並みにしたがってただ街を歩くだけではない。「意識的に」街を探り、「漂流」するための方法となり、活動、実践であった。自発的に〈わたしたち〉の環境を押し広げていくような「状況の構築」であった。ドゥボールは、このような「生の瞬間的環境」を具体的に作り上げる。シチュアシオニストの歩くという身体活動は、自己が外部環境へと拡張していく「ユニット」を作り、地図作成を行う。ドゥボールにとって重要なキーワード「雰囲気」が、消える地点に感応しながら「ユニット」を作り、地図作成を行う。その地図は自己の内部環境の表現となる。言い換えれば、その実践は、都市を自分たちの着心地のいいものにするために、自分たちで「着る＝切る」ことだったのであり、自分たちの手で「染め」ていくことだった。ここでまたたび、都市という住環境を通して、「着ること＝切ること」へ〈わたし〉は向かっていく。

わたしとわたしたちと

人は生きているかぎり、〈わたし〉への執着や煩悩に囚われがちである。言葉（「名言」）、それが元になった「二元対立」的な認識に縛られて、日々あがいている。生きるということは、「人」という脱げない服を着ているということではないだろうか。〈わたし〉からいったん離れて衣服を解体して、一本の糸や繊維を纏うことを実践し、布そのものを意識して「着る」こと。自然の馨に耳を傾け、音が立ち現われ、〈わたし〉を忘れつつ本来

の〈わたし〉や〈わたしたち〉に目覚める瞬間に気づくこと。そのような瞬間を都市に見出すべく、意識的に探索して都市を着る＝切ること。こうした試みは、脱ぎながら着る／着ながら脱ぐような、自由な実践的着脱行為となるだろう。情報や意味から解き放たれ、他生物と分かたれることなく一つの大きないのちの中で繋がり、個ではなく共に生きるべき地図を描いていく。そのとき「こころ」と「からだ」はバランスのなかで解き放たれて「清浄」となり、「静態的な自然」ではなく、「躍動的な自然」を取り戻し、わたしたちはその只中にいて「着ること」そのものを体験することができるのではないだろうか。

注

＊1　Barthes, Roland, *The Language of Fashion*, Translated by Andy Stafford, Edited by Andy Stafford and Michael Carther, Berg, 2006 [2004], p. 98.

＊2　Derrida, Jacques, *The Animal That Therefore I Am*, Translated by David Wills, Edited by Marie-Louise Mallet, Fordham University Press, 2008 [2006], p. 5.

＊3　Knight, Kathryn, 'How The Zebra Got Its Stripes', *Journal of Experimental Biology*, 15 February, 2012. https://jeb.biologists.org/content/215/5/iii（二〇一九年九月二五日最終確認）

＊4　Derrida, Jacques, *Op. cit.*, pp. 29-35.

＊5　拙著『闘う衣服』（水声社、二〇一一年、一七–三七頁）の序論「人は服を着る動物である」を参照。ファッションは唯一無二の個としての表現と共同体の一員としての表現が拮抗して〈わたし〉をめぐって現象する。

＊6　Derrida, Jacques, *The Beast & the Sovereign Volume 1*, Translated by Geoffrey Bennington, Edited by Michel Lisse, Marie-Louise Mallet, and Ginette Michaud, The University of Chicago Press, 2011 [2008], pp. 25-26.

＊7　*Ibid.*, p. 68.

＊8　Berger, John, 'Why Look at Animals ?', Penguin Books, 2009, pp. 38-53.

＊9　Pryor, Felix, ed., *The Faber Book of LETTERS*, Faber and Faber, 1990, pp. 217-218.

＊10　Wilde, Oscar, *An Ideal Husband*, The Hokuseido Press, 1985 [1913], p. 75.

＊11　『コカコーラ・レッスン』思潮社、一九八〇年。

＊
12
唯識論では一般的に漢字の「心」を用いるが、本章では、「体（てい）」と区別するための「からだ」、「からだ」とともに論じるものとして「こころ」を平仮名で対応させている。

＊
13
多川俊映『唯識こころの哲学』大法輪閣、二〇一二年、一五七─一六二頁。

＊
14
原典は『唯識三十頌』第十七頌、西暦五世紀頃。

＊
15
袈裟についての基本的論文は第五章を参照。

第二章

北園克衛とファッション

潜水服を着てヒヤシンスの畑に寝ながら五分間を経過した。と言ふことはひとつの文明である。

日本語の「服」という言葉は、現在では「洋服」の意味で使うことが自然になった。洋服＝欧米文化、と単純に考えてみれば、日本人の「洋服」への接し方は、戦前、戦中、戦後を通して、好奇心、躊躇、憧憬、抵抗など複雑な感情が入り混じり、また変化を余儀なくされてきた。

本章ではそのような時代を生きたひとりの詩人北園克衛（一九〇二―七八）とその作品を取り上げる。北園は、詩のほか、エッセイや小説など書き言葉での表現にとどまらず、絵画・写真・イラスト・装幀など多方面で活躍し、その創作の美学やスタイルは、現代でも再評価され続けている。いまでいえばマルチ・アーティストだが、生涯自分を「詩人」と名乗ることに固執し、また衣裳を「もっとも憧れる形」と述べていた。この時代の洋装文化受容の背景を一人の詩人を通して読み解きながら、人と衣服／ファッションについての関係や意味を再考する。

26

1 視覚詩のなかのファッション

風俗としての洋装

日本人が一般的に洋服の存在をはじめて知ったのは「ペリー来航」だといわれている。実際に着用されるようになったのは「文明開化」以降で、洋装＝鹿鳴館のイメージが一般的に強い。「明治に洋装というものはあったが、洋装の風俗はなかった」[*2]といわれるように、このときの洋装はごく一部の特権階級が享受する装飾的な服装を意味した。日本社会においては男性の方が早く普及したが、明治四（一九三七）年に軍服に洋装が採用されてからは急速に定着した。女性は、ファッションとしてあるいは生活のなかに洋装が馴染むには、昭和の時代を待たねばならなかった。着物の女性と洋服の女性が街中に混在していた時代もあり、庶民の間に本格的に浸透するのは大戦後となることは第三章でも述べる。

洋服が特別な装いであった時代、モデルは異国から来た大使夫人や貴族階級の日本女性で、大正時代に入るとカフェの女給を筆頭にバスガイドや看護婦などの職業婦人になる。明治後期から大正時代にかけての「モダン・ボーイ」や「モダン・ガール」の流行は、まだ一部の人々に限られたファッションとはいえ急速に広がりそのインパクトは大きかった。大正一三（一九二三）年、関東大震災の体験をきっかけに、洋服の機能性が説かれるようになる。「婦人公論」や「婦人倶楽部」など大正初期から創刊されていた婦人雑誌は、「はじめて洋服を着る婦人の心得」[*3]などの特集記事を組みはじめるのだった。

「圖形説」[*4]と時代考証

本節では、「圖形説」という視覚詩のシリーズ作品の中から、特にその時代の風俗を表現していると思われる

二作品を取り上げる。「圖形説」は二篇から構成されており、ペアになっている「貴婦人」と「美麗な魔術家」を紹介する。

同時代の詩人伊藤信吉（一九〇六—二〇〇二年）は、この「圖形説」という作品群を、「これも『ポエジイ』の一形態にちがいないが、私どもが一般にいう『詩』ではない」と、全集の解説で感想をもらしている。「圖形説」は、今読んでもあるいは眺めても、たしかに解読に困難を要する作品かもしれないが、「読む」よりも「視る」あるいは「感じる」詩というべきだろう。作品が所収されている詩集『白のアルバム』は、「現代の芸術と批評叢書」というシリーズの一冊として刊行され、その編集企画の中心人物であった詩人春山行夫（一九〇二—九四年）が「北園克衛について」と題した序文をこの詩集に寄せている。春山を中心とした詩の運動の核になった「意味によって詩を書かない」という宣言をこの序文のなかでも繰り返す。

文学に於いて、書かれた部分は単に文学に過ぎない。書かれていない部分のみが初めてポエジイと呼ばれる。

「書かれていない」（＝言葉で意味を伝えない）要素から「詩ではない」という判断を下した伊藤はその時代の読者の代表かもしれないが、「書かれていない部分」に「ポエジイ」が生起する春山の解釈に光をあてたい。同時に「ポエジイ」の意味のうち「詩情」という「こころ」の働きにも焦点をあてたい。

明治、大正、昭和という三つの時代を生き抜いた物書きの間で、世界の芸術運動と共時性をもった形で新しい創作を進める潮流が生まれる。北園も積極的にそのなかにおり、構成主義・表現主義・ダダイズム・未来主義・超現実主義など前衛芸術運動での方法を次々にその詩作活動に実践として取り入れた。「私ども」が持っている歴史と断絶して、新しい詩をつくろうとするグループの誕生である。

鈴木貞美は、日本のモダニズムの一九二〇年代説を八〇年代には掲げていた海野弘の功績をとりあげ、日本における新しい言語表現の運動とその時代についての関係を論じている。この時代からはじまる「リトルマガジン」と呼ばれる詩誌の夥しい数の刊行は、それが世界的に大きなうねりであったことを示している。日本は、大

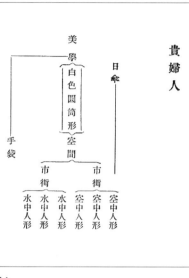

図A

図B

震災をきっかけに、併存していた「江戸」と「東京」がまるごと新しい文明に改造されるという勢いに飲み込まれていく。新しい文学の潮流は、拡大化する身体＝「モダン都市」とその風俗をテーマに、新しい芸術形式を積極的に詩作に組み入れながら、個の内面を描いてきた「旧弊なるものとしての抒情詩」を乗り越えて行くというものであった。身体が「都市を着る」ことによって「わたし」の意識が変わっていく。言語も文化も翻訳され、海を越えて広く行き渡る。

A　「貴婦人」

作品の背景を述べたところで作品の分析に入ろう。

「貴婦人」（図A）は、いうまでもなく貴婦人を描いているが、その実験的な造型詩の対象は、「婦人」でも「女性」でもなく「貴婦人」という言葉が指し示すものである。上流階級の意味も担う「貴」が添えられることで、「身分の高い婦人」の意味に加えて、その婦人に「洋」の香りが漂う。北園のほかの作品でも「貴婦人」という言葉はいくつか確認される。「ゲンスボロオの貴婦人」（「サボテン島」）では、画家ゲンスボロオの絵の中の女性の優美な衣装のイメージを表現する

のに効果的に使われる。洋装がなかなか「風俗」にならないのは、ファッションというシステムが階級社会を頂点に形作るヒエラルキーとして成立し発展した現象だからだろう。「婦人」は同時期に頻出する「マダム」という別のことばでもよかったのかもしれない。

作品のなかの「日傘」や「手袋」もその時代の流行を示す重要なアイテムである。頭部の「美學」から腕が伸びて下降しその先にある「手袋」、ヴォリュームのある足下から支えられるように伸びて上昇する「日傘」。同義語の「パラソル」や「手套」も北園詩によく登場する言葉だ。「圖形説」の新しい読み手である金澤一志は、中心にある「空間」を都市生活の空間としてとらえるところから「貴婦人」の読みをスタートし、「市街」を闊歩するモダン・ガールたちを背景にしたひとりの女性像の光景が浮かんでくると言う。「水中人形」はおそらく水着姿で、また時代背景から「ジムナスティックに向かう構成主義の傾向が発端」という考えから「空中人形」は「体操服」と解釈している。[*9]

「ひとりの女性像」という前提では、「円筒形」は「ボディ」を示していると考えられる。和服の時代が長いこともあり、日本人女性のウェストは洋装と違ってくびれを強調しない。そんな日本的なからだをデフォルメして描いているのかもしれない。洋装になると身体のフォルムは顕著にあらわれる。全体をひとつの図と考えれば、言葉の位置付けからも「白色円筒形」は「からだ」の表現と解釈できる。「モダン都市」に立つ「安定感」のあるボディ。ややアンバランスな違和感も醸し出している。頭のなかの「美學」によって景色として成立する身体表象は、文字や記号（約物）という衣装によって作品となった。

洋装がなかなか普及しなかった理由として、日本の女性にとってそれは「新しい服」というよりも「珍しい服」だったからという説がある。[*11] 着物の持つ長い袂や帯からは解放されても、身体を矯正するコルセットやバッスルなどの下着の過剰なフォルムは装飾性を超えて滑稽にも映る。身体を拘束する下着で成り立つ衣装スタイルが動きやすいものとは思えない。雑誌や映画のなかの洋服を着てみたい好奇心は芽生えても、生活のなかに取り入れるにはそんなに簡単ではなかったのではないか。断髪や袴でさえも過激だとして悪女のレッテルを貼られる

図1
『婦人グラフ』の「現代婦人職業百態」の連載では様々な働く女性が写真付きで紹介されているが、この写真は女流飛行家の回（1927年5月号）

ような時代で、貴族階級の日本人においてすら、洋装はパーティなどの公式な社交場でしか着用されなかった。機能性や合理性の面を考えても欧米のファッションを受容するには、労働や運動をするための「ユニフォーム」の登場を待たねばならなかった。つまり「水着」や「体操服」という、明確な目的でデザインされた衣服の存在は、洋装の大衆化への入り口に大きな貢献を果たした。

その時代の洋装（スカート）を指して、「彼女らは街頭の飛行船だ」と表現したのは日本における未来派の祖述者といわれる詩人神原泰（一九三〇年の彼女の風景）だが、そう考えると「空中人形」は「飛行服」と解釈することも可能なのではないか。この作品が準備された昭和初期には、仕事着のユニフォームとして、男性と同じ飛行服（つなぎのズボン）を着た女子練習生の記事が大きな話題となった（図1）。ちなみに乗馬にはじまり登山などが女性のするスポーツとして認められるようになると、何を着るのかというその衣服の方に注目が集まったのだという。

さて、「貴婦人」についてまとめておこう。北園はその裾広がりの下半身部分を社会のヒエラルキー構造に見立て文字で埋めている。上から下に降りて行くファッションの流行理論を詩のなかで描写したユニークな手法と発想で書かれた作品である。「手袋」を着け「日傘」を差しストリート（市街）を歩く白い衣装の「貴婦人」は上流社会に属している。洋装は、水泳着・体操服・飛行服などの活動的な働く女性によって支えられている。時代の社会構造を視覚詩として読むことができるのである。

最後に「白」という色について、この作品との関係を説明しておこう。このシリーズ作品は一九二七年頃に書かれたものを

原型にしていると言われるが、それは「白色詩集」[12]という作品を差しているのだろう。「白い住宅／白いテーブル」にはじまる時代の風俗描写は「白」という色を中心にして書かれている。三連目に「日傘をもつ白い手袋／白い衣装」、八連目に「近代型貴婦人装置」がある。「白」は欧米人の肌の色をも示唆する。この作品ですでに「圖形説」[13]の「貴婦人」設計図案を準備していることがわかる。

北園克衛はかつて、自分ほど「白」を使った詩人はほかにはいないと、その色への特別な思いを語っていた。[14]「白い」という形容詞を使用する頻度は高く、自らを「世界的な「白」の詩人である」と述べている。「白」は「鍵」の役目をする言葉で、何かを否定する場合や「無」の意味に使うこと、また自分の詩の中ではすべての色を「白」と同じように使いたいとも語っている。徹底的に「言葉」を「素材」として扱い、詩の中でその「形／体」を純化させる北園克衛のスタイルにとって、重要な役割を果たしている言葉でもある。

B 「美麗な魔術家」

次に、「貴婦人」と隣り合わせた作品「美麗な魔術家」（図B）をとりあげる。「圖形説」にロマンティックな響きを残しているのはこの作品のなかの「★夜會服」のフレーズだと金澤は述べるが、詩作をはじめた一九二二年に書かれた「ある夜の舞踏會」を下敷きにしているという。以下に引用する。

　……貴婦人の肉色の衣はひるがへり／豊満なる肉はその下に蛇のごとくのた打ちまはり／ナメシ皮の靴は、[15]リスのごときこうかつなるこびを売る／ああ大都会の高樓の乱舞／腐れたるバナナの興奮……

「肉色の衣」はすぐあとの「豊満なる肉」と呼応し、北園詩の別作品から「桃色の貴婦人」（「記號説」）というフレーズも確認できるように、肌色に近いピンク色の衣装を表現したものであろう。「肉」「のた打ちまわり」「こびを売る」「乱舞」「腐れたる」など生々しくダーティなイメージを喚起させる言葉を並べて、夜の舞踏会での貴婦人の奔放で誘惑的な様子を表現している。まさにそんな「貴婦人」は男性にとって「魔術家」ではないか。

作品「美麗な魔術家」へ戻ろう。「この作品の上部下部構造を壇上・客席と見て、全体を奇術などの舞台とすることもできるかもしれないが」「一人の女性を中心にした室内光景としたい」という金澤の説に首肯したい。

一人の女性であること、つまり「魔術家」＝「貴婦人」説を示すのに有効な材料として、同じ『白のアルバム』内の「記号説」にある「★」で区切られる最後の連がある。

夜會服／夜會服／夜會服／夜會服／夜會服／面白くない

「夜會服」の繰り返しと「面白くない」の組み合わせにその糸口を見出すことができるが、さらにもう一つ「レセプション」（《火の菫》）という北園作品を加える。正しくは、北園がその作品について説明した文章を解読してみる。

「レセプション」は招待会という意味で、秋から冬にかけてそういう小さな音楽界が催されたりする。そのときのスケッチと言ってもよい。「睫の長いマダムが砂糖のように笑う」というのは美しい婦人が、非常に艶やかに誘惑的に笑っていた、という程度である。「曖昧なかん高い孤独」というのは、そうした華やかな場所で昂奮していながらも、なんとなくそぐわない自分の孤独な気持ちを表現したもの。[*17]

「艶やかで誘惑的な笑い」は魔術になるが、その場面に居る自分は「なんとなくそぐわない」で「孤独」すら感じている。つまり「面白くない」のだ。

夜会服は通称「ソワレ」とカタカナでも表記されるが、色は黒と相場が決まっていて、単調なデザインではなく技巧的な衣裳なので、服が「面白くない」と考えたとは思えない。気持とは裏腹に魅惑されてしまう「魔術家」としての女性を表現しているのではないか。それは、洋装に代表される近代化や欧米人に対するアンビバレントな態度とも読める。憧れと戸惑い、甘い誘惑と居心地の悪さと。言語を徹底的に記号ととらえた北園は、ただ徒に「意味のない詩」を書いたの表現のなかに感情を切り捨て、

ではなく、目指したのは「無価値の価値」の表現だった。だからといって「こころ」をおろそかにするのではな

く、実験的な詩のなかにも抒情的な要素が見え隠れする。

「魔術家」＝「夜會服」を着た「貴婦人」のモチーフが続いていることが確認できた。夜会服は正装だからなおさら長さはマキシだろう。「★夜會服」

から七センチ上の裾に生きている。「貴婦人」のモチーフが続いていることが確認できた。夜会服は正装だからなおさら長さはマキシだろう。「★夜會服」は地面

の下半分だけを女性の像ととらえると「美麗な魔術家」は非常にバランスが悪い。四本の「軟い足」でやっとそ

の豪奢で重いドレスが支えられる。あるいは金澤説に倣って「キュビスム的な映像表現が彼女に四本の美しい脚

を与えている」としておくべきだろうか。「身体に密着するもののなかで近代の最も尖鋭な美を持つものは婦人

靴」と考えていた北園が、「軟い足」と言い放ったまま足元のスタイリングを未完成なままにしているとすれば

違和感をおぼえる。あるいは形容詞「軟い」が地面に並ぶことで逆に身体を拘束する豪華なローブと美しくも窮

屈で歩きづらい靴が対照的に「見えて」くるのかもしれない。「書かれていない部分」に現前化するポエジィが

イメージを鑑賞者／読者の脳裏へと映し出す「詩」。

　残る難問、上部構造の解読を試みよう。「花束」は会場に飾られているシーンとするよりは、女性が胸のあた

りに抱えていると考えるほうが自然だろう。そうなるとやはり全体で「ひとりの女性像」ということになる。

「水中人形」は超難問だが、【　】付きなのでメタ言語として扱われているはずである。何かの名前かもしれない。

「貴婦人」での「水着」の解釈をふたたび思い出せば、配置や【　】の役割を考えても、やはり繋がりは不明で

「無価値」の表現なのかもしれない。「天空にさわぐ空虚の人魚」（「SUR UN PARISSIEN」）という表現が同詩集内

にも見つかったので、水中人形＝人魚ならば、また不思議な魔術を持った女性のイメージに貢献できそうである。

虚空の女性の耳のあたりに人魚的なものが浮かんでいるのだろうか。

　本章では二作品のみ取り上げたが、北園克衛にとって詩集『白のアルバム』は、スランプになれば立ち返り、

詩作の新しい発展のパターンが見つかる、名実ともに原点となる重要な詩集である。その「アルバム」にある

「圖形説」の造形詩は、風俗文化を単に描いた新しい実験作品という評価にとどまることなく、背後にある時代

背景を映し出しており時代考証という点でも重要な作品である。

2　詩人のファッション論

本節では、北園克衛が雑誌などの印刷媒体で書いていたファッション評をいくつか取りあげて、引き続き当時の洋装受容を探っていきたい。「ファッション評」とひとくちに言っても、「衣服、ファッションに関する覚書」のようなものから、立派な「服飾文化論」あるいは「今年の夏の流行事情」[20]のようなジャーナリスティックなもの、無意味にも響く散文詩のようなものまで様々である。

ここでは、衣服やファッションの流行を扱った文章からとりあげる。単発で書いたファッション論や、紀伊國屋書店の月報上の「SEASON の手帳」や鉄道雑誌『旅と読物』の「DANDY」など連載としてまとまって読めるものから抜粋する。

A　「夏の銀座」

一九三三年に刊行されたエッセイ集『天の手袋』のなかの「エスキイス」と題されたパートに収められている。初出は、銀座の町を背景にした文章がほかにもあるので、詩人左川ちかと銀座で共同編集していた雑誌『ESPRIT』[21]の可能性が高い。まず「夏の銀座」のなかの一節をあげてみよう。

クレエルの巴里の屋根の下が上演されて以来、銀座の通りには鳥打帽のふえたことは驚くべきだ。殆ど歩いている青年の六〇パアセントはカスケットなのである。これを上演以前の二〇パアセントに比較して驚かぬ人があるだろうか？

平易な文章でわかりやすい。当時洋装文化は、欧米の映画俳優などを通して触れる機会が多かったことは次章

で扱う小説『女家族』にも見られる。また統計的なデータを出してくるところなど、なるほどと納得してしまいそうになるが、これには続きがある。

と、ある友達に僕は興奮した振りをして言つてみたのである。處が彼は平然と答へた。『それや夏のせだよ』

僕は無意味にやられてしまつた。

フィクションとして文章を終わらせようとしているのか、意味が不明である。「詩」と考えてもいいのだろうか。友人の答えもまた意味不明であり、無意味といいながらもその言葉に「やられて」しまう。ファッションに関する文章のなかで北園は「無意味」という表現を使う傾向があった。ほかに夏を扱った文章に「そろそろ「水」と「背中」の季節がやってきた*²²」ではじまるので、そこから類推できる。

しかし「セ」は「せい」で、早口に耳に入ってきた音であらわしているのかもしれない。

このエッセイのなかの「あるひは銀座」と題された部分には、また風変わりな友人を登場させて流行について語らせるユニークな文章もある。とりわけ身体についての描写が興味深い。

彼女たちは最う昔の婦人達のやうに膝を重心にして歩くようなことをしない。彼女たちは全く歐羅巴の女達のやうに重心を腰部に置て歩く。これが彼女たちのポオズをシイクにまたデイナミツクにしてゐるのである。それが彼女達の高いヒイルを完全に有効なものとする事によって、歐羅巴の長い傳統を溯つてしまつたと言ふ事が近代文明の特質である理知主義の価値を實證するものだ。

歩行の変化まで観察し描写しているのは「僕」である。しかしこのあと「僕」は、「多分ひとは、僕を無禮な奴と言ひ廣めることであらう」と自省的になる。風俗を語ることは「無禮」なことなのかもしれない。服を通して体を見ているからだ。そして、またふたたび「無禮な友達」が登場し、「近代の最も尖鋭な美」を持つ「婦人靴」の称賛をさせ文章は終わりに近づいていく。一人称、三人称(「友達」と「ある人」)と、語り手をスライドさせる

ことによって、新しいこの文化＝洋装をできるだけ客観的に捉えようとしている。「僕」は「驚」いたり、「やられた」りするも、「無禮」なのかもしれないと省みたり「近代文明の価値」を説こうとする。また、たくみに一九二〇─三〇年代のモダン都市の流行を紹介し、無意味な虚構作品のようにして読者に想像の余地も与えている。

B 「TOPを行く」

銀座で発行されていた流行文化誌『ESPRIT』[23] の最終号のなかで、ここでは小栗喬一郎の名前で執筆しているミニコラム集がある。北園克衛は本名の橋本健吉、亞坂健吉をはじめ、カットを書くときによく見られたローマ字表記（Kat や Le Katué など）にいたるまで確認されているだけで十以上のペンネームで仕事をしている。[24] 軽いタッチで文化を語るときにこの名前を用いる傾向がある。

片手で読める長方形のこの雑誌は広告からみても文芸誌ではなさそうだ。チョコレート、香水、口紅、レインコート、目薬と全体で三八頁の雑誌のうち五頁が宣伝広告。衣・食文化や音楽・演劇にいたるまで最先端のモードを扱う流行雑誌の装いである。写真は表紙を入れて合計七枚、うち六枚は欧米人のモデルで撮影されている。ちなみに残り一枚は筆者の一人杉田千代乃自身の写真で、断髪に洋装スタイルである（杉田は日本での女性アマチュア無線資格第一号者として紹介）。

北園のコラムに移ろう。まずレイアウトがユニークで、見開き一枚二頁分を4×5のマス目で区切り、それぞれの四角の中に文章を埋め込んでいく。「★」ではじまり、文字は縦書き、ページは開いた状態で右から左に進み、不揃いに出来上がるマス目の左の余白部分は全体をゆったりした空間に仕上げている。

内容は、海外でのトレンド・アイテムの紹介文を集めたといった様子。列挙してみよう。「チェツコスロヴァキヤの硝子工が作ったガラスの婦人用手袋」「ニユヨオクのL・シムプソン嬢のロココ風デコレイションの自動車」「木の幹を薄く剥いだもので造ったバッグ（クリスチアン・サイエンス・モニタア紙による報告）」「パリのボン・マルセ百貨店で売り出している軽金属のパラソル」……とまだまだ続くが、読み始めたときはほんとうに海の向こ

うで流行している新しいアイテムかと思ってしまう。宝石や衣裳、化粧品、カメラ（写真機）にいたるまで、非現実的な物語をともなって空想上の産物であることが示される。読者は一六種類もの流行商品の説明を読み終わる頃、もしかすると実在する商品なのかもしれないという考えがふとよぎる。

この種のものは未だ日本へは一箇も来てゐないかもしれないが、早晩やって来ることであらう

実際は素晴らしくセンシブルなものださうである

當分是以上のものは現れないだらうと言はれてゐる

固有名詞を使うことでまことしやかに語られる。新聞・雑誌、百貨店、法学者、映画監督、化粧品会社、ハリウッド女優、一貴婦人の名前など、片仮名で表記されるが、最後まですべてが真偽の程がわからない。ファッションは一時的に絶対的な「新しさ」を価値とする。北園克衛にとってファッションとは新しい言語表現を造るための「容れ物」や「形式」だったのかもしれない。ジャーナリズムにもポエジィを編み出し、散文詩を仕立てたようにその言葉は響く。詩の深刻さと遊びのバランスも絶妙で、それはファッションの要素そのものでもある。

C 「六つの角度」

戦後すぐに刊行され、詩人長田恒雄が編集した『新女性手帖』[*25] で、北園は「六つの角度」と題し文章を執筆している。女性向きで教育的配慮のある企画から、散文としても読みやすい内容。テーマは「衣裳」「食物」「住宅」「趣味」「結婚」「政治」の六つ。北園らしいスパイスの効いたエッセイになっている。「衣裳」をテーマにした箇所ではかなり本格的な服飾文化論を展開している。

衣裳選びは十分に注意しなければならないと説くことから文章ははじまる。なぜなら、衣服が「その女性の趣味、教養、経済を無言のうちに示す」からであり、しかしあまり注意をしすぎるとエキセントリックなものにな

る危険性があるという警告もここで一筋の光が差し込んだ。「衣裳の柄の好みや生地の趣味にも階級があり、職業がある」という指摘である。「エレガンス」とはなにか、「衣裳を正しく着るには建築や工藝と同様にその下地をしっかりとして置くことが大切である」と江戸風俗を引き合いに下着の重要性について語って、洋装を念頭に置いて「コルセット」の話題にも触れている。「流行雑誌やパタン・ブックのサンプルはあまりにも誇張しすぎている。これは一流の店になればなるほどむしろ甚だしいのである」――と、行き過ぎる雑誌メディアの情報をうのみにしないよう読者に促す。本人は「シンプルな装い」を謳っている。

ロラン・バルトは、「衣服は飛び切りの詩の対象となるはずだという期待はもっともである[*26]」と語っていた。モード雑誌の言葉がレトリックに乏しく文学から借りてきた決まり文句でできていることを説く。「詩」を作ってはいるが、月並みな「詩」以上のものは作らないのだ。北園がジャーナリズムについても心のある詩人であったことを押さえておきたい。簡単にメディアの欧化政策に踊らされてはならないのだ。

前節で述べた紀伊國屋書店の月報に連載していたエッセイ「Seasonの手帖[*27]」では、編集者としての北園のジャーナリズム観が見られる。

ジャアナリズムというのは本来、今日の文化的価値の標準をつくっていくところに存在理由があったはずですが、現代の日本のジャアナリズムは、いつも昨日の価値の標準を追っかけているに過ぎません。

「ビッグネイム」や「卑俗な常識家」を追う強い批判の後に続く文章で、おそらく現代のジャーナリズムに対してもあてはまるだろう。「つくっていくところに存在理由」を求める態度は、詩作やファッション評にも一貫している。外国のジャーナリズムを意識的に取り入れながら、日本の新しいジャーナリズムを創造していこうという使命に燃えていたのだろう。

D 「今年の水着その他」[28]

　三省堂から刊行されていた雑誌『ECHO』で、小栗雋一郎のペンネームで執筆している。目次の「今年の流行事情」からタイトルが変更になっている。エッセイは断章形式で、

　光る海、目に青葉、月の夜のポムパン、亜熱帯の風はソオダ水の泡の中にも光る。そして街の飾窓には海と山のグヅスが氾濫する。

　――はじまりはまさに詩で、北園克衛らしいモダニズムの響きをともなったスタイル。つづいてサンダル・パラソル・水着などの「海と山のグヅス」のリストアップがはじまる。水着の流行色とデザイン、素材について、水着の取り扱いが語られたあと、夏を演出する小道具の小物類について饒舌に語りはじめる。海岸帽、パラソル（北園はほんとうにこのアイテムあるいは言葉が好みのよう）、ビイチ・コート、ビイチ・バッグと続く。

　前節で紹介した「夏の銀座」や「TOPが行く」に比べると、歯切れが悪い。たとえば提案は、「賢明なことと思ふ」「あまりおすすめ出来ないものと言はなければならない」「海のモオドの傑作と言って良いと思ふ」「新しいロマンチシズムを感じない譯にはゆくまい」「黙殺する譯にはゆかない」など、まわりくどい表現でページが占められており気弱な印象をぬぐいきれない。新しい欧米文化へのためらいは隠せない。終盤になってやっと筆が乗りリズムが生まれて内容も面白くなってくる。

　平凡なデザイナは海の物に魚類や海草や波の模様をデザインしたがるのは極めて滑稽である。といふことを殆ど例外なしに彼のデザイナ諸氏は氣づかないらしい。その結果海のアトモスフェグをすっかり平凡にしてしまっているということは驚くべきものがある。多分、これはデザイナの生活の貧弱さの反映であるのかもしれない。

　平凡なデザイナは海の物に魚類や海草や波の模様をデザインしたがるのは却って海の風景を戯畫化してしまふばかりである。

批判のターゲットは、デザイナー自身の生活にまで及ぶ。Cでもその傾向があったが、むやみやたらに外国文化を取り入れようという態度には批判的。自分の確固たる美的感覚や審美眼からはずれるものに対しては黙って通り過ぎるわけにはいかない。そんな世相を嘆いてもいるのだろう。ここで毒舌ファッション評論は息をつき、最終章では潮が引いていくような静かな海の散文詩で終わった。

E 「DANDY」連載

戦後まもなくはじまった鉄道雑誌『旅と読物』での連載は「DANDY」と題された。[*29] ペンネームはふたたび小栗隼一郎である。一九四八年八月第一回目は、「みだしなみ」というタイトルのファッション概論。季節の詩的描写からはじまり、全体を通して読みやすい内容である。タイトルが示すように男性のファッションがテーマなので肩の力が抜けているのだろう。洒落た流行論という仕上がり。

「香水」「ステッキ」「靴」「室内着」「手袋」「鞄」と回を読み進めていくうちに、男女両方ともに楽しめる「お洒落の心得」のスタイルになっていく。やはりファッションは女性もののほうが色彩豊かで文章のなかにイメージを織り込みやすいのかもしれない。

鉄道雑誌なので一般的な読みやすいスタイルの文章だとはいえ、突然に、

ある婦人は夏になると、その日その日のコスチュムによって飲み物が違っているのだった。たとえば深紅のリボンの帽子の日はメロン・ソオダ水を、黄いろい衣裳の日にはピンク色のフルウッジュウスを、といったように。

やはり詩の女神が顔を出す。美しい散文詩になる。

しかし、厳しい眼差しを持ったファッション評論家であることも忘れていない。たとえば「香水」編では、アメリカの映画女優が気分やするこことに反論を投げかける指摘がたびたびなされる。たとえば「香水」編では、アメリカの映画女優が気分やアメリカ文化を無条件に受容

図2
北園克衛名で「季節の洋装」の連載
がはじまった号の『オール女性』
（1946年7月号）のモダンな表紙

服によって香水を選ぶという話が出てきて、グランの「ミツコ」・シャネルの五番・ランヴァンの「アルパージュ」など香水の名前を連ねる女優に対して、「全部パリの一流の香水店の名前だが、いかにもアメリカ式の香水趣味であきれたものである」と言い放ち、「それから、あ、もう書く場所がない！」と、唐突にエッセイを締めるなど痛烈なユーモアも感じられる。

男性の洋装の重要な小道具であるネクタイについては、「われわれはあまりに實業家の國アメリカの映畫を観すぎている。日本人はあまりに絵を描いたように、機械的にネクタイというものを、そのネクタイの結び目に現すべきである」と述べて、画一化して行く日本のファッションの状況に異議を唱える。

香水にも特別なおもいがある。「いろいろ試して自分が一番気に入ったものを見つけるのもいい」が、「季節や場所や服装によってそれぞれ違ったものを用いる人もある」と助言し、ファッションの醍醐味である「遊び」の要素を語る。

この連載は戦後すぐに男性向けに書かれたこともあるが、戦時中の画一化したファッションをどうにかしたいという思いにも満ちている。「ステッキ」の回では、「それにしても長い戦いの歳月は、このなんとはなしに古風で粋な趣味を忘れさせてしまったようである」と、若い二〇代三〇代がステッキをもたない現状を嘆き、「ステッキというのは、いわばもう一人の自分のようなものだ」という比喩を交えながら詩的に展開していく。モダニズムのにおいのする戦前の街に郷愁をおぼえつつ、戦後の新しい風を賢く取り入れていこうという宣言。時間を遡り、夏目漱石が愛用した戦前の香水を紹介、与えられたものではない自分の眼で探した「新しさ」の提案。それは甘

い香りのする「ヘリオトロープ」という香水で、北園詩に頻出する言葉でもある。

重さ、色感、リズム、形態から、できるだけ広い範囲に言葉を蒐集し整理する。言葉は物質化した形で記号のように使用する。北園克衛は詩の体系ともいうべき在庫目録のようなものを作っていた。これはまさにバルトが衣服のコードに取り組むときに行った一覧目録の作成と分類の仕事と酷似している。この言葉のリストは、新しいパターンが作られる毎に作り変えられていく。

最後に、本編では大きく取り上げなかった雑誌『オール女性』でも生地と材料の重要性、デザインにとってのカッティングや縫製の重要性についても説き、時と場所による衣装の分類なども試みている（図2）。

3　結び——北園克衛と「和装」

海を渡ってきた新しい文化や言葉は、大戦を挟み目まぐるしい変化にさらされた。戦争が弾圧し使用禁止となるも、戦後ふたたび街にあふれだす。「マヌカン」を「衣裳人形」と訳すセンス、「肌着」と訳した'chemise'を別の作品で「衣裳」に換えるエスプリ、当時詩人に流行した外国文化の当て字のルビを自ら主宰する詩誌では固く禁じたり……、言葉はいかにも詩人にできるだけ印刷物として詩集を残すように助言していたという。北園は若い詩人にとって生き物である。今読まれなくても百年後に読み直されるかもしれない。書き言葉は生き続け、その時代時代によって新たな価値を生む可能性を持つからである。服もしかるべし。

　　　　菫の垂れた鉛
　　　の車
　　星の縞
わたしは切断

fancy は切断

泡の

または綿の

よろめく圓筒に突き刺さる

骨の翼

影響の輪のないトルソオ

（中略）――「黒い鏡」より

一九五一年に刊行された『黒い火』[30]のなかに収められた詩の一つである。「トルソオ」（胴体）を軸に、色や模様が身体に描かれていく。「切断」という行為によって人は世界を分節化し、意味が生まれる。からだに縫い目はない。裸になれば一目瞭然。服や言葉が身体を意味付けして、輪郭やパーツを形作っているのだ。

北園克衛が好んでいたといわれる茶色にまつわるエッセイがある。これは戦後に書かれた。戦争の落とした影をぬぐいきれないままとはいえ、新しい日本・日本人・日本の服を創っていくことをあきらめないという希望に満ちている。

最近のデパアトの紳士服部や街のメンズウェアにはブラウン系統の生地が殆どない。まるで色盲の世界に迷い込んだとしか考えられない単調さである。たぶん現代の男子服には流行も趣味もなくなってしまったのかもしれない。（中略）ブラウンは決してフォオマルな服装の色ではない。しかし、日本人の皮膚によくマッチするばかりでなく、独特の品位とタフネスとをあわせもつシックな色である（シックな色ブラウン[31]）。

北園の作品は、リリカル・実験詩・和風と三種に分類して読まれることがある。決してこれまで正当な読み方をされることがほとんどなかった「和風」の作品群に対して、新しい読み方を提示している文章を二つ紹介して、

44

本章を終えることにしたい。

戦後の北園が自信をもって「郷土詩」にたびたび言及していることからは、純和風の「郷土詩」をナショナリズムとは完全に区別された詩群として認識していたことがうかがえる。『郷土詩論』は「郷土詩」という実験を推進されるために書かれたものであるから、この文章は時局の変化によって北園のライフスタイルが転回させられてしまった、のではなく、郷土詩のために自ら「変へた」と読むしかない。[*32]

北園克衛に「郷土詩論」や「風土」「家」というような詩を書かせてしまう大きな要因の一つには、こうした現実把握の力の乏しい低下にあったのだと僕は思っている。(中略)せっかくのミーイズムを頑固一徹に通すはずだったリアルなスタミナが切れてしまっているのだ。北園克衛はあくまでも想像のなかの幻想の「風土」「家」を自分の理想の共同体として弱々しく持ち出して描いてみせたにすぎないのである。[*33]

北園克衛の好んだ実験的虚構性は、和装も洋装と同じ線上にならべられる衣装だったのではないか。丁度、女性が和装と洋装を自由に着用し、画一化するまではその時差を楽しんでいるかのように（図3）。ファッションは、言葉であり、その語彙は古くなれば辞書の貯蔵庫に還って行く。じぶんの眼で発見する新しさ、無価値の価値。ファッションを語るとき北園はよく「シャルマン」という言葉を使った。これはフランス語で「魅力的な、素敵な」を意味する形容詞の charmant の片仮名表記だが、詩の作品のなかにもよく登場する。「パラソル」の代わりに「貝殻」でも「ヘリオトロオプ」でも「菫」でもよかったのかもしれない。

図3
大阪商船株式会社（現三井商船）の広報誌『海』（1937年1月，第64号）表紙には新しい洋行の時代の華やかな近代的風景のなかに一人後ろ姿の和装の女性が混じって描かれている．

けれども、どんな言葉を持ってくるのであれ、「いま」「ここ」で、もっとも「新しい」「シヤルマン」を創造しなければならなかった。つまり究極的にはどんな言葉を用いてもかまわないのだ。北園克衛はファッションという表現形式を借りて詩を作った。あるいは詩の中にファッションの方法を取り入れ実践していたといったほうがいいかもしれない。

詩とファッションの創作活動。新しい形＝無意味な意味を「着る」ことで、わたしたちのトルソーは、着せ替え可能な、ぼんやりとした輪郭の、いまここにある乗り物にすぎない、怒濤の時代環境の波に漂流し、行きつ戻りつ、回帰しながら、続いていく。

上衣の襟が不器用な羽根のやうに働くのだつた。ある種類の天使は純白な羽根がその背中についてゐる。そのために非常に適切な生活を生活するものである。ところがぼくらのやうに羽根が胸の上に生えてしまつた者は天使であることが一層みぢめにするのだ。僕らはこの不倖な羽根がじやまになつてなんでもない石につまづいて下らなく倒れる、僕らはみすぼらしく立ち上がる。やつと飛び立つたと思ふがいゝ。すると最う何も見ることができない。眼には廣漠とした青い空があるばかりだ。不倖な羽根かまたしても僕らを逆に吊り上げてゐるのだつた。[*34]

戸惑い・ためらいは好奇心・遊び心の内にある。モダニズム詩人も、振り子のように「服」の前で揺れている。

注

＊1　北園克衛『サボテン島』アオイ書房、一九三八年。

＊2　村上信彦『服装の歴史3』理論社、一九六九年、一四頁。

＊3　当時は「女性」と「婦人」の付いた雑誌名が混在している。女性史では、「婦人」は人間的な尊厳をもった存在との認識のなかで広がり、やがて近代日本ではより普遍的存在として「女性」へと推移していくが、女性解放運動とともに女性自身鹿野政直『婦人・女性・おんな――女性史の問い』岩波新書、一九八八年）は三つの用語について説明、人によって使い方ははっきりしていないようだ。

が「女」を好んで使うようになったと認識されている。

＊4　北園克衛『白のアルバム』厚生閣書店、一九二九年。

＊5　村野四郎（著者代表）『全詩集大成　現代日本詩人全集13』創元社、一九五五年、三九九頁。

＊6　鈴木貞美「海野弘『モダン都市東京』が切り拓いた地平」『Bookish』4号、二〇〇三年。

＊7　澤正宏・和田博文編『都市モダニズムの奔流』翰林書房、一九九六年、一三一—二五一頁。

＊8　鈴木貞美編『モダン都市文学X　都市の詩集』（平凡社、一九九一年）の「まえがき」から。

＊9　金澤一志『北園克衛の《圖形説》』日本記号学会第二三回大会関連展示資料、二〇〇三年。

＊10　島森路子『広告のなかの女たち』大和書房、一九八四年。

＊11　村上信彦は「キモノ」がいかに日本の女性の衣生活を長く支配したのかを女性解放という面からも考えている（『服装の歴史1-3』理論社、一九六九年）。

＊12　金澤一志、前掲資料。「近代型貴婦人装置」という指摘がある。

＊13　北園克衛『白色詩集』『文芸耽美』五月号、一九二七年（北園克衛未刊行詩篇』『現代詩手帖』一一月号、思潮社、二〇〇二年、七八—七九頁）。

＊14　北園克衛『白』とわたしの詩「かんざき」七月号、一九七四年（現代詩手帖』一一月号、思潮社、一九九〇年、七四—七六頁）。

＊15　北園克衛「ある夜の舞踏會」『鹿火屋』四六号、一九二二年（北園克衛未刊行詩篇』『現代詩手帖』一一月号、思潮社、二〇〇二年、七八頁）。

＊16　北園克衛『私の処女詩集』昭森社、一九六一年。

＊17　北園克衛「私の短詩」一九五一年（黄いろい楕圓』宝文館、一九五三年、一九四—一九九頁）。

＊18　北園克衛『天の手袋』春秋書房、一九三三年、二四〇頁。

＊19　北園克衛『火の童』昭森社、一九三六年。

＊20　北園克衛が関わった雑誌について整理しておきたい。北園のライフワークに同人誌『VOU』の編集・発行があるが、一九三五年に創刊され大戦を挟んで復刊して北園が亡くなる一九七八年まで続いた。他編集・発行を中心に行った雑誌は、伝説的な前衛詩誌『GGPG』にはじまり（二号から）『新領土』『新技術』『cendre』と名を変え発行）。そして『紀伊國屋月報』まで最終的には『レセンゾ』（レイアウト担当）『白紙』『MADAME BLANCHE』などがある。『VOU』と並ぶ仕事に紀伊國屋書店のPR誌の編集がある。『L'ESPRIT NOUVEAU』から『薔薇・魔術・学説』（レイアウト担当）、休刊をはさみ一九三〇年から三十年間関わった。エディトリアル・デザインだけでなく、文章の寄稿を含めると、様々なジャンルで夥しい数の印刷物に作品やエッセイを書き散らしていたようだ。この雑誌については書誌学的に重要な確認が

なされた話題になった。その経緯がよくわかるのが曾根博義氏のエッセイ「紀伊國屋書店のＰＲ誌」（『舢板』六号、二〇〇三年）である。佐々木桔梗氏の『日本の肉筆絵入り本 北園克衛を中心に』（書肆ひやね、二〇〇三年）で確認できる。

＊21 通巻4号刊行。最終発行が一九三四年四月、エスプリ社発行。佐々木桔梗『北園克衛とモダニズム雑誌群』プレス・ビブリオマーヌ（『色都市』別冊）、一九八一年。

＊22 北園克衛「Season の手帳」『紀伊國屋書店月報』七月号、一九五一年（『黄いろい楕円』に所収）。

＊23 「ＴＯＰが行く」『ESPRIT』四月号、一九三四年。

＊24 金澤一志「ペンネームのことでも」『KitKat＋』0号、キットカットプラス編集局、二〇〇二年。

＊25 長田恒雄編『六つの角度』『新女性手帖』出版文化集団、一九四六年。

＊26 『黄いろい楕圓』（宝文館、一九五三年）に一九五〇─五三年までのものが掲載されている（二三七─二六〇頁）。

＊27 Barthes, Roland, Système de la mode, Seuil, 1967, p. 240.（佐藤信夫訳『モードの体系』みすず書房、一九七二年、三二六頁）。

＊28 「今年の水着その他」『ECHO』三省堂、一九三六年。

＊29 『DANDY』「旅と読物」鉄道協力会、一九四八─四九年。

＊30 この詩集では、北園スタイルである格助詞「の」による線行の方法論確立について焦点が当てられることが多いが、戦前にモダニズム詩人として活躍した詩人による「戦後詩」としての読み直しが必要だと金澤は言う（『北園克衛的なるもの1』『現代詩手帖』思潮社、二〇〇三年）。

＊31 戦後の未刊行評論を集めた「破片と水晶」のなかの「色と生活」11から（鶴岡善久『北園克衛全評論集』沖積社、一九八八年、八九─九〇二頁）。

＊32 金澤一志「『VOU』と『VOU』のあいだ2（承前）」『C/O』care of press、二〇〇二年。

＊33 奥成達「北園克衛『郷土詩論』を読む21」『gui』vol. 21-57、一九九九年。

＊34 北園克衛「日日の貝殻」『天の手袋』春秋書房、一九三三年、二五七─二五八頁。

林芙美子『女家族』にみる日本の西洋文化の受容

本章では時代を遡り、日本の衣服が洋装化していく様子を、引き続き文学から眺めてみたい。明治・大正・昭和を生きた日本の女流作家林芙美子（一九〇三―五一）の小説『女家族』を取り上げ、日本の西欧文化の受容について衣服を中心に考察する。掲載誌では、洋画家森田元子（一九〇三―六九）による挿画からも当時の働く女性、通称「職業婦人」の簡素な洋服が確認される（図1）。林芙美子は波乱万丈の人生を送ったことがよく知られており、ここでは詳しく触れられないが、複雑な家族環境や激動の時代を生き抜いてきた女性である。同時代の婦人雑誌もあわせて参照しながら、背景となる時代や社会、都市の風景も探ることにする。

珍品＝洋装と和装の併用

東京の一軒家が舞台。家族構成は、母（雪江）、戦争未亡人である長女（時子）、次女（るい子）、三女（秀子）と長女の娘（麗子）の女五人。父は七年前に他界、長男はスマトラで戦死している。新しい時代への期待と敗戦国としての日本社会の現実の狭間に生きて揺れうごく女たちの心情が、リズミカルな会話展開を通して描写される。ある日曜日、るい子と秀子は炬燵にあたって「寫眞ブック」（アルバム）のなかの両親の結婚記念の写真を見ているシーンからはじまる。大正一一年撮影と記されたその写真の父親の衣装は、懐中時計・シャツ・帽子・靴の洋装と紋付き袴に羽織といった和装が入り交じっている。描写は――「縞の鳥打ち帽子をかぶり、紋付の羽織を

図1
遺作となった『女家族』（1946年8月号の『婦人公論』、林芙美子の追悼号になった）
挿画では職業婦人の簡素な洋装が確認される.

着てゐるのだが、袖が短いために、シャツの袖口が、二寸ばかりもはみ出てゐた。父は医者のはくやうな靴をはいてゐた。濱縮緬の帯をぐるぐる巻きにして、時計の鎖がさがってゐる。父は、鼻下に髭をはやしてゐた。まるで仁丹の廣告のような、立派な男ぶり」（一二二頁）。広告写真のような父の風貌に次女のるい子は吹き出してしまう。「珍品ね」という台詞を吐く。

るい子は「立ち入り禁止区域」というあだ名で呼ばれ、秘密主義で自由奔放なタイプの二四歳。縁談がもちあがっているが、妻子持ちと恋愛している。我が儘で母や姉とも折り合いが悪く、妹の秀子が一家のまとめ役を買ってでている。るい子は、「いまごろ、お見合ひなんて……馬鹿にしてるわ。（中略）お見合ひなんて、私、売り物ぢゃないことよ」と見合いを厭がるのに対し、長女の時子は好きな人の一人や二人はあるだろうが、結婚は別物だから「向かふを売り物だと思へばいいぢゃないの」と妹に苦言を呈する。そして、見合い相手の男に対して、妹が父の写真に対して言った珍品という同じ表現を使う――「一人前の男のひとが、今日まで、好きな女もなくて、見合い結婚を望んでるなんて、いまどき珍しい珍品だわ」（一五七頁）。時子は、夫が戦死し実家に戻り娘を育てているが、洋裁の内職をしている。時子は「珍品」にさらに「珍しい」という形容詞をつけて、結婚を合理的なものと見るように妹を諭そうとしている。

　見合い相手である關は、呉服屋の息子で銀行員をしており、野菜作りとヴァイオリンを趣味にしている。いつまた戦争が起こるかもわからない不安な時代、母親と秀子は「一年分の野菜を作る銀行員」の關を気に入っている。時子はるい子に「お芝居か、映畫でも観に行くつもりで、出掛けてみたらどうなの……気樂に行つておよば

れして来ればいいぢゃないの。こっちから断つたつていいんだもの……」（一五九頁）と、ミシンに油を差した手を拭きながら、見合い場所である銀座の資生堂へ行くことを促す。結局るい子は見合いをすっぽかし家出をしてしまう。

銀座はこの小説でたびたび登場する戦後復興期の日本で新しい時代を感じさせる憧れの場所。たとえば、この小説の書かれた時代の雑誌『主婦之友』に、「憧れの銀座詩画帖」*2という特集頁がある。

「行つてかえつてまたもどる／銀座八丁のショウウィンドウ／どこに　何があることを／知つているだけそれだけで／心ゆたかな　銀座娘（一銀座娘）、スターの集まる喫茶店／ここキャンドルの廣い窓／ビルの間もれて　青空が／いつも明るく　花やかに（「スターの集まる喫茶店」）、外國（あちら）の品が　夢のせて／いっぱい並んで招いてる／あのネクタイはあの方に／きつと似合うと思うけど／月給日まで　日が遠い（「お酒落横町」）など、すべて銀座の風景を描いたイラストが付いている。たとえショーウィンドウの舶来品を購入できなくても、その華やかな街へ出掛けるだけで、銀幕のスターに会うことができたり、恋を待つているような明るい町だと誌面で歌われている。

秀子は姉の見合い相手として關の写真を眺めていたときから、まだ見ぬ男に対して父性愛のようなものを感じている。時子は關を珍品と言つたが、父のように大真面目、「周囲にみかける男たちのやうに、てかてかしたお酒落でもない」、新しい時代を迎えようとしている社会のなかで珍しい存在であり、「珍品」とは結婚相手にふさわしい男の呼び名のようであつた。

ミシン

母雪江は三人の娘にそれぞれ好きなものを習わせて、結果として娘たちの仕事にもつながつている。時子は洋裁を、るい子と秀子は邦文タイプだつた。「まさか、出戻つてきた時子が、趣味で習わせてゐたミシンで、生活を支へるやうになろうなぞとは、夢にも思わなかつた」（一六六頁）という母雪江の言葉にもあるように、現在の

女家族＝滝澤家を一台のミシンが支えている。*3

秀子とるい子は外に出て会社勤めをしている職業婦人だ。*4 新しい時代の解放的な響きをもつこの職業婦人という言葉は、弁護士になりたかった夢を父が死んでからは捨て、実家に戻った後も家族を支える長女の時子が、自由で気楽そうな妹たちをうらやむような際にも使われる。「何一つ女らしいことも出来もしない癖に、一人前になったつもりでゐるのよ。世間の男が、面白半分に、からかってるのを知らないんだわ。だから、私、会社勤めの職業婦人って嫌いよ」（一六八頁）とるい子に言うシーンがある。

この時代の洋裁は高収入を得ることのできる女性の仕事だった。たとえば『洋裁の時代』*5 では当時の内職の仕立代と男性の初任給を比較している。この小説が執筆された一九五一（昭和二六）年の銀行員の初任給は三〇〇〇円、公務員が五五〇〇円。「これで、お仕立て代はいくら？」「さァ、いくら取るのかしら、三千圓位じゃない？」「高いわねえ……」（一三二頁）という秀子とるい子の会話からも、男の初任給額は女が一枚の外套を縫うのと同じあるいはさほど変わらないことがわかる。洋裁は女性が十分自立できる職業であった。るい子は、給料から食費のみを入れ、秀子は給料の全部を母へ渡して小遣いと電車賃を貰っているが、長姉の時子の稼ぎは二人の給料とは雲泥の差だと推測できる。

『主婦之友』には、「内職増収の体験（東京）」*6 という頁があり、読者の投稿の他に仕事の広告なども掲載されている。戦時中の物資不足の時代は針仕事は必要に迫られたものであったが、戦後はその技術を職業として十分活かすことができた。たとえば読者の投稿によれば、「この仕事を始めたのは、たった一人の子を戦争に送り出した昭和一八年のことでした。子供は終戦まもなく無事帰還しましたが、子供に少しでも経済上の負担をかけないために、つづけてやっております」と裁縫仕事の重要性は体験談を通して語られる。

ミシンは高価であったから、大事に使うために事細かな工夫が説かれた特集記事も掲載されている。『婦人倶楽部』の付録内では一〇頁にもわたる分量で、ミシンの部位の名称から故障時の対処の仕方まで丁寧に解説されており、「ミシンの知識がないために、一寸した故障がわからずそのままにしておいたり、機械を無理して部分

品を損めてしまったりしては、本当にもったいないことです」[*7]と、自分でメンテナンスするように勧めている。

また、ミシン会社の広告もこの時代の婦人雑誌には頻繁に掲載される。

時子の身体は常にミシン台を軸に家の中を運動する。「ミシン台にとりついたまま」「ミシン台を離れ、ああと溜息をつ」き、「ミシン台を手荒く片づけ」て部屋を出て行く。るい子が時子をおもしろおかしく真似するときにも足踏みミシンを動かすような足の動きをしている。製作するのが西欧化スタイルの衣装なら、それを製作する日本人の身体もミシンを通して西欧化していく。

『洋裁の時代』によれば、内職は「主たる収入」である場合と「家計補助」の場合とがあったようだ。「ミシンの内職で、家族の生活の大半をささえてゐなければ、滝澤の家はいまごろは、もっとひどくおちぶれてゐるはずである。時子はるい子に似て、とても勝気だったので、どんなに気分の悪い時でも、ミシンを踏まない日はなかった」(一四一頁)とあるように、女性だけで営まれる家族生活にあってはその生活費の足しになる副業ではなく、常にミシンを踏んで働いて稼ぐ主収入であることがわかる。女家族の稼ぎ頭の長女は父の役割をしている。「仕事の手順で、食事が遅れる場合も、みんな姉を待つために、母がわざと、食事をゆっくり支度」(一三〇頁)するという描写もあり、るい子はそんな家が気に入らなかった。父の位置が長女に変わった以外は、封建的な旧い体質の日本の家庭の風景はなかなか変わらない。

更生服

時子が注文を受けて製作中の「ラクダの外套」が部屋の壁に掛かっている。るい子も秀子もその外套を羽織ってみたい衝動に駆られる。「でも、型が気に入らないわ。せっかくの布地、時子姉さんの手にかかっては、修道院みたいになるわね……」(一三一頁)。手に届きそうにない高価な服であることに対して負け惜しみを言いながら、るい子はどんな女が着るのだろうと空想せずにはおれない。秀子も、いつになったら、こんないい外套が着られるのだろうと、もう何年も着ている古い自分の外套をみじめに思う。

「いっそ、あれを裏返して、型をかへてみようかとも考へるけれども、さうするには、裏地を新しく買い変へねばならない」(一四四頁)という秀子の台詞からもわかるように、この時代は古着を利用して新しい服に仕立てることは珍しいことではなかった。

『主婦之友』誌上の「洋裁の誌上講習」では、外国人デザイナーによる日本人向けの洋装が紹介されている。和服布から作られる洋服は、アメリカ人デザイナーが日本婦人向けに作ったスタイルであり、「フランス風の上品なツーピースドレス」や「プリンセス型の清楚なワンピース」として紹介され、詳しい型紙とカラーのデザイン画が裏表紙を彩る。「乏しい衣生活の中にも新春らしい装いを工夫していただきたい」「デザインは、どれも和服から更生しやすい型ばかりです」と唱われ、戦時中リメイクに慣れた日本人が更生服の感覚で気軽に洋装を楽しめるような提案がなされる。

を説くための婦人雑誌の目玉は、別冊になることもある付録の型紙であった。和服をつぶして洋服に仕上げたり、デザインだけ新しく変えたり。その方法

「女家族」は非常につつましい生活を送っている。日常着は大変地味だ。るい子は空色の「ジャケツ」、秀子は紺の上着を着ているが、二人は揃いのグレーのスラックスをはいている。るい子は妹に、「世の中じゃ、つまらない女が、素晴らしい身なりをしてるけど、金次第だわね。秀子ちゃんも、早く、お金持ちの旦那さまをみつけることだわ……」(一三二頁)と言う。夜遅く酔って家へ帰り母親に頬をぶたれたるい子は、次の日に控えていた見合いの場所へは行かずにあてつけのように家出をする。三人姉妹の中では新しい女として描かれる。けれども裕福な家庭に嫁に行き素晴らしい身なりをさせてもらうしかないという受動的な女性観を拭いきれないでいる。こころの方はどうだろうか。内面は和風の情緒を抱える女性の正直さが、男性の洋装化とは違い遅れた理由なのではないか。社会も、受容の自然なスピード＝和装と洋装の共存をながらく許したのだ。

「女のお勤めってものは、秀子ちゃんのやうな、おとなしい人には無理かも知れないわね」という台詞にもあるように、女が社会に出て働くことの厳しさも語られる。「みんな、いいなりしたのが、わんさとゐるんだもの、

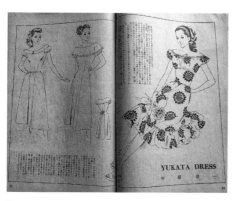

図2
中原淳一「YUKATA DRESS」(『スタイル』1948年7月号)

私だって、時々、真面目に勤めてるのが、馬鹿馬鹿しくなる時もあるのよ。時には、誰も知らない賑やかなところで、ストリップでもしようかと思ふ時あるわ。いっそ着ているものを脱いでしまいたい——実際ストリップはこの小説が書かれた一九五〇年頃に日本で大流行していた。人は少なくとも社会では服を着ないわけにはいかないし、服を着ていないと無防備であることがわずらわしい。姉の時子は「天衣無縫よ。少し、世の中へ出て揉まれてみるといいんだわ」(一六八頁)と、呑気な世間知らずの職業婦人であるるい子に嫌みを言っていた。

新しい服は古い布地で作られる。経済的に余裕がなければ自作しか方法がない。この小説の書かれた頃の婦人雑誌は「ぬうところの少ない夏の流行婦人服」「経済裁(断)の三ヤールの婦人服」「浴衣一反で作った涼しい姉妹お揃い服」など、「経済」がキーワードだ。今でいえば古着やリサイクルは単なる流行になってしまう。戦後代のファッションデザイナーとしても人気の高かった中原淳一は、を引きずっている貧しい時代は、何を着るのかは切実な問題であり、だからこそ身なりによって人は容易に判断されてしまう。新しい時くつろいだ湯上がりに着る華やかな形の日本衣文化を残そうとしている。「ゆかたは日本のきものの傑作である」と述べ、必ずしもゆかたで作らなくてもいい「ゆかたの感覚で着るどれす」を提案している(図2)。

既製服が足りない時代、女性は手に針を持ち、あるいはミシンを使い、型紙を用いて服を作る。編み物も同様に流行していた。小説の中でいつもミシンを踏んでいるのは時子だが、三女の秀子はよく編み針を動かしている。冒頭ではソックスを編んでいたし、結婚の申し込みを承諾するときにもできあがったばかりの手編みのジャケ

ットを羽織って出掛ける。現在でもポピュラーなセーターやカーディガンのようなニット製品に加えて、ジャケットなどの重衣料も手編みされた時代。婦人雑誌はたびたび編み物の特集頁を組み、付録の別冊になることも多かった。

身支度

　母の雪江はつねに娘の「身支度」^{*10}について心配している。見合いの前日は二人の娘達に着せる服装のことをあれこれ考えて時間が過ぎていく。それは婚姻のために必要となる結納のお返しや結婚衣装にまで至る。「もし、結婚がうまく、まとまるとして、式服は和服にして、すべて貸衣装で間に合わせるとしても、先方へ持って行かせるものとしては、新しい箪笥と、寝具だけは、何とか買ってやらなければならない。迎えようとしている先方は呉服屋なので、あれこれと、新しい着物をつくってやる必要もあるまい。何しろ、女手一つで今日までやって来た身には、娘一人をかたづけるという事は、大変な出費であり、箪笥と寝具さへも、なかなか思ふやうにはつくれない」（一五五頁）──先方に会う前から身支度の取り越し苦労ぶりだ。新しい時代はすぐそこに来ているけれど、母は婚礼に関して伝統的な日本式にこだわっていることがわかる。また、「昔と違って、新時代なのだから、いい縁さへあれば、みんな他へ片づいてくれるといいのだ」（一五五頁）と言いつつも、なかなか新時代というわけにはいかないのだ。

　一方、關に会いに行くことになった秀子の身支度も十分な時間をもてない。狭い我が家にあっては遮られがちで、なかなかその場所は空かず自由に使えない。日々の身支度の場所＝鏡台の前は、たかったが、時子は鏡台のそばのミシン台の前に坐ってゐるし、るい子は、長火鉢の前で、ビギンザビギンを鼻歌でうたひながら、足の爪を切っている。秀子は何処へも坐りやうがな「多少のおしゃれはして行きい」（一九〇頁）い。少し残ったやかんの湯を洗面器にあけて、鏡も見ないで蒸しタオルで、顔や首や腕などの体を丁寧に拭くという簡単な支度だった。家族のもめ

　秀子は三姉妹のなかで最も遅く生まれてきたが、それゆえ新しい時代に最も近いのかもしれない。

事を仲裁し給料を全額家に入れながら、料理作りを「うっとり」楽しめたり、休日の留守番を一人で引き受けたり、編み物にも夢中になれる。縁談のような特別な機会でも「この間、編み上げた水色のジャケッ」を着て「自分で、古いのを裏返して縫った、灰色のスプリングコートを羽織って」出掛ける。地味で堅実な中にも、生活を自由に楽しみ、新しい時代のなかでバランスを取った理想的な女として描かれている。

戦後は日本女性の美点が失われておりもっと内省的であれと婦人雑誌では若い女性へ苦言が呈される――「戦争からこのかた、何といふ乱脈さであらう」と嘆き「派手で享楽的な」新しい女の態度に「憤懣」する一方、「地味な姿態」だが「一つのことを深く正しく判断して進んでいく」ことのできる「初々しい娘らしさ」を持った女性の存在を喜んでいる。

秀子の婚約者關はどうだろう。支度なんてどうでもいいことを秀子に告げ、「お母さんがそんなにおっしゃるのなら、一度、僕はお母さんにお目にかかりたいですね。――女の人は、年をとると、はたの事も考えるのはあたりまへなんですよ。家の母だって、口では無欲な事を云ってはゐますが、やっぱり、はたの事は気にかける性分だから。僕と貴女とで、うまく、考えればいい。いっぺん、これは、小畑のおじさんを引っ張りだして、一度、みんなでお目にかかって、話しあへば何とかなると思ふ。『珍品』の關は、二人の母の顔をつぶすことなく仲人にも気を配り、結婚成立に向けた賢明の策をうかがう。古い身支度にこだわらないが新しい考えを急に取り入れず、まわりに気を配り現実を臨機応変に調整して事を進めるべく、過渡期にある時代の日本の理想的な男として描かれる。

新しい女

　鏡台の前で顔にクリームを塗って念入りにマッサージし、美しく化粧してるい子はデートに出掛ける。この時代のクリームとはコールドクリームと呼ばれる化粧品のことで、メイク落としやマッサージ、ナイトクリームとしても使用できる万能なもの。また美白ブームは現代と同じだが、高価な輸入品の美白化粧品などが不足してい

る時代、白い肌になるための必死の工夫が婦人雑誌で提案されている。たとえば美白にいい食品や、白い肌を作るための黒砂糖を使った洗顔法など、女優が使う化粧品を紹介するところも、現代の女性ファッション誌と大差はない。

るい子は身支度を終えると、ハンドバッグから煙草を出して一服つける。恋愛している大坪、見合い相手の關の二人の男性以外に煙草を吸う人間は、女家族のなかではるい子だけだ。彼女のバッグにはいつも煙草が入っており、身支度の必需品。喫煙シーンもたびたび描かれる。一方、秀子を見初めた關は、秀子が煙草が嫌いであることを知り、好意的な感想をもらしている。小説が書かれた一九五一年は新しいデザインが評判になった「ピース」が爆発的に売れ、喫煙がさらに拡がった時代でもある[12]。

新しい女として描かれる次女のるい子の身支度は、いつも手際よく首尾よくこなされる。母と喧嘩して家を出る際には、一寸した身のまわりのものをボストンバッグ一つにまとめるといった手軽な身支度だ。男の仕事が終わるのを待って自分の手荷物をロッカーに預けて身軽になり、映画を見て時間を潰した後、大坪と行きつけの居酒屋で会う。自分の身を引き受けてくれることを期待していた男は、ひどくうろたえて、しどろもどろになっている。大坪はるい子の当分の生活費は準備してきていたが、るい子の希望でそれはその日の宿屋の代金に消えた。

るい子は大坪に決断を迫るが、暖昧さを慎重さで繕い、身勝手な男の煮え切らない態度に別れを決める。「さっき起きて、身支度をすると、ハンドバッグから櫛を取り出してかきつけ、コンパクトで鼻の頭を叩いた」(一七六頁)――このようなるい子の身の振る舞いは潔く見え、それは身支度の手際の良さからもうかがわれる。大坪との別れを決めた後は家へ帰るに帰られず、友人の家にしばらく寝泊りする。

秀子の縁談話は母との間でのみ慎重に進められている気配を察し、姉妹たちは気が気でなかった。妹の幸福を願う気持ちと、息苦しい家から一足先に逃げられることへの羨望も入り交じり姉妹の激しい口喧嘩が始まる。

「何だったら、この家を売って、みんなで分けて、解散してもいい事よッ」(二一六頁)と、るい子が口火を切る。

長女時子は常に正論を吐いているようにも見えるが、自分の要求を押し通すことはなく、至極現実的である。

まさに「私は一家の家長みたいなもの」である。一方新しい女＝次女るい子は別れた男の子どもを妊娠していることが発覚、一人で産み育てる覚悟をして「私は私の巣をつくる」と家を出て独立する宣言をする。もともと家に執着がなく封建的な家を嫌って自由になりたがっており、家を売るべきだと提案をする。末っ子の「秀子ちゃんだけでも幸福になってほしいわ」（三二二頁）という言葉は結婚の夢を妹に託しているようにも響き、「みんな、自分の運命ってあるものなのね」と「自分の運命」という言葉をもって個人を尊重しようという姿勢を表現している。「このまま、みんなで一つ家にゐたところで、みんな生埋めのような状態になることが果たしていいことか。るい子は自分の希望や主張は合理から成り立っていると信じて疑わない。新しい女は新しい家を求めてやまないのだった。

ニュールック

　フランス人デザイナーのクリスチャン・ディオールの「ニュールック」と呼ばれる新しい女性服のシルエットは、一九四七年に発表されて以来日本にもアメリカ経由で少し遅れて入ってきた。日本の女たちもこのパリの新しいファッションに夢中になった。五〇年頃からは当時最大の娯楽であった映画のなかのファッションに興味と関心が向けられ「シネモード」として大流行する。林芙美子は昭和七（一九三二）年にパリに滞在していた。多くの映画を鑑賞し、ファッション雑誌を購入している記録が日記に残されている。[*13]

　小説のなかでも洋画がたびたび登場する。叔母が出した結婚広告によって貧しい娘が医者と結婚し砂漠を旅する『憂愁夫人』（セルジュ・ド・ポリニイ監督、一九四六年）を観た三女秀子は、冒険が自由にこころみられる国フランスに憧れを抱く。『自転車泥棒』（ヴィットリオ・デ・シーカ監督、一九四八年）は、るい子が見合いの当日に新宿で恋愛相手の大坪に会うまでの時間潰しに観る映画で、捨てられて侮られているような自分の現在の境遇を、映画と重ね合わせながら観ている。

図3
『1933年スタイルブック』婦人画報新年臨時増刊号
大判でカラー頁も多く，外国のミシンの広告宣伝ページからはじまる．

妊娠が発覚して会社をやめたるい子は、弁当を持ってオフィス街の公園で時間を潰すのが常であった。それを知って心配し休みを取って一緒に出掛けてくれた秀子のやさしさに触れ、救われた気持ちになる。そのときも二人で映画を観ようということになった。有楽町の映画館へ入って『レベッカ』（アルフレッド・ヒッチコック監督、一九四〇年）を観る。家政婦をしていた貧しい娘が大邸宅の主人と結婚をする映画。「こんな、夢のやうな事は、まづ、日本にはない事だわね。外国だからあるンでせうね」（二二七頁）とるい子はささやく。秀子はるい子の人目につくやうな美貌を認めているが、こんな映画のように報われるとどんなに素敵だろうと姉を想い、「自分達の年齢が、この戦争をとほってきて、みんなみじめに、じめついて来ているのを悟るだけの映画」（二二八頁）だと思う。

新しい時代といっても、現実は映画のなかだけのこと、日本には、少なくとも自分の住む世界にはないことを憂う。二人の服装は着古したネイヴィブルーのスーツで、いかにも職業婦人の姿である。そんな地味な若い姉妹には街の洋装が憧れの世界の住人として映る。「もはや戦後ではない」時代をむかえるため、準備を整え、ファッションも新しい時代へ突入していく。洋装や自動車は素敵な憧れの西洋文化の象徴であった。るい子のこんな台詞からもそれはよくわかる――「私、毎日、ここへ着て、

寝転んで、綺麗な自動車の通るのみてるの……。西洋人の生活って、私達のやうに、みみっちくなくて、素的なのね。外面的には、幸福な人種ね。私達も、こんど、生まれ変わる時には、白人種に生まれて来ることだわ……」（二二七頁）。

「外面的には、幸福な人種ね」という言葉は、外面がいかに大事か、金次第で何でも揃う世の中を嘆くようだ。時子の仕事に利用しているスタイルブックを眺めては「素晴らしいニュールックのスタイルが、並んでゐる。美しい女優の寫真が・違ふ世界の女達のやうに、ほほゑみをかけてゐる。一度だって、こんな美しい洋服を着るやうな事はないのだ」（二三一頁）と、所在なく頁をめくるしかなかった。スタイルブックとは大判のスタイル画集で、西洋のファッションがカラーで紹介され、洋裁の資料集としても使われていた（図3）。ニュールックは銀幕や誌面のなかの新しい女であり、女家族たちには遠い憧れであった。

結び——女家族

母と喧嘩し家を出たるい子がなかなか帰ってこない間、母も姉妹も複雑な感情を抱えていたが、心配せずにはいられない。五日後に家に戻ってきた際にも、手放しで暖かく迎えるというわけにはいかないようだ。「みんな、おなかのなかぢゃァ、よろこんでるのよ。（中略）肉親ってものは、おせじが云えないのね……」（一八六頁）——三女秀子が割って入り、やさしい言葉をかけるのだった。

小説の冒頭でも、自由のない家を煙たがるるい子に対して秀子は「いまんところ、滝澤の家は、女ばかりで、一番、気楽な時代じゃないの？　お母さまも、お父さままで男はこりごりだって、とても、いまは気があって、のんびりしていい」（二二七頁）と姉になだめ聞かせている。「外面」を取り繕う必要のない、好きな事を思い通りにお互い言い合える、活気に満ちた女家族の光景は、この小説の最大の魅力でもある。

前節で述べたが、るい子は個人が生きられる新しい家を求める新しい女として描かれてはいるが、家や結婚に対する考え方は制度にいまだ縛られている。この時代、家とは制度であり、家族はその制度を作る構成員であり、

図4
1931年12月パリ14区の古書店前で洋装で
佇む有名な写真

制度は紙の上のもので実態や中味がなくても形式として存在している。[*14]

恋愛相手の大坪を忘れられない心情は拭い切れず、相手の家庭を自分が壊すことはできないという心にある真実の声に耳を傾けていく。るい子の友人は、実のところるい子が結婚という制度に固執していることを指摘し、つねに控えめでおとなしかった妹は姉が古風な考えをなぜ疑わないのか痛快な問いかけをする。読者にとって最も「新しい女」が抱える矛盾と葛藤。家探しは困難を極めていく。「新しい女」とは、イメージなのかもしれない。身なりや振る舞いは外国風で、購入したり作ったりからだは繕えても、こころの方はどうなのだろう。結婚神話やしかるべき身支度はこの時代に限ったものではなく現在も根強い。

本小説は絶筆に終わっているが、男と別れて一人子どもを身籠もったるい子はどうなっていくはずだったのか。それとも実家に戻り女家族で喧嘩しながらも仲良くやっていくのか。

新しい女として生きるため一人新しい家を作っていくはずだったのか。

林芙美子は画家の夫と子ども（養子）、そして実母や養父の生活まで筆一本で支えた。海を越えパリの空の下では叶わぬ恋もしたが、家族を捨てる選択肢は持てなかった。一人っ子で雑談を言える兄弟姉妹はなく、幼いときから働き、のんびりと過ごす娘時代もなかった。放浪するように職場を転々とした体験から、身支度は簡易で手際のいいものだったに違いない。一九三一年から秋から三カ月程暮らしたフランス・パリでは「流行マガジン三部」や「コルセット」[*15]を購入している。着物で暮らした異国の地、新しいファッションに触れてどのような気持で過ごしたことだろう（図4）。小説を通して、当時の日本人の西洋文化への憧れを描くとともに、手放しで受容す

るにはためらいや抵抗を隠しきれない現実感覚を、女家族のそれぞれの思いで語らせている。

注

＊1　『女家族』は、林芙美子の絶筆作品で『漣波』（中央公論社、一九五一年）に収録されている。林芙美子にはもう一つの絶筆作品として『めし』が知られている。一九五一（昭和二六）年四月から朝日新聞紙上で連載され、後に成瀬巳喜男が原節子を起用して映画化された。『女家族』は、その一足早い同年一月から『婦人公論』紙上で同題の連載小説が始まり、こちらも一九六一年に映画化された。

＊2　『主婦之友』一九五一年七月号、一一五―一二二頁。

＊3　アンドルー・ゴードン『ミシンと日本の近代化――消費者の創出』大島かおり訳、みすず書房、二〇一三年。アメリカがオリジナルである「シンガーミシン」は日本ではヨーロッパを通して輸入されて大きなシェアを獲得するが、大戦を経た後は日本製の「ジャノメミシン」に取って代わられていく。洋装化が早かった紳士服は既製服市場の定着も早かったが、女性や子ども服は家庭で裁縫されることが多かった。家計を助けつつ、お洒落や流行を楽しむこともできた。内職仕事の需要が高まると共に普及したミシンの存在は、女性の自立に大きく貢献した。

＊4　わたしたちの歴史を語る会編・著『婦人雑誌からみた一九三〇年代』同時代社、一九八六年、一一〇―一二一頁。一九三四年から女性も働いた、国を支えるべきだとされた。

＊5　『婦人公論』誌上で働く婦人に関する記事が増えてきたという。昭和初期の不況と戦争の長期化によって、タイピストや事務員として女性も働いた、国を支えるべきだとされた。

＊5　小泉和子『洋裁の時代』ＯＭ出版、二〇〇四年、五一頁。

＊6　『主婦之友』一九四八年新年号、五四頁。

＊7　『婦人倶楽部』一九五二年二月号付録、六三頁。

＊8　『主婦之友』一九四八年新年号、四五―五〇頁。

＊9　『主婦之友』一九五一年七月号付録。

＊10　身支度に関する資料としては『婦人倶楽部』の付録として、書籍の体裁で発行された『新時代　縁談と婚禮一式』（一九三〇年一月、大日本雄辯會講談社）が参考になる。調度品や衣装などの値段を掲載している結婚費用について書かれた章には「身分、家柄、財産、風習などから、色々と考慮を廻らして、禮に缺けず、俗に媚びず、虚榮に走らず、識者の笑を招くことなく、寧ろ稱讃を博するよう、時代にふさわしい改善味を加へて、大いに有意義に行ふことを理想としたいものであります」（三二九頁）とある。

＊11　『婦人春秋4』一九四六年、三六頁。

＊12　『日本のレトロ』織部企画、一九八七年、八六頁。

＊13　今川英子編『林芙美子　巴里の恋』中央公論新社、二〇〇四年。

＊14　本小説が執筆される五年前には「民法改正要綱」が発表された。新憲法では、夫婦の権利の平等と個人の権威の尊重を基礎にして家作りの提案がなされ、戸主を筆頭とする封建制の廃止を意味した。成年に達すれば、父母と別居して独立して生計を営む際には、新しい戸籍を編成することも認められる。『婦人之友』誌上では、大学教授や議員などを集めて「家を語る」というテーマでこの改正案をめぐる座談会が開かれている（一九四六年、第四〇巻第一〇号、三―一五頁）。新しい法律で個人の自由に対する考え方の発展があっても「習俗として残るものはなかなか変わらない」、「主として経済力がなくて、ただ道徳力だけでは「家」といふ制度の出来ることも制度をもちつづけて行くことも出来ない」という議論に留まっている。

＊15　一九三一年九月に起きた満州事変後日本円は暴落して林芙美子は慎ましく生活していたようだが現地の雑誌や下着は贅沢な買い物である。一円が一二・五フランで、当時日本の公務員の初任給は七五円とのこと。『林芙美子　巴里の恋』中央公論新社、二〇〇四年、七、一四、四五頁。

第四章 現代イギリスファッションにおけるキモノ文化受容

洋装は少し位よごれていてもよい、よごれているとかへって顔とか脚とかが、なまなましい本来の気を吐いて見せるが、和装のよごれはすその方から木枯らしが吹き、しぐれの雨がしょぼつく

——室生犀星「着物」[*1]

前の二つの章で日本に本格的に洋服が入って来る時代について文学の分野から眺めた。逆に、日本の民族衣装である着物が外国に出ることはあったのか。あったとすればいつどのように渡ったのか。本章では、まず欧州における受容の歴史的な流れをおさえた後、現代イギリスファッションを例にとり着物の変化・発展について考察する。

着物の近代化＝キモノを視野に入れ、近年のイギリスでの展示作品を紹介する。最後に、実際にどのように着物が着用されているのか、その現状を調査する。着物を市場に送り出す人々や、着用者とその着用方法に焦点をあてる。日本の民族衣装が国外へ渡ることは、他国にとっては新しい美意識や価値観の導入となり、また本来の日本の着物の方もデザイン・技術・着用法などの面で異文化からのきっかけとなる。双方向的に発展していく衣装'Kimono'の可能性を考えながら、着物をとりまく現代ファッションの環境と文化的な有り様について探ってみよう。

1 欧州へ──着物の輸出

一八五一年にヴィクトリア女王の命により、ロンドンのハイドパークで世界初の万国博覧会が開かれた。その後一八六二年にサウス・ケンジントンで大博覧会が開催される。一九世紀の万国博覧会はフランス開催のイメージが一般的に定着しているがイギリスが旗揚げの役割を担っていた。

イギリスでのこの二度目の博覧会時に、江戸後期の日本の陶器や茶道具などが欧州ではじめて紹介されたようだ。[*2] 着物も何らかの形で一緒に渡ったのではないだろうか。第一回の博覧会時と同様、産業革命後の最新の技術や科学文明の産物を紹介することが内容の中心だったが、この一八六二年の大博覧会はウィリアム・モリスの装飾的デザインや最先端の写真技術や音楽文化など芸術方面へも展開している。日本の幕府や藩が正式に万国博覧会に参加するようになるのは一八六七年の第二回パリ万博からである。

一八七四年にロンドンのリージェント・ストリートにリバティ商会が設立され現在のデパートの基礎を作る。一八九〇年代には、パリを中心に華開いたアール・ヌーヴォー様式を紹介し、それを後押ししていく形でテキスタイルを中心にした商品が販売されるようになっていく。リバティは、東方の手工芸品としてのシルクをその展開の主軸に置いて、ペルシャ・インド・中国・日本から生地を輸入し、絹や絹の商品化に乗り出していく。商品を魅力的な芸術作品のように展示する手法でリバティは成功をおさめるが、ラファエル前派やモリスらの自然主義的絵画芸術運動の流れとも連動していた。

日本のキモノは、リバティで取り扱われて販売された。「ティー・ガウン」(図1)という商品名で室内で着用されるドレッシング・ガウンとしての販売が主であった。リバティは東方のシルクをその経営の主軸に置いていた。この時期積極的に輸出していた日本の商店は、絹を衣装の形で製品化するという戦略で海外進出を軌道にのせていく。[*3] プライヴェートな空間で着用する特別なねむり衣として人気を得るようになる。ファッションに興じ

る上流階級のあいだで、高品質で肌触りよく光沢のある神秘的な東洋の室内着は不動の位置を獲得していく。江戸か

また、パリで流行していたデザイナーのポール・ポワレのキモノスタイルがイギリスにも入ってくる。[*4]江戸か

ら明治期にかけ日本も積極的に参加するようになったパリの万国博覧会以降、フランスでは日本の絵画や工芸品

を通してその美意識や芸術様式がジャポニスムとして流行し、アール・ヌーヴォーが生まれて華開く時代。絵画

に着物姿の女性が多く描かれることもあってファッションの分野にも自然に伝播し、ポワレのデザインもジャポ

ニスムの影響を受けていた。

図1

Tea Gown designed by Charles Worth, 1900

©Victoria and Albert Museum

パリ万博のファッションパビリオンは、イギリス人デザイナーのチャールズ・ワース（ウォルト）が企画担当

者の一人として携わっていた。その頃すでにウォルトはパリ発の世界的ファッションデザイナーとしてメゾンを

開いて大成功をおさめていた。今日のオートクチュールの基礎を作ったとされ、ファッション史にも大きな発展

をもたらしたデザイナーとして知られている。パリ・コミューンが立ち上がり政情不安となった一八七一年頃に

は店を畳んでいる。ポワレはそのイギリス人デザイナーの下で働いていたことがあった。英仏服飾文化交流史の

なかで大きな貢献をするべく、ジャポニスムという運動は重要な位置を占めた。

先述したように、キモノは西洋ではまず室内着として着

用された。ティー・ガウンあるいはドレッシング・ガウン

と呼ばれるこの贅沢な寝間着はプライヴェートな場で身に

着けられるが、そのとき女性はコルセットと呼ばれる下着

を装着しない。西洋服飾史の必要悪でもあった身体美の徹

底的追求の果実でもあるこの下着から、ヨーロッパの女性

が解放されたのには、キモノの存在が大きく貢献している。

一方、着物はエキゾティックで神秘的でエロティックな衣

装でもあった。からだと自然に調和して着心地がよく、ま

た特別な気分にもなれる衣装として欧州で受容されていく。

ジャポニスムが西洋絵画に及ぼした影響は、モチーフの主客転倒（人物ではなく、キモノ絵柄や屏風や家具の美しさを詳細に描く）、独特の色彩表現やアシメトリーな構図、自然と調和するデザイン、などがあげられる。[*5] 絵画至上主義からの脱却として、当時台頭していたアール・デコのムーヴメントとも連動していく。日本の美意識や表現形式は、欧州が抱えていた閉塞的状況や既存のスタイルの限界を乗り越えるきっかけになって受容され、絵画芸術からファッションの分野に伝播するのは自然の流れで、衣装のスタイルもその影響を受けていく。日本女性が描かれただけでなく、西洋人が着物を身につけている絵画も多く描かれた。

ジャポニスムのファッションは、一九〇三年にポール・ポワレが発表したキモノコートがその代表としてあげられる。たっぷりととられた特徴的な袖（キモノスリーヴ）にゆったりとしたシルエットのからだを締め付けないドレスは、新しいデザインとして流行する。少し遅れてマドレーヌ・ヴィオネのバイアスカットが登場し、これはキモノの直線裁断から発想を得たことでよく知られている。

はじめてジャポニスムという言葉がフランス語の辞書に登場したのが一八七六年、[*6] 万国博覧会での浮世絵に描かれた日本女性やピエール・ロティの文学作品『お菊さん』、[*7] また川上音二郎・貞奴一座の舞台の観劇を通して、日本の民族衣装が知られるようになり、後期印象派の西洋絵画にも着物姿の日本女性が描かれる。絵画や工芸品のスタイルがジャポニスムとして受容され、アール・ヌーヴォーの名の下で芸術運動に発展し、ポワレもその流れの中でファッションの分野の中心的人物となっていく。日本の民族衣装が受容されるのは欧州の熱狂的な日本趣味からであり、それはイギリスにも及んでイスラム圏やロシアを含んだ東方文化の一つとして捉えられていた。

ここで、万博の前の日本の鎖国時代の前後に遡る東西文化交流について、少々補足をしておきたい。長崎や鹿児島など九州地方を中心にオランダやポルトガルとの貿易が栄えた時代である。

江戸期に入り海路で大阪堺の港から江戸に舶来物が到着し、宗教や文化が伝播するとともにその交流がさかんになった。幕府がオランダ総督に着物を献上し、それはオランダの美術館に「ヤポンセロッケン」という名で現

在保存されている。また、西欧への日本文化の紹介者として重要人物の一人に、ポルトガル人――イエズス会宣教師で日本に長く居住したルイス・フロイスがいる。フロイスは一六世紀に日本の衣装について下記の指摘をしている。日本の着物と帽子は同じデザインで男にも女にも用いることができ（性差を超える）、一年を通して流行に惑わされることがないこと（不易流行）、また袖が長く全体としてからだにゆるやかに身につけられ（自然との調和）、上着よりも下着や裏地に良いものを身に着けること（新しい発想や手法）など。すでに西洋の衣服との違いを認識し、またそれに感嘆もしていた。

2　展示1：近代化とキモノ

イギリスで現在どのようにキモノが位置付けられ、また実際にどのように受容されているのかを見ていこう。

近年の美術館での展示からその内容を紹介したい。

日本の伝統文化としてのキモノは、ロンドンのヴィクトリア＆アルバート美術館（以下V&A）で紹介されている。V&Aでは Toshiba Gallery という日本コーナーで数点ではあるが常設展示されている。来館者らは漆の工芸品や茶道具、日本刀、根付けのコレクションなどとともに着物を鑑賞することができる。二〇〇五年から二〇〇六年にかけて、この Toshiba Gallery のスペースを使い、八カ月間（入れ替え二回）着物を特別展示していた。'Fashioning Kimono', と題され、キモノの近代化に焦点を当てた内容になっている。

色柄デザインが欧米の影響を受けていると見られるもの、鮮やかな色彩の大柄な模様のキモノが印象的であった（図2）。このようなキモノはまず輸出向けに製造されたのだろう。薔薇を大胆に配したキモノは幾何学的な配置で明らかにアール・デコの影響を受けていることがわかる。アール・ヌーヴォー風の濃い桃色の葡萄の蔓模様などもその顕著な例である。また明治以降化学染料が導入されることで、これまでなかった濃い桃色や日本の古代紫とは違う鮮やかな紫色の表現が可能になる。本国イギリスの紫色の画期的な染め技法も紹介されていた。

図 2

Kimono, Japan Made, 1912-1930
©Victoria and Albert Museum

このようなデザインは、外国人好みの色柄であるというだけにとどまらない。国内向けの新しいキモノのデザインとしても製作されるようになり、主に大正時代に流行した。もともとアール・ヌーヴォー様式は日本の調和的自然観や美意識から新しく生まれた芸術様式である。アール・デコはその発展的なスタイルでファッションの流れとも並行していたが、日本にとっては本来逆輸入されたものだから、自然に受け入れられただろう。世界大戦前、海を超えて文化や芸術が自由に交流していた華やかな時代が、着物を背景に想像できる。幾何学模様、非対称性、大胆な線の取り方などの特徴は、一方向的ではなく双方向的な影響のもとに生まれたデザインなのだろう。

日本の民族衣装であるキモノが歴史的に大きく発展する重要な双方向的な時代ともなっている。

さらに、戦時中に作られたキモノも展示されており充実した内容になっていた。着物の輸出が一時停止となることもやむを得なかった時期に、コレクターらによって幸い欧州に渡って日の目を見た着物である。日本の近代化は日本の衣装の近代化でもある。その激動な変化の途上に作られた着物。たとえば男児や男子のキモノの裏地や襦袢に自国のプロパガンダを謳う模様、戦意を鼓舞するようなデザインなども施されている。富士山や零戦といった日本の象徴である絵柄を配し、勝利を願うスローガンのような文章が布に書かれたものもある。裏地や襦袢は直接肌に触れて内側に着用するものだ。キモノを媒介に国のイデオロギーが身体化されていく。眠るときに着用する夜着という中綿入りの男児のキモノにも顕著にあらわれている。とりわけ男性のキモノに多かったこのような図柄は、女性の衣装にも施されることがある。戦車が刺繍されている帯も現存、日本国民としての態度を、女の腹にもしっかりと据えおくべきだと衣装に語らせている。

日本人の扮装が大きく変わっていくのは戦後の本格的な洋装化であるが、その直前に国民国家の精神を凝縮さ

せたようなキモノが作られていたことは注目に値する。衣装における近代化＝洋服の時代が到来するにあたって通過せねばならなかった出来事として、研究者が記録したり、国外で紹介される*10。「着るもの」をシンプルに意味していた着物はめまぐるしい変化を余儀なくされた。大きな意味や重要な役割を担わされることで、幸いにもこの民族衣装のもつ可能性は拡がったのだろう。

戦争とキモノという観点から見て興味深い写真について紹介しておこう。二〇一五年六月に掲載されて話題になったヒトラーのキモノ姿である。イギリスの『デイリー・メール』紙で初公開となった。一九三六年の日独防共協定締結時に着用したと推測されており、ナチスの鷲と鉤十字の紋も確認できる。かつてオランダ国王が着物を献上された際にも、天鷲絨でフリンジを施して西洋風にアレンジされた。このキモノも幸福な異文化交流とは簡単に言えないながらも、誇り高き民族衣装として外交の場面で重要な政治的役割を果たしていたのだ。

3　展覧会2：アートとキモノ

次にキモノがアート作品として紹介されていた展覧会を紹介しよう。イギリスのロイヤル・アカデミー・オブ・アーツで二〇一〇年に開催されていた'Aware: Art, Fasion, Identity'*11 では、世界から様々な作家の作品がテーマ別に展示されていた。

その詳しい紹介をする前に、時代の流れに沿って、着物を背景にした日本の現代ファッションの展開を確認しておきたい。近代化を余儀なくされた戦後、一九七〇年代に入ると、欧州のモード界でデビューする日本人デザイナーらが活躍するようになる。森英恵や高田賢三、後半には三宅一生、山本寛斎、川久保玲、山本耀司が登場した。日本人デザイナーのファッションはたびたび芸術性をもった作品として批評され、やがて美術館や博物館で展示されるようになった。同時に新しいキモノやキモノスタイルを提案するような作品も生まれ、民族衣装の伝統や歴史に裏打ちされた形で、欧米のマーケットで新しいファッションとして展開されていく。

日本人デザイナーは欧州のファッション界においてアバンギャルドな位置付けを得ると、国際的な活躍の場を確保する。[*12] キモノスタイルも洋装と融合し、生地・染色・色柄の伝統的手法を新しく表現することで、欧米のファッション界に歓迎されその存在が認められていく。つまり、日本の民族衣装が新しい形で固有の文化として継承されていくのである。特にイギリスでいえば、三宅一生は一九九三年に王立芸術大学から名誉博士号を、二〇一二年にはデザインミュージアムから二〇一二年度のデザイン大賞を授与されている。また、山本耀司の特別企画展が二〇一一年（三月二二日〜七月一〇日）にV&Aで開催された。

さて、展覧会の内容に戻ろう。会場となっている美術館の母体である Royal Academy of Arts という芸術組織は、一七六八年に創設された英国王室の権威的なグループである。その組織に所属する作家のイメージを衣装で表現したのが、グレイソン・ペリーの「アーティスト・ローブ」と題された作品。会場に入るとまず目に入る装飾的なシルクの衣装で、丁寧に華やかな刺繍が施されており、日本の伝統的なキモノからインスピレーションを得て制作したもの。ペリーは陶芸家としてもよく知られているが、一つずつ異なる個性的な焼物／磁器のボタンが衣装に施されていた。女装パフォーマンスをすることでも知られており、女性の人格になるときはクレアという名前で活動する。現代イギリス人作家が作品のなかで表現したキモノスタイルは英国の伝統や文化性とも結びついた。

イギリスを舞台に活躍する、キプロス島出身でトルコ系の血を引くフセイン・チャラヤンが、日本の文楽に感銘を受け、その伝統芸能の考え方や手法を取り入れたインスタレーションを発表していた。チャラヤンは建築的で構造的な衣装をデザインすることで知られているが、本展では「存在することの息子 Son of Sonzaisuru」と題された作品で、黒子である人形遣いの存在感や、風を受けて舞う白いドレスの衣装を通して、舞台空間が開かれ拡大していく過程を見せる。キモノを作ったり使ったわけではないが、その精神性や空間性からインスピレーションを受けている。文楽においては、頭（かしら）は本来不動で、心中劇の舞台では人形の表情や衣装の躍動感は豊かに表現される。見えないはずのものが見え、見えているものが見えない——衣装と身体の関係を日本の

図3
'Kimono Memories of Hiroshima'
©Marie-Ange Guilleminot

伝統芸能の手法を用いて問題提起する。

広島でのフィールド調査の後、戦争遺留品をモチーフにして着物柄をデザインしたインスタレーションも見られた。フランス人作家によるもので、「広島の着物の記憶 Kimono Memories of Hiroshima」と題され、遺留品の着物や帯、バッグなども陳列、作家と作家のデザインした着物を着用した日本人らを撮影した写真もあった（図3）。その写真作品は、日本人は皆後ろ姿なのに対して、外国人の作家本人だけがひとり前を向いている。そして観覧者を凝視し、不思議な微笑みを浮かべている。配色は淡いピンクと白が中心で、同じデザインの帯も展示されていた。その会場は静かで一種独特で不気味な空気を放っていた。まず洋服とは明らかに違う和服の構造に対して外国人は驚きをおぼえるに違いない。通常の着物の制作と同じように直線裁断できるような反物に図柄を白抜きで配置している。キモノは西洋人にとって極東日本という異界への入り口である。遺留品をモチーフにしていることから、死者の世界への入り口という意味でも、このインスタレーション作品は二重に異化された世界を作りだしている。

本節の冒頭で日本人デザイナーの活躍について簡単に触れておいたが、日本のファッションの高度なデザイン性や芸術性が語られるとき、同時に敗戦国としてのトラウマティズムが語られることが多い。[13]山本耀司の日本固有の伝統的な色合わせやキモノスタイルのシルエット、三宅一生の実験的でインダストリアルなデザインの発想は、日本のキモノの平面裁断の手法を駆使したものだが、そこには光と影が表現され、健やかに育つ新しいジャポニスムの背後に、被爆国としてのトラウマが映し出される。川久保玲と山本耀司のパリ・コレクションのデビューの際にも、穴が開いて破れた黒い衣装作品を評して、「焼け野原になった日本の生き残り、原爆国の風景」などと記述されたことはよく知られている。広

島出身の三宅一生の戦争体験のエピソードも語られることが少なくない。「広島の着物の記憶」という作品名からも明らかなように、「着物という衣装を通して、人は記憶を生きながら、同時に癒されていくべきか」という問いが投げかけられている。

4 Kimono：イギリスでの受容の現状

イギリスでは現在どのようにキモノが受容されているのだろう。着る人に焦点を当て、その現状を紹介し考察していきたい。まず、ハイファッションの世界での影響として、イギリス人デザイナーのヴィヴィアン・ウェストウッドの作品。キモノを大胆にデフォルメした作品は、ウェストウッドが元々西洋の古典的な衣装を再現しながらその解体美も表現するデザイナーであることを想起させる。キモノシャツと呼ばれるメンズウェアでは、デニムに絣の文様が描かれており、日本の伝統柄である雲龍紋をあしらった衣装も確認できた。これらは直接キモノを使うのではなく、着物の伝統柄に注目して取り入れるアップサイクルの好例。ファッションシーン全体が、時折ジャポニスムをキーワードに流行することもある。欧州のオートクチュールのデザイナーでは、アルマーニ、プラダ、ヴェルサーチ、ゴルチエなどがキモノ風のファッション作品を発表していた。グローバル化したキモノという日本文化＝民族衣装が無国籍化していく現象とも言える。

次に、受容の実態について考えていきたい。まず、Takayo さんという日本人が始めたキモノのレンタルビジネスの例を紹介する。日本と較べると、イギリスでは子どもの誕生日を重要視するため、お祝いのための出費は惜しまない。たとえば「ドレスコードはジャパニーズの誕生会を開いてみませんか」と提案をする。衣装レンタルだけではなく企画を持ち込みスタイリングまでを引き受けている。一着浴衣で三〇ポンドほどなので日本円で五〇〇円ほどになる。決して安い金額ではないが、現在ビジネスとして成功し、ファッション誌などでも取

首都ロンドンに見られる小さなキモノビジネスを通して、実際どのようにイギリス人がキモノに接している

材され注目されている。いわばキモノは、このときコスプレの衣装のような存在である。日本を離れることで、キモノの国家性・民族性・文化性が過剰に強調されている。

次に、ロンドンで Furuki Yo-Kimono Vintage という名で展開する日本人のキモノディーラーのストールを紹介したい。アンティークマーケットやヴィンテージフェアに定期的に出店することで顧客と出会い、またファッショナブルな町の店舗の一画でキモノコーナーのセレクションを担当している。ストールの顧客を紹介してみよう。

英国紳士のアイテムでもある山高帽やパイプ・ブーツと合わせて着こなしている男性は、鮮やかな紫色も個性的な顔立ちに似合っているように思われる（図4）。キモノは西洋風にリメイクしているようだ。文化の融合が

図4
男性顧客
撮影：Furuki Yo-Kimono Vintage（2010）

新しい衣装のスタイルとなった着こなしの成功例であろう。

売れ筋は気楽に組み合わせられる羽織が人気。内側には単色の衣服を着て派手目の羽織と合わせるのが定番の着方のようだ。洋服と組み合わせても抵抗がなく、羽織るようにコートとして着用し、自分のスタイリングで気軽に楽しんでいる。お洒落な日常着として着用し、セミフォーマルなパーティなどでも活躍する。羽織は、外国人にはとっつきやすいキモノとなる。年齢や性別を選ばず、中に何を着ても良いのでシーズンも選ばないこのキモノは、着物本来の持つ強みでもある不易流行性が活かされる。

また、固定客には業界人も多いとのこと。日本独自の文様やプリントに着目し、商品企画に取り入れようと購入していく。近年の傾向で、キモノ全体のスタイルよりも伝統的な日本独特の模様に関心が集まり、古典的な柄の着物が個性的で新しいデザインとして映るようだ。異国趣味のオリエンタリズムや日本趣味としてのジャポニ

図5
女性顧客
撮影：Furuki Yo-Kimono Vintage（2010）

スムとしてキモノを提案するというよりは、キモノの一部分であるパーツやピースを実験的に洋服に融合させていく。民族衣装のもつ文化性が薄まり、その表象から離れることができれば、キモノは場面を選ばず自由に着用できる衣装となる。新しいファッションの一スタイルとして違和感なく受容されている。

インタビューから引き続き紹介しよう。結婚式の当日に室内で横になったりメイクをするときに着用するキモノ＝ドレッシング・ガウンが欲しいという目的で一人の女性が現れた。華やかな襦袢や、色柄は地味でもエレガントで高価なキモノを選んでいったとのこと（図5）。同様な需要は続いているようだ。かつての室内着としてのキモノの役割あるいは受容していた一九世紀末から二〇世紀初頭のティー・ガウンという、眠りと覚醒のあいだの橋渡しをする。エキゾチックでエロティックで着心地のよいプライベートウェアとして再燃しているのかもしれない。この現象は興味深い。ファッションとは、流行のスタイルが回帰する現象であるが、着用方法が流行として繰り返すこともある。

結婚式の控え室で着用されるとは何ともロマンティックな話だが、裏方にあってもキモノが特別な仕事を担っていることに相違はない。身体を締めつけないゆったりとしたシルエット、美しい染色や豪華な刺繍をほどこした高品質のシルクの衣装、ヨーロッパにはないキモノ独特の着心地もまた求められているのだろう。ここでファッションの世界ではすでに古着文化が根付いていることも付け加えておこう。高価な「骨董品」よりは手の届きやすい「古キモノ」を購入することで、抵抗なくこの日本の伝統衣装をファッションとして楽しむことができるのだ。

Furuki Yo-Kimono Vintage のストールのキモノがファッション雑誌に掲載されたことがある。このページを担当したスタイリストは、「セクシーな気分になれるもの」としてキモノを探しに来たという。ミステリアスでエロティックでもある極東の衣装という存在も根強いことがわかる。着付けの方は日本の正統的なそれとは程遠い。肩脱ぎながら、ルースに羽織り、また裾も大胆に開いて、肌の露出度も高い。果たしてこの着こなしを日本人は真似することができるだろうか。辛うじてからだに纏って引っかかった布がキモノの片鱗を残している、もはやキモノではない別の衣装のようである。

本節の最後に、舞台衣装としてキモノを着用している例を紹介しよう。キモノパフォーマーとして活躍しているイギリス人で、古い日本と新しい日本の両方を同時に愛しているアキンボ・ムーンチャイルド。芸者に憧れ、日本からキモノを取り寄せ、自分の舞台で着用している（図6）。新しい日本の原宿ファッションなどにも大いに興味を持っているが、二〇〇〇年初頭のイラク戦争勃発の期には、自らの反戦意識や批判的態度を表現したパフォーマンスのなかで迷彩柄のキモノを着用している。キモノの文化性を強調しつつ、無国籍化する現象がここでも確認できる。

かつて日本のパフォーマンスアートのイヴェント『縛りの夜』を、アキンボと合気道をたしなむスイス人の日本人類学者と共にイギリスで主催したことがある。キモノを脱構築化し、着付けそのものを見せるショーを行った。いわゆるキモノのワークショップはロンドンの日本愛好家のあいだで時折開催されているが、たいていは、美しい民族衣装着用の異国文化体験にとどまる内容である。『縛りの夜』では、キモノ

図6
アキンボ・ムーンチャイルド
撮影：Nick Ensing（2011）

図7
自作のキモノを着るアキンボ
東ロンドンの自宅にて（2015）

とは何かを問い、着ることと脱ぐことの両方を見せられるような、キモノという衣装の構造も明らかにして、新しい表現を試みる内容であった。ちなみに同イヴェントの他の出し物は、イギリス人のプロの縄師によるパフォーマンス、フランス人による漁網を小道具にした暗黒舞踏などもあった。

アキンボは自分で着物を縫っている。居住地区の図書館のソーインググループに半年間通い、はじめて自分で一からキモノを作ったこともある（図7）。参加者はアキンボ以外はすべて中高年の女性だったとのこと。マーケットで見つけたキモノの型紙をもとに、他女性メンバーに助けてもらいながら仕上げている。

かつての日本は、自分の着物を自分で縫うことはふつうだった。日常生活で手に針と糸を持つという日本人の身体感覚はすでに失われて久しい。大柄な体型にも合[*14]

アイデンティティが多様化する現代は、様々な役割を日々演じているかのようである。服を着替えるように、場面に合わせて服を選び着用することで意識され作られる。モノの文化性ももはや希薄になっている現代。いわゆるグローバル資本主義社会は、着用者に[*15]

「どう演じるのか／どう見せるのか」という難題を与えながら新しい衣服の購入を強いているとも言えるだろう。

日本には、男性が女性の化粧を施して女性の衣装で演じる歌舞伎などの伝統芸能があり、江戸時代から現在にまで続く長い歴史がある。欧米のバーレスクなどの舞台は比較的歴史的に新しい文化だ。アキンボは舞台人であ

う華やかでかわいらしい仕上がりのキモノは、ステージではインディアンのような自作のかぶり物と組み合わせたいと、アキンボは今後の展望も持っている。

役割を着替える。〈わたし〉は、常に揺れ動く不安定な存在であり、

るとともに同性愛主義者の男性である。キモノは彼にとって「ジェンダー」と同時に「ナショナリティ」を表現することのできる衣装である。それは女性のこころを着ることであり、憧れる日本人の精神性に触れる、媒体のような役割を担っている。つまり、何かを纏わなければ、からだは持て余す空虚な容れ物であるかのような。着ることの重要性と根源的な問いを投げかけてくれる、イギリスで見つけたキモノであった。

結び――キモノのみらい

人は裸のまま生きられない。衣服を着用して生活する社会的な動物である。自然を加工変形させることで文化が生まれるなら、裸体に服を纏うことも文化だろう。文化としてのモノ＝衣服は、新しい環境世界を作っていく身体の延長となる。モノは身体化すると同時に、わたしたちの身体もまた文化的な刻印がなされ、文化的産物となるのだろう。[*16]

からだを基準に服を合わせるというよりは、からだを服に合わせるよう強いるのがファッションである。身体が再びデザインされていく。それは精神の変容を伴うこともある。グローバル資本主義社会の時代、大量生産されるモノは、遠く速く商品として流通する。民族衣装もまたファッション化し無国籍化していく一方で、生産地や生産者から離れれば離れるほど伝統や文化性が過剰に強調されるのだ。キモノもしかり。

日本国民国家のシンボルであるキモノは、グローバルなファッション商品となる。身体に辛うじて乗っているパズルの一ピースのようである。戦時中はスローガンＴシャツのような役割を担って、強制的に日本を重ね着する窮屈な時代も体験した。正統な着付けが壊れてしまったキモノは、身体と共謀し、エロティックな表現を生む。そのとき、冒頭で紹介した室生犀星がかつて語った言葉を借りるなら「汚れてもいい洋服」としてキモノは変身するのかもしれない。

伝統と前衛の両方を背負って海を越えて旅する衣は他にもあるだろうか。国際化を基盤とするグローバル化は、

地球上を自由に行き来しているように見える一方で、文化性や国籍を放棄することで成り立つ側面も大きい。クローゼットに埋没すれば他の洋服たちと一緒に並んだ一枚のキモノ。リフォームして機能性を施し洋服に変形するべきか、箪笥のなかに大事にしまい込んで時々正統な文化を着こなすなすべきか。日本人も日本人を演じなければならない時代なのかもしれない。

注

* 1　『生きたきものを』中央公論社、一九六〇年。
* 2　本章の服飾史に関する記述は、主に下記二冊のイギリス人によって記された書籍に拠っている。
　　『ファッションの歴史』山内沙織訳、上・下、パルコ出版、一九八五年［一九七五］。Laver, James, A Concise History of Costume, Thames and Hudson, 1969.
* 3　日本の絹がいかに戦略的に輸出されていたのか、他アジア諸国との差別化がはかられていたことがわかる。周防珠美「明治初期の輸出室内着──椎野正兵衛商店を中心として」『Dresstudy』51、京都服飾文化研究財団、二〇〇七年。
* 4　イギリス人の視点から服飾文化を論じているが、この時期は特にパリモードの影響を看過できないことが明記される。Wilson, Elizabeth & Lou Taylor, Through the Looking Glass: A History of Dress from 1860 to the Present Day, BBC Books, 1989.
* 5　ジャポニスムが西洋にもたらした価値観や美意識はオリエンタリズムという言葉で表現されるものとの差異に留意しながら論じられている本書より抜粋している。稲賀繁美『絵画の東方──オリエンタリズムからジャポニスムへ』名古屋大学出版会、一九九九年。
* 6　西洋ファッションにおける日本の影響の歴史的な研究とその展示は、世界的にも深井氏の仕事によるところが大きく本章もその成果に大きく拠っている。深井晃子『図録 モードのジャポニスム』京都服飾文化研究財団、一九九四年。
* 7　彼らの舞台は文字通りイメージとしての日本を送り出すための舞台装置であったことがわかる。言うまでもなく視覚的に衣装はその重要な小道具となる。白田由樹「川上音二郎・貞奴が演じた「東洋」──一九〇〇年パリ万国博覧会における日仏の位相から──」『人文研究』第六四巻、大阪市立大学大学院文学研究科、二〇一三年。
* 8　すでにこの時代から日本の着物についての鋭い描写が確認できる。ルイス・フロイス『ヨーロッパ文化と日本文化』岡田章雄訳註、岩波文庫、一九九一年［Fróis, Luis, Europeens et Japonais, 1585］。
* 9　関連図録も発行されており、Jeffrey Montgomery という有名なスイス人の日本民芸コレクターのキモノがメインである。当時ロンドンで筆者は研修しており美術館所蔵の別のキモノも合わせて閲覧する機会があった。Van Assche, A. M., Fasioning Kimono:

* 10 *Dress and Modernity in Early Twentieth Century Japan 5 Continents*, 2008.
乾氏はヴィクトリア＆アルバート美術館でも調査をしていることが確認できる。乾淑子『図説　着物柄に見る戦争』インパクト出版会、二〇〇七年。

* 11 本章では記述しなかったが、オノ・ヨーコによるインスタレーション映像 Cut Piece も展示されていた。舞台に座した彼女の衣装に観客が自由に鋏を入れて切り刻まれて行くスリリングな内容。Orta, Lucy, et al., *Aware: Art, Fashion and Identity*, Damiani, 2011.

* 12 本章で取り上げている日本人ファッションデザイナーの展開については同展覧会のカタログに詳しい。Fukai, Akiko et al., *Future Beauty: 30 Years of Japanese Fashion*, Merrell, 2010.

* 13 この観点から論じた日本のファッションについては、本書の英語での論文 III Costume and Trauma を参照。

* 14 日本人はかつて麻を栽培し、その繊維から糸を紡ぎ、織物を作り、着物を縫ってきた歴史がある。池田孝江『服装の生活史』大月書店、一九七五年。

* 15 ドゥボールはすでに六〇年代よりこのような時代が来ることを語っていた。Debord, Guy, trans. Knabb, Ken, *The Society of the Spectacle*, Bureau of Public Secrets, 2014 [1967].

* 16 モノの身体化およびフェティシズムについての考え方は以下に大きく拠っている。田中雅一・稲葉穰編『コンタクトゾーンの人文学第II巻――物質化／物質文化』晃洋書房、二〇一一年。

袈裟とファッション

本章は仏教の僧侶によって着用される袈裟という衣服について考察する。これまで「人を着ているとは言えないだろうか」という問いを立てながら、人間の衣服が文化として空間や時間を越えて、流行現象を伴いながら変化・発展していくことを探ってきた。袈裟の歴史を概観すれば、あらゆる事物がそうであるのと同様に、袈裟もファッション化しているような現象が垣間みられる。僧侶の衣装の構造を知り、道元（一二〇〇―五三）の開山した日本曹洞宗における袈裟の継承について考察する。食事とならび「着ること」も仏弟子にとって重要な修行であると捉えた道元禅師は、『正法眼蔵』*1 という書物のなかで、特に「伝衣」「袈裟功徳」*2 という巻で袈裟について説いている。人間にとって衣服の持つ根源的な価値について袈裟を通して考える機会にしたい。

1 袈裟について

袈裟とは

袈裟とは、仏教徒の着る衣のことである。律衣や如法衣とも呼ばれる。律とは仏弟子としての個人生活あるいは団体生活におけるこまかな生活規定を記したものである。つまり、それは仏弟子らしくない行いをした際に釈

尊が直接注意を促したり罰を加えたりした事実を詳しく記録したものであり、言い換えれば、釈尊や仏弟子たちの正確な生活記録でもある。漢訳されている有名なものには五大律（四分律、五分律、十誦律、僧祇律、有部律）がある。

袈裟の成立は仏教の成立とほぼ同じ頃で、二五〇〇年の歴史を持つといわれる。師匠から弟子に法（仏法）が伝えられるように、袈裟も伝承されていく。仏教者は生涯に一度の伝法式ではじめて師匠から袈裟を与えられる。師匠と弟子が一対一で向かい合い一週間かけて執り行われる他見を許さない儀式の中である。衣とともに法を受け継ぎ、袈裟は仏教者の象徴的な役割をも担う。仏教で最も重要な「法」は目に見えず実体はないものだが、衣装によって体現されるのだ。法を授ける証としての「存在」として、これは証契ともいわれる。

袈裟の起源

袈裟は釈迦以来二五〇〇年あまり続く伝統的な方法によって縫われる。割截衣とも呼ばれ、基本は截縷と呼ばれる布を接ぎ合わせて方形の衣服を作り、合わせて一枚の布に仕上げる。はぎれがなければ布をいったん裁断してから作製される。布は反物では高価であり貨幣のような交換価値を持つ。装飾品としての値打ちを断ち切るように、布を裁断して小さくすることで人の欲しがらないものにする。それは人の思惑を断ち切ることでもある。

袈裟の起源については、以下のようなエピソードがよく知られている。仏教が誕生した頃のインドはさまざまな宗教が盛んであった。仏教僧団を他と分けるための衣服を作ることが必要となった。釈迦の説く仏教に帰依していた王（ビンビサーラ）が、馬を降りて丁寧に挨拶した相手は仏教徒ではなかった。紛らわしさを避けるために、異教徒と仏教徒とを見分ける衣を着用するように王は釈尊に命じた。これが仏教教団の構成員を示すための衣裳＝ユニフォームのはじまりである。

釈迦の弟子で甥でもあるアーナンダがインドの美しい田園風景から袈裟のイメージを得たことから始まる。田んぼの稲穂が豊かに実る様子を袈裟の意匠に取り入れた。福田衣という呼び名はこのことに由来する。形状から

考えて、稲作文化と袈裟は切っても切れない。暑いインドの国では、気候風土を考えれば理解し易いが、人々は縫合も裁断もせず直接体に巻きつけるように一枚の布を身に着けていた。日本の仏教は、発祥地インドから中国を経由して伝わったので、この衣服の着用の仕方も多少変化する。宗教服は教団の衣装として統一されるユニフォームとなる。そのモチーフは自然を模倣したデザインから生まれた。

言葉の由来──「色（しき）」

袈裟は、サンスクリット語でカシャーヤといい、元々インドでは色をあらわす言葉である。「袈裟色」などというふうに使われて濁った色という意味を持つ。原色ではない混合色で、具体的には赤褐色のような色である。いわば袈裟色とは「汚い」色のことを指し示している。袈裟のことを「壊色布（えじきふ）」や「間色衣（けんじきえ）」あるいは「染衣（ぜんえ）」と呼ぶのも、この色の特徴に由来する。

截縷（せつる）から成る構造がそうであったのと同様に、本来この衣装は人の欲しがらないものでなければならない。見た目に美しく澄んだ色であってはならない。仏教で「色（しき）」という言葉は特徴的な意味を持つ用語であり、袈裟の言葉の由来が読みは違っても色に関連していることは興味深い。

インド仏教教団では、タブーとされる色が五色あった。青、赤、黄、白、黒の基本色で、これを五正色（せいしき）と呼び、原色のような目立つ色を避け、原色しかない場合は布を染め直す。色は富や権力の象徴と結びつきやすい。明るく派手な色は人の好むところとなり、そのような色を「壊す」ことで、人の思い慮いを断ち切るのである。また袈裟は複雑な色相を持つことが多い。元来、袈裟には用いられないことになっていた（詳しくは次頁の資料を参照）。

法衣には用いられないことになっていた（詳しくは次頁の資料を参照）。仏弟子が自ら布を染めることもあるため、結果的には色が定まらず、はっきりとした色名であらわせない表情をしているからである。

衣財全体を染めることを「染浄（ぜんじょう）」というが、それに対して袈裟の一部に小さな汚点をつけることを「点浄（てんじょう）」という。点浄は、袈裟という衣服にとって重要で特徴的な行為で、他（在家・外道）の持ち物と区別するために付

① 鉢（P patta ⑤ pātra）の音写。鉢多羅，波多羅，鉢和蘭などの略。意訳は応量器，応器とも。僧尼が常に所持し，僧団で私有物と認められた食器。材料・色・量ともに規定の法にかなうところから，応量器と漢訳する。鉄製・陶土製が定めで鉄鉢・瓦鉢と称し，木製は外道のもの，石鉢は仏のものとして禁じられた。日本の禅門では仏が木製を禁ずるのは，一に垢，二に簡（他と簡別する），三に因（制戒）の三つの意味があるが，木製でも漆を塗れば仏戒にかなうものとして，今は多く木鉢を用いる。

② 袈裟 インドの猟師などが着ていたボロの衣を Kaṣāya（カシャーヤ）とよんでいたが，仏教はそれを取り入れた。インドの僧団で制定された法衣をその色から袈裟（迦沙，迦羅沙門，頼沙）と称した。カシャーヤは染衣，間色衣，赤血色衣，壊色衣・不正色衣とも漢訳され，汚れて濁った色（赤褐色）を意味する。

③ 五正色（五色・五大色とも）青・黄・赤・白・黒の基本色。インドの仏教教団では法衣に用いてはならない色とされ，華美な色とされた。中間色の五間色（緋・紅・紫・緑・壇黄）も不可。白衣，白衣舎

④ 三衣 用途から生じた名称 衣・三衣・沙門衣・僧衣・比丘衣・苾芻衣・守持衣・三領衣
色から生じた名称 袈裟・染衣・不正色衣・壊色衣・間色衣・別色衣・濁赤衣・赤血色衣・黄褐色衣
形から生じた名称 方服・方袍・田相衣・割截衣
功徳から生じた名称 法衣・法服・道服・功徳衣・仏衣・如来衣・離染服・出世服・離塵服・蓮華服・慈悲服・解脱服・福田衣・無垢衣・除熱悩服・吉祥服・如法衣・忍辱鎧・無相衣・無上衣

⑤ 安陀衣 ⑤ antaravāsaka の部分的音写。内衣・中宿衣・裏衣・中著衣・下衣と漢訳される。一重，五条で，作務・旅・ひとりでいる時・臥床などのとき用いる。禅宗の絡子がこれに相当。

⑥ 鬱多羅僧（伽）⑤ uttara-āsaṅga の音写。上衣または上著衣，三衣のうち，中位であるから中価衣，比丘集合のときに着用するので入衆衣ともいい，聞法・説法・食事・坐禅などの時に用いる。一重で七条の布片でつくられる。

⑦ 僧伽梨（胝）⑤ saṃghāṭi の音写。比丘の三衣のなかで最大のもの。両重で，九条から二十五条まである。条数が多いので雑砕衣ともいう。説法や托鉢のために王宮や聚落に入るときには必ずこれを着ける公式の服。入王宮聚落服ともいい，上・中・下品にそれぞれ三品があるので九品衣ともいう。

⑧ 糞掃衣 ⑤ pāṃsukūla の音写で，衲衣・衲袈裟ともいう。ぼろきれの衣。塵芥の中に捨てられたぼろを拾ってつづり合わせてつくった衣。初期の修行僧はこの衣をまとっていた。衲僧

⑨ 衣財・衣体（材質）
「袈裟をつくるには麁布（目の粗い布）を本とす，麁布なきがごときは細布をもちゐる。麁細の布，ともになきには絹素（しろぎぬ）をもちゐる，絹・布ともになきがごときは綾羅等をもちゐる，如来の聴許なり。絹布綾羅の類，すべてなきくには，如来また皮袈裟を聴許しますん」『正法眼蔵袈裟功徳』

⑩ 袈裟の量 度分法（直接法）→肩から踝上四指まで。局量法（間接法）→舒肘・拳肘・磔手（張手）・指（第一関節の指巾）・豆・麦

⑪ 縁・葉・壇隔（一長一短→五条衣 両長一短→七・九・十一・十三条 三長一短→十五・十七・十九条 四長一短→二十一・二十三・二十五条）

⑫ 偏袒右肩 インダス文明以来のならわしらしい。現在，スリランカ・ミャンマー・ヴェトナムなどでは正式な服装の時には肩を覆っている。通肩（通両肩）は両肩を覆う着用法である。

⑬ 直裰 上半身を覆う褊衫と下半身を覆う裙子をつなげたもので，中国の南宋代（1127～1279）に初めて作られた。「褊衫および直裰を脱して手巾のかたはらにかく。」『正法眼蔵・洗浄巻』

⑭ 褊衫 僧祇支（saṃkakṣikā の音写で，掩腋衣・覆膊衣と漢訳する。腋と左肩を覆う長方形の下着）と覆肩衣（右肩を覆う）を縫い合わせ，それに袖や襟をつけたもの。

⑮ 裙子 下半身の下着。大きさは長さ四肘，巾二肘。

⑯ 「予，在宋のそのかみ，長連牀に功夫せしとき，斉肩の隣単をみるに，開静のときごとに，袈裟をさゝげて頂上に安じ，合掌恭敬し，一偈を黙誦す。その偈にいはく，大哉解脱服 無相福田衣 披奉如来教 広度諸衆生 ときに予，未曾見のおもひを生じ，歓喜身にあまり，感涙ひそかにおちて衣襟をひたす。『袈裟功徳』

資料 三衣一鉢

注：幣道紀老師作成（2012年5月神戸ファッション美術館で開催された日本記号学会大会の講演時に参加者に配布された）

ける印を意味する。なぜ、いわば汚点のようなものをつけて「浄める」のだろうか。新しいもの（布・衣）に対して、遠慮して差し控えようという姿勢の表われであり、少し汚してから身につけるという心構えを表していると言う。

ファッションは「新しい」という価値が一時的に絶対となる現象[*6]であるが、新しさを追い求めることは自ずと競争をまねくため人のねたみやそねみを生みやすい。汚すことによって浄めるという逆説的な行為は、新品に謙虚であれという、いわばこころを鎮めるための浄化作用なのだ。

袈裟の構造は「体」「色」「量」と呼ばれる「素材」「色」「布の分量」それぞれ三つの側面からなっており、さらに着用法を含めて四つの視点から説明する。本節では「色」を中心に紹介した。前頁の資料を参照しつつ、以降「体」と「量」についても触れていくことにしたい。

2　清浄ということ

糞掃衣と「体」

道元は「糞掃衣」を袈裟のなかで最も清浄なるものと記している。糞掃衣とは人が捨てて顧みない布で作った袈裟を示し、サンスクリット語の「パームスクーラ」[*7]の音写である。「パームス」は汚物を、「クーラ」は土手を指し、汚物が集積したという意味になる。衲衣あるいは衲袈裟ともいう。「衲」とはぼろきれの衣で、塵芥のなかに捨てられたはぎれを拾って綴りあわせて作る糞掃衣の特徴を表現している。

道元は『四分律』をもとに一〇種類の糞掃を定めている。[*8]　①牛嚼衣＝牛のかんだ衣、②鼠嚙衣＝ねずみがかじった衣、③火焼衣＝焼け焦がした衣、④月水衣＝女性の月経で汚れた衣、⑤産婦衣＝産婦が汚した衣、⑥神廟衣＝神廟に供えた衣、鳥などがくわえてきた持ち主の

ない衣、⑦塚間衣＝墓場で拾った死者の布、⑧求願衣＝願掛けのために使われた布、⑨王職衣＝朝廷の位階にしたがって決められた布、⑩往還衣＝死者に着させて火葬場まで行き、帰る途中で捨てた衣。

以上、挙げた一〇種類の布は、人が忌み嫌う、いわば「不浄」の布である。捨てられた布の中から、穴が開いていない、洗えば汚れが取れそうなものを選んだり、すり減った布の場合は合わせて刺子にして補強して用いられる。

だからといって、袈裟を身に着けるのは、わざとみすぼらしい格好をするためでも美服のためでもなく、仏道の修行のためである。袈裟とは、弊衣と美服の境界を超える存在でなければならない。袈裟を搭け（着用し）て三世諸仏の皮肉骨髄を正伝する。つまり、この身は仏と同じ身体であること、また仏と同じ衣裳を着ているという表現行為でもある。

ここで袈裟の素材＝「体」について述べておこう。基本的には、袈裟には麁布という目の粗い布を用いる。それがなければ絹、それもなければ綾織の布、それもない場合は動物の皮でもいい、と道元は記している。糞掃衣に関しても同様のことがいえるが、材料が何からできているのかは問題ではない。それをどのように調達したかが重要になってくる。仏教の「少欲知足」＝「選り好みをしない」こと、できるだけ身近にあるものをたとえば檀那から施されたものなどをありがたく用いる。

ファッションとはいかにも好みの問題であるが、この点からいえば、袈裟はファッションから外れた衣服である。袈裟にとって要になるのは何か。それは「清浄」という価値になる。洗ってきれいにすることは文字通り清浄になることだが、それだけではここでいう「浄」には遠い。清浄とは「名利を棄てる」*11ということであり、言い換えれば、いかに衣服に執着しないかということだ。人の好みそうもない濁った「色」であり、麁布を使うことを基本にしても選り好みをしない（あるいは糞掃衣のように人の執着から離れた）「体」でできている。袈裟を構成する重要な要素となる。

三衣一鉢と「量」

道元禅師は糞掃衣を袈裟のなかで最上の衣財としたことは前述したが、日本であるいは現代において、このような捨てられた着物を見つけることは困難だ。仏教はインドよりまず中国へ渡り日本へ入ってきたが、国やその気候風土によって、袈裟も少しずつ変化しながら受容された。現代のファッションと同様、衣服が海を渡ることによってその形や用途は変化していく。

亜熱帯のインドでは一枚の布をまとえば生活に事足りる。しかし、中国大陸に渡れば冬の厳しい寒さが待っており、また日本の気候には四季がある。着用する衣服の枚数に加えて、着用方法も季節に応じて変わる。

三衣一鉢という仏教の言葉は・出家僧が私有財産を持たないことを表わしており、三枚の衣と一つの鉢があれば足りるとされる。「鉢」は、僧尼がつねに所持して僧団で私有物と認められた食器のこと。この器は、材料・色・量ともに規定の法にかなうという意味で「応量器」と漢訳される。

「三衣*12」は、僧侶が護持することが許される三衣の袈裟を意味する。三衣は布団や枕としても用いられ寝具にもなる。いわば「衣服」に留まらない、あるいは「衣服」を超えている衣である。三種類とは、安陀衣、鬱多羅僧、僧伽梨で、それぞれサンスクリット語から部分的あるいは全体の音写と中国の漢字にあてた形で日本では表記される。内側から順番に着用される。三衣の特徴を記しておこう。

安陀衣＝内衣、裏布ともいう。下着に相当し、一重、五条（一長一短*13）から成っている。作務、旅、一人でいるとき、臥床などのときに用いられるので、私的な室内着と言っていいかもしれない。インドではこの安陀衣をからだに直接あてて一枚着用する。中国や日本においては気候や環境の違いから自然にすたれてだんだん用いられなくなっているらしい。現在禅宗では、首から胸元に掛ける小さなサイズになった絡子がそれに当たり、日常に身に着けられる。

鬱多羅僧＝上衣ともいう。三衣のうち、中位（二枚目）に身につける。聞法・説法・食事・坐禅などの時に用

いる。ふだん着であり、一重の七条（二長一短）の布片で作られる。

僧伽梨＝三衣のなかで最大であり、両重（裏地付）で九条から二十五条のものまである（九品衣）。公式の服として用いられ、いわばよそいきの服である。説法や托鉢のために王宮や聚楽に入るときに必ず着用する。九品衣とは条の数によって袈裟を三つに分け、それぞれ三つずつに分類されるため、合わせてこのような呼び名がある。それぞれ、九、十一、十三条衣＝下品、十五、十七、十九条衣＝中品、二十一、二十三、二十五条衣＝上品となる。

以上、「量」の観点から袈裟を見てきた。平安・鎌倉時代を通じて布は米に換わって流通する価値を維持していた。「お布施」という言葉からも明らかなように、人々は反物を寺院に寄進することで信仰や感謝の意を表わした。僧侶はこのお布施として受けた衣財から袈裟を仕立てて身に着けた。パッチワークのように端切れを継ぎ合わせて条にし、複数の条を縫い合わせて方形にすることを基本構造とする。また糞掃衣を模したようなパターン（山形模様など）や意匠も生まれてくる。[*15]

仏教者は生と死を同等のものとみなす。法そのものである袈裟を身に着けるということは、からだに浄／不浄あるいは聖／俗といった二項対立的な価値を超える存在を纏い、その精神を着て生きよということなのだろう。

3　ころもとからだ

身に着ける＝搭袈裟法[*16]

『四分律』によれば、袈裟は「三輪を覆う（両膝と臍の三点を隠す）」ように身に着けなければならない。つまりからだのおよそ三分の一が隠れる。本来の袈裟のように、単なる装束ではないことを意識して、実用的な衣服として着用された。大切なことは身だしなみを整えて搭けることである。また、身だしなみとは、見た目の問題に

留まらず、自分の内面も清浄であることが表われる。

インドでは袈裟は一枚で実用的な僧衣であり、出家という世俗の世界から離れることを袈裟一枚で表現した。

一方、中国では寒冷の東アジアである気候条件とも関連して、袈裟は装束衣としての特徴が強い。実用的な衣服というよりは、重ね着した一番上に着用される、見せるアイテムとして発展した。中国における仏教が国家権力のなかに生きざるを得ない運命にあったことも手伝って、袈裟は装飾的になることも多かった。華やかな装束として存在し、また象徴的衣服としての傾向も大きかった。鎌倉仏教以前の法皇の時代には、立場上袈裟はとりわけ華美にならざるを得なかったようだ。

中国から仏教が伝来した日本は、教義のみならず袈裟のあり方も中国の影響が大きい。

着用法について簡潔にまとめておこう。着用法は、二種類ある。「通（両）肩（けん）（搭（た））」と呼ばれる両肩を覆う方法は、仏像などに多く見られる。条数の多い袈裟を着用する場合は正式な場面であることが多いので「通肩」となる。「偏袒右肩（へんだんうけん）」は、右肩を袒ぐ（はだぬ）着用法であり、こちらの方が一般的である。修行僧が目上の人に対していつでも役に立てるよう、働きやすい格好が重んじられたことから生まれた。それは右利きの人が多いからでもあるが、インドでは左手は不浄とされるので、左側を隠すという行為とも解釈される。

「梵漢兼挙（ぼんかんけんこ）」という言葉がある。音はサンスクリット語に写してから中国の漢字に当て、日本語ではそのまま音は使用するという意味である。この言葉と同様に、袈裟も仏教伝来の過程において変化しながら受容されてきた。着るということは人間の生活に根ざした身体的行為である。たとえ袈裟が宗教服という特殊性を具えていても、そのまま継承される要素もあれば、気候や風土によってその土地に合った形に変わっていくことも免れない。新しい形が定着していくと、その国固有のスタイルや意匠を生むこともある。袈裟に対する思想や態度についてもしかりである。また、袈裟という衣服はからだを隠すことを主に目的としている。衣服とは身体を保護し、差恥心の表われでもある。袈裟の着用法は、人間と布との関係における基本的な有り様も示している。

袈裟の伝承

冒頭でも述べたように、袈裟は伝法衣（でんぽうえ）ともいわれる。師から弟子へ、法を伝えた証として授けられる特別なものである。このような特徴から、袈裟が権威的な意味を帯びたり権力と結びついたりする現象も生じる。

中国禅の開祖達磨大師（釈迦から二八代目）の袈裟を六代目の大鑑慧能禅師（だいかんえのう）が引き継いだといわれている。初祖菩提達磨の伝法の象徴としての袈裟は慧能禅師が相伝しているとして、その袈裟が利用されることも少なからずあった。荷沢神会（かたくじんね）は自身の師の袈裟の正統性を喧伝し強く主張した。[17]逆に、慧能禅師を第六祖と位置付けるために、その袈裟が利用されることも少なからずあった。

平安時代までは、文様のない一種類の生地で製作され、デザインは中国的な美意識に貫かれたものが多い。これは大陸への留学経験が重要視された時代であることを物語っており、袈裟にもそれが顕著に表われている。たとえば、禅宗の九条袈裟は、台形で中央付近に三角形の生地を挟み込む形になっており、着用するとゆったりとしていてやや裾広がりになる。袈裟がはだけないように紐を結び留めるための象牙や鼈甲（べっこう）で作られた環も現存している。

文様は柿の蔕（へた）や花折枝文様なども取り入れられ、世俗の染織品の流行とも対応している。

やがて日本らしいデザインである藤の花房や桐竹鳳凰麒麟（夢窓疎石）[18]も登場するが、これは、滅宗宗興など中国への留学経験をもたない僧侶がいたことを推測させる。流行のスタイルは移り変わるものである。袈裟は、着用法に大きな変化はないが、デザイン面などにおいては時代の傾向や好みを反映したファッション現象を帯びることもあったと言えよう。

鎌倉時代に生きた道元禅師は達磨大師から数えて五一代目にあたる。正式な釈迦の袈裟が唯一いまに伝わっているのが禅宗であるという誇りのもと、袈裟とは師と弟子が向き合って伝える相伝の証だとして、書物でもその重要性を説いている。その経緯は、中国曹洞宗の僧である如浄禅師（にょじょう）のもとで修行した体験[19]によるところが大きい。日本の仏教界で袈裟の精神的重要性が語られるようになるには、道元禅師を俟たねばならなかったのである。

結び──こころとことば

衣服の詩

言語も衣服も「身に着ける」という表現が用いられる。からだというモノを媒介にして、目に見えない法や仏のこころを表すのが袈裟という衣服である。からだに纏って着ることを繰り返しながら、そのこころを装いつつ人として執着を脱ぎ、仏となり、生きていく。

道元禅師が仏道修行において袈裟の重要性を目の当たりにしたのは、南宋の時代、如浄禅師の下で修行していた時であった。一日のはじまりである暁天坐禅終了の合図の板が鳴るとともに、袈裟の包みを開いて頭上に載せ、合掌して敬い、一つの詩を唱える儀式がある。その最も肝要な箇所を、以下に引用する。

予、在宋のそのかみ、長連牀に請功夫せしとき、斉肩の隣単をみるに、開静のときごとに、袈裟をささげて頂上に安じ、合掌恭敬し、一偈を黙誦す。その偈にいはく、

大哉解脱服　無相福田衣
披奉如来教　広度諸衆生。ときに予、未曾見のおもひを生じ、歓喜身にあまり、感涙ひそかにおちて衣襟をひたす。（『袈裟功徳』二十二）

僧侶たちが袈裟を敬う姿に感動して涙を流した場面の描写だ。「大いなるかな解脱服／無相福田の衣／如来の教えを身につけたてまつり、広く諸々の衆生を度さむ」という詩を三度唱えた後、合掌し、立ち上がって袈裟を身に着け、作務に向かう。「衆生」とはいのちあるものすべてのものを指し、「度す」とは迷いや悩みから悟りの境地へ達するという意味である。拝むべきものとは、ふつう頭上にあり、権力的な存在である。袈裟をその位置に載せるということは、袈裟を重要視する象徴的行為だといえよう。詩は呪文でもある。その詩を唱えるという

[92]

袈裟とファッション

日本曹洞宗開祖道元の袈裟は、熊本県の広福寺に大智禅師（六代）の相伝を経て継承され、約八〇〇年あまりの時間を超えて現存していると言われている。平織りの麻素材で、縦糸緯糸ともに黒に限りなく近い濃紺＝青黒色である。*22 この袈裟は、山城の生蓮房の妻室が、自分たちで育てた麻の繊維を潔斎して織り上げて越州の永平寺に献上した衣財を、道元自ら裁縫して一生涯搭けたと言われるものである。二十五条袈裟で、分類としては「上品」*23 となる僧伽梨であり、嗣法の証として弟子の懐奘にまず継承された。

袈裟は如法衣である。正伝の仏法を嗣ぐことは、正師の衣装の伝承を象徴としている。聖性を表現している布であり、仏教者の特権性もあわせ持っている。

袈裟は宗教服であるから、権力的な要素も自ずと示してしまうのでないかという問いも生まれる。しかし道元は言う、「仏子とならんは、天上人間、国王百官をとはず、在家出家、奴婢畜生を論ぜず、仏戒を受得し、袈裟を正伝すべし」。*24 仏教とは、本来の自己に目覚めることを目指すものであり、真摯にそれを求めて修行に励めば、仏袈裟を着ることができるのだ、と説く。厳しいカースト制のインドにあって平等性を釈迦が強く説いたことに由来している。

身体を保護するという根源的な理由から始まり、国・民族・宗教・階級・職業などをあらわすユニフォームとしての役割を、人の衣服は持つようになった。また、社会が発展するとファッションの流行現象からは逃れられず、いわば布というモノに過剰な意味が付着する。新しさを絶対的価値にもつファッションの世界のなかでは、衣服の持つ継承すべき価値は軽視される。民族衣装などの伝統的な構造・装飾・着用法は過去の遺物のように扱

ことは、袈裟の奥義や呪術的な力を聴覚の音のリズムからも体感する行為になるのではないか。

帰国後、道元は如浄禅師の教えに従い、世俗化した当時の仏教を批判し、仏陀本来の精神に立ち返ることをところに決める。その手がかりの一つとなるのが仏僧の身に着ける袈裟であった。

われたり、意味が形骸化して記号を遊ぶような現象＝コスプレやフェティッシュな存在となる。

政情不安となった鎌倉時代、人々に求められた新しい仏教は次第に俗化して、仏教界も政治的な血なまぐさい闘いに巻き込まれていく。道元禅師が貫いたのは、釈迦から達磨大師そして翁師如浄が受け継いだ清浄なる仏教者としての姿勢――根本となる潔白で厳格な正伝の仏法を遵守して伝承していくことだった。道元が袈裟にこだわっていたとすればその理由は袈裟が護持している思想であり仏法そのものなのである。

衣服は共同体に属したものであると同時に自己を表現する手段でもある。現代において人は様々なアイデンティティを脱ぎ着するかのように衣服を脱ぎ着しているのかもしれない。ファッションという情報を剥ぎ取って衣服そのものを語ることができるだろうか。袈裟という衣服の存在は力強い。信仰や思いを織りこむように手を使ってこころをこめて丁寧に縫い上げられる。着る人の持つ思想や生き様が継承される。尊敬の念をもって伝えていく服。それを使命として受けとめる服。正伝の仏袈裟は相伝書が存在していなければただの麁末（そまつ）な布にすぎない。

袈裟とは超越した衣服である。人が規定する二項対立的な価値である、きれい／きたない・良い／悪い・新しい／古いなどを超えて行く。めまぐるしく消費する現代ファッションのシステムから自由である。わたしたちは何を着ているのか、服を通して身に着けているものは何なのか――その問いの答に奥行きをもたらす可能性を孕んでいる。ファッション研究に光をもたらしてくれる、いわば、こころとからだがその布を通して、一つになるのである。

注

*1　本章では岩波文庫版に所収されている「伝衣」を主に参考にする。道元『正法眼蔵（二）』水野弥穂子校注、岩波文庫、一九九〇年、二四七－二八一頁。

*2　「伝衣」も「袈裟功徳」も、仁治元（一二四〇）年開冬日（一〇月一日）の土衆となっているが、「伝衣」という情報が日付としては正確で、後に永平寺へ移って増補したものが「袈裟功徳」とのこと。水野弥穂子『正法眼蔵袈裟功徳』を読む』大法輪閣、二〇〇七年、六－七頁。

*3　仏教の開祖釈迦牟尼世尊の略尊称、紀元前六二四－五四四年（南伝説）、紀元前五六六－四八六年（北伝説）、紀元前四六六－三八六

年（宇井説）。

*4　沢木興道監修、久馬慧忠編『袈裟の研究』大法輪閣、一九六七年、一五頁。

*5　久馬慧忠『袈裟のはなし』法藏館、二〇〇〇年、七—一二頁。

*6　ロラン・バルト『モードの体系』佐藤信夫訳、みすず書房、一九七二年。

*7　水野弥穂子、前掲書、一七一—一七七頁。

*8　同書、一七七—一八一頁。

*9　松村薫子『糞掃衣の研究』法藏館、二〇〇六年、五七—八四頁。

*10　水野弥穂子、前掲書、一八一—一八七頁。

*11　沢木興道監修、久馬慧忠編、前掲書、四一頁。

*12　同書、二八—三三頁。

*13　条とは細長い帯状の一枚の布を指す。「一長一短」とは長い布片と短い布片一枚ずつをつなぎ合わせて一条にするという意味。

*14　現在は法衣店などでも製作販売されるが、この慣習は残っている。

*15　松村薫子、前掲書、一二五—一三二頁。現在でも袈裟を縫う会として引き継がれている福田会の例では「山、雲、四角」が挙がる。

*16　沢木興道監修、久馬慧忠編、前掲書、一九〇—二〇二頁。

*17　山川暁『高僧と袈裟』（特別展覧会図録）京都国立博物館、二〇一〇年、一一—一四頁。

*18　同書、一四—一六頁。

*19　道元「伝衣」、前掲書、二七五—二七六頁。留学の折、毎朝袈裟を掲げて頂上し詩を読むことに感動する場面が記されている。

*20　現在熊本県立美術館において、相伝書とともに委託保存されている。川口高風「道元禅師の広福寺蔵 『二十五条衣』について（上）

*21　『傘松』八四六号、大本山永平寺傘末会、二〇一四年三月、一五—一八頁。

*22　カタログでは糸の色は「黒」と書かれている。山川暁、前掲書、八四—八五頁。

*23　「八月に入ると、二人は身を清め、仏壇に参ったのち、いよいよ仕事に取りかかった。丹精こめて育てた麻を刈り取り、皮をはぎ、水にうたせてつけて、叩いて、繊維を取り出し、二人がかりで糸に紡いでいった。十一月半ばのある日の早朝、静は宇治川に下りて身を清めた。帰宅すると、仏壇に灯明をあげ、『般若心経』を唱えた。今日からいよいよ布地に織る作業に入る。静は酒と塩で身を清めた。機も酒と塩で清めた。九条家から賜った例の伽羅を長持の底から取り出し、織り機のおいてある部屋に焚き込めた。静はそこにこもって一心不乱に織りはじめた」（大谷哲夫『永平の風』文芸社、二〇〇一年、三九八—四〇三頁）。

*24　道元「伝衣」、前掲書、二八〇頁。

智慧としてのファッション

——こころは服を着るからだ

自分を意識して世界と繋がる——まさにこれはファッションのことを言っているように響く。じつは「自分」「意識」「世界」という三つのいずれの言葉も、仏教から由来した用語である。本章のタイトルにもなっている「智慧」もそうだ。仏教者の修行において肝要となる概念で「慧」が「簡択」を「智」が「断疑」を意味する[*1]。

平たくいえば、分類して選び、その是非を断定するということ。

一日のはじまり、何を着ようか、わたしたちは考える。ファッションがカジュアル化して長いから、現在はリラクシングウェアが充実していて、寝ていた衣装で家に一日居ることも珍しくないかもしれない。しかし少なくとも外へ出るときは、服を新たに選ぶに違いない。あれこれ迷うことも多いはず。最後はコレ！あるいはコレとコレ！などと決めなければならない。そのとき、選ばなかったものと〈わたし〉は、断たれてしまっている。

本書のうち日本語パートの最終章にあたる本章は、ややカタイ言葉からはじまったかもしれない。これまで服を着るという行為から何が読み取られるのかを考えてきたが、ファッションというシステムのなかで、着る人であるわたしたちのからだを軸に、衣服のもつ可能性についても語ることにしよう。

前章で扱ったわたしたちの裂装は、いわば超越する衣服であった。現代ファッションの研究の限界を克服する光になるのではないか。そんな直感から研究を開始した研究対象であることは述べたが、本書所収の英語パートのなかでもIV章でさらに展開している。からだを考えるときこころの声も聞かなければならない。第一章の第二節で紹介して

おいた仏教における「こころ」の捉え方の一つ「唯識論」にもまた力を借りようと思う。

本章では、現在英国と日本をベースに作品を制作し発表している新進気鋭のメールアート（郵藝）／コラージュ作家のニコラ・オーリック（Nichola Orlick, 一九八六―）の作品を紹介しながら、人が衣服を着ることとその可能性について考えていこう。

身体とことば

身体とことばをテーマに作品を作ってきたニコラは、二〇一四年夏ロンドンのテート美術館の 'Source.' と題された公募展で、一九六〇年代から七〇年代中心のコラージュ作家に混じって作品が展示された。曽祖父が南九州の出身で当時の藩の代表の一人として渡英、公式に留学していたのかは判然としないが、英国人女性との間に生まれた祖母はそのまま英国に留まり、ニコラはその孫として生まれた。祖母の意向で美しく正しい日本語や日本文化を身につけるよう教育され、大学では日本の人類学を専攻し、現在は日英を行き来する生活を送っている。

早速一つ目の作品（図1）を見てみよう。ファッション雑誌のモデルのような女性の後ろ姿に重なるように、白い菊の花が頭部になっている身体が買い物籠を持っている。手が大きいので男性かもしれない。後ろ姿の女性とは別の個体なのか、あるいは影のような存在なのか。からだ／服のパーツの切れ目の部分に、新聞や雑誌で切り取ったことばが縫い目のように貼り付いている。

頭部には、「呉服」「着物」「洋服」と並んで「青物」ということばが見られる。「着」と「青」は文字としてよく似ているから、注意深く見ないと見逃してしまう。菊の葉の緑色と重なるように、背の部分に柑橘類のライムやレモン＝青果が装飾品のように乗っている。籠のなかには何が入っているのだろうか。両方の足下に [soap]「off the list」という言葉が見られる。イギリス人の日常になくてはならい買い物リスト [shopping list] を示唆するようなことばである。石鹸はリストから除き、「青果を買い物している人」と言ったところか。日本の下町の風景のような写真のコラージュでできた太めのズボンと西洋人らしき女性との間には、天草四郎の横顔が見

図1
ニコラ・オーリック　無題（2014）

え隠れしている。ニコラの曽祖父と同じ九州で活躍した、江戸時代の歴史上の人物でキリシタンである。

人間の身体に切れ目はない。ロラン・バルトは、モード雑誌のことばを集めて分類し体系化して、衣服を記号現象として分析した。どこからどこまでが足なのか臀部なのか。胸部と腹部もそうだが、デジタル情報のように、からだははっきりと分かれてはいない。たとえば、身体は「ブラウス」や「スカート」など服のことばで、上半身や下半身のように言語化される。ニコラの作品は、肉の塊ともいえる人のからだが、社会化され世界と繋がっていく過程で意味が出現していることを物語る。

衣服を着るとき、人種・民族・ジェンダー・職業など様々な社会的な意味＝アイデンティティを纏っている。英国人の血と、遠く離れた国であってもからだの内に流れる日本人の血。影のような身体は白い菊と日本の町を身に着けているが、「long wear」「tailored」「silky story」という英語の言葉でからだは区切られている。外界を切り取り、意味付けする。〈わたし〉は世界と繋がっている。人のからだに合わせて生地から仕立て制作されるシルクの衣装＝「着物」の物語。高級なオートクチュールである日本の民族衣装は長く着用されて次世代に継承されていく。着物は日本人の「こころ」を表現してくれるのだろうか。頭の中にある日本語が遥か彼方にある空想の中の外国のことばとしても霊のように並んでいる。

二つ目の作品（図2）に移ろう。古い日本家屋と瓦のコラージュが帽子やケープの上着になっている。スカートの折り目からはたくさんのスピーカーが垣間見える。突き出しているゴジラの存在。ゴジラは「recent explosion」＝最近の爆発（噴火）ということばからも示唆され、中央部分に位置する「夏葉書（富士山と花火）」とも対応している。高温の炎が上がり爆発するイメージ。

手で高く掲げているのは「食パン」と「だご汁」という文字。日本の日常的な食べ物。祖母の味なのだろうか。掲げる（志向する）ものは気取

だご汁とは、南九州でよく知られた小麦粉で作った団子を入れた味噌汁のこと。掲げる（志向する）ものは気取

図2
ニコラ・オーリック　無題（2014）

らない日本食であり、くすっと笑える親しみやすい庶民のことばである。イギリス的なユーモアにも繋がるだろうか。西洋の女性のからだと日本のことばを繋いでいるのは、日本でも現在あまり見かけなくなった白くて細い紙縒。

腕には「delivering」「travelling」ということばが確認できる。葉書のモチーフと併せて、この作品はメールアートになっている。瓦は厚くて重い。自身の背に「日本」がアンバランスに重くのしかかっているのか。目を覆っている「創業」の文字は、オリジナルでありたい、じぶんの眼で見極めたい、そんな願望を表現しているのかもしれない。足下の「open here」という文字はまるくやわらかい裾のラインを作る。バラバラなモノが乗っかり熱く重く黒い服の下は果たしてどうなっているのだろう。

広く速く遠くに繋がる最新の情報媒体＝インターネットの通信方法に対して、時間もかかり通信費もかかる郵便にこだわって作品を作るのはなぜなのか。こころの中の日本は遥か遠くの国。空を飛び、海を超え、時差のある、憧れの国。封筒に貼られた切手の消印はロマンティックな旅の刻印となる。デジタル情報は行き来できても、からだそのものはインターネットで送ることはできない。日本語と英語のバイリンガルを活かし、細やかな表現やユーモアの入り交じった作品。ここ＝英国とそこ＝日本を結ぶのは郵便であり、手の先を動かして紙を切ったり貼ったり繰り返し、自由な時間と空間のデザインをしている。

こころと世界

冒頭で、自分を意識して世界と繋がることは、ファッションを表現していることと似ていると述べた。本節では仏教の考え方や用語を借りながら、「意識」についてしばらく考える。

仏教あるいは「唯識論」では、すべては意識＝こころから成り立っていると考える。その意識は八つの階層から成り、一個のからだを構成する。「前五識」と呼ばれる眼識・耳識・鼻識・舌識・身識は、わかりやすくいうと五感にあたる（身識は触覚のこと）。前五識を支えているのが「第六意識」で、知・情・意を司り、それぞれ判

断・感情・意志にあたる。これらをあわせて「表層意識」という。

見えている「表層意識」の下に、見えない「深層意識」が二つ存在している。その一つ「第七末那識」は自我で、執着や煩悩と結びついている。残る「第八阿頼耶識」は自分の行為の経験の痕跡で、生まれる前から染みているものも含まれ、大きくて測りしれない貯蔵庫のようなイメージとして捉えられる。二つの深層意識はお互いにその拠り所となっていることが特徴である。

平たく言えば、人は聞きたい音しか知覚していない。外界すべての音を聞いて認識せねばならないとしたら、気が狂ってしまうだろう。つまり、選びつつ、捨てているのだ。日常に見慣れたはずの風景のなかで突然新しい事物を発見することがある。また同じ一枚の絵があったとしても人によって見方がそれぞれ変わる。それは五感である前五識が第六意識の働きによって知覚するからである。興味や好みや必要性によっても変化する。

表層意識は、深層意識の第七末那識の性質である自己中心性によっても左右される。自分に都合のよい話しか覚えていなかったり、鏡を見ても自分の欠点に気付かなかったり。よく見られたいという煩悩が強まると、逆に欠点ばかりに目がいくこともある。さらに下部の第八阿頼耶識は、人は自覚することができない意識であるという。いまの個人の行為の経験だけでなく、民族や人種としての共同意識や、生まれる前の祖先を遡り脈々と流れている太古の意識も含まれる。

阿頼耶識は善でも悪でもどちらでもなく、「汚れ」ということばで表現されることがある。仏教では人はみな仏であり、凡夫として人間が持つ汚れがあるからこそ「清浄」を志すことができるのだという。あらかじめ清浄さを内に持っている、あるいは清浄さに抱かれている存在という考え方である。意識は階層ごとに単純な運動をしているのではなく、それぞれが複雑に関係しあって、こころという現象を生み出している。

アイデンティティとオリジナリティ

次に、ファッションと意識について考えてみよう。人は服を着るとき、こころにどのようなことが起こってい

るのだろうか。着るものを選ぶ時、自分の美意識によって色・形・素材・スタイルを選ぶ。その日の気分も関係してくるに違いない。また、その美意識は個人のもののようでいて、はっきりと自覚できない誰かの何かの意識も働いているかもしれない。教育を受けなくてもパジャマを脱いで外へ出て行く子どものように。

美しくありたい、自分らしさを表現したい、という欲望は、健全な自我の表れだろう。作品の人物の眼に「創業」という文字が貼りついていた。オリジナルや純血とは何か。人は誰でも物事を見る時バイアスがかかってしまう。本物とは何か。深層意識のなかにある、制御することのできない、自分では測りしれない嗜好。たとえば日本人の考え方の傾向が自然に顕われたり。美しさもわたしらしさもしっかり自分で決めているようでいて、ダイナミックで流動的で移り変わり易いものなのかもしれない。

さらに言うならば、わたしたちは個性を表現したいと願う一方で、人から理解されたいというこころも同時に働いている。あえて変人として笑われたいわけではない。個性や新しさにこだわってばかりいると、奇怪な扮装になってしまう。たとえ奇妙でも全体のバランスが表現されていないと、一歩先のモードとして受容されない。

繰り返せば、ファッションは、個としての自分と共同体に帰属する一員である〈わたし〉とが桔抗するところにこそ生まれる。

世界とはいま目前に見ている外界のことを言う。仏教では、自分を離れて世界は存在しないという考え方をとる。つまり、世界とは、内面のこころがあたかも外に実在するような形となって現れたもの。

ファッションは、〈わたし〉のからだを媒介に世界を表現する絵画のようなもの、あるいは世界そのものが〈わたし〉なのだ。自分の内面の「こころ」や「意識」が外界に表れる。からだはどこに？ここで再び仏教のことばを借りれば、「自分が客体化」されて「対象化され」その「対象化をしているのも〈わたし〉」。細胞分裂を経て、捨てながら選び、選びながら捨て、〈わたし〉は服を通して、生まれる。見るのも自己、見られるのも自己。わたしが〈わたし〉を見つめる。「智慧」を通して服を着ることによって、辛うじてこころとからだが繋がる。そこに座っている、人らしき存在の〈わたし〉──立ち上がって、歩きはじめる。

結び──自由なコラージュ

Clothes speak ──衣服は語る。意図しなくても、自ずと着ているものが何かを語っている。人は衣服を着る動物である。

服を着替える、流行を享受する、他の動物はそんなことはやらないから、そのとき〈わたし〉は人になる＝人を着る動物になる。動物を追う、ゆえに〈わたし〉は動物になる。〈わたし〉は人を脱いで動物になる。そのとき動物に還るのか。裸であることが恥ずかしいのは、服を着なければならない社会のなかに居るからだ。恥ずかしいとおもう〈わたし〉を発見する〈わたし〉。差恥心という言葉も概念も相対的なものでしかない。人の社会にあっても、動物という世界にあっても。

阿頼耶識を深くたどっていくとどこに辿り着くのだろう。意識の眠りにぶつかって生きとし生けるものと融合し未分化な一つに統合されるのかもしれない。動物的なことは本能的なこと、装飾行為もしかり。雌を誘う雄の虹色に輝く翼は生殖行為に結びつき、からだを飾ることは社会的な行為でもある。動物と分かれたがったり、動物に還りたがったり、もちろんそんなことは動物の方では知ったことではない。「人間は、みずからの他者を自己に関係づけながら自己の外部へと排除する構造を必要としている」[*4]。追いつつ、どっちつかずなまま、揺れている。さ迷うこころを包みこむように、今日の服はからだを前へ送り出してくれる。

共同体に帰属する〈わたし〉は、時には他グループと差異化するためユニフォームを着る。帰属意識を衣服の記号性で高める。時代とともに発展した社会は、衣服の「新しい」という情報を一時的に絶対的な価値としてファッションを造る。高度消費社会のなかでは、衣服の記号性は遊戯ともなって、意味内容が剥ぎ取られ「スタイル」になる。

一人の数学者は言った──人は動物だが、単なる動物ではなく、渋柿の台木に甘柿の芽をついだようなもの、つまり動物性の台木に人間性の芽をつぎ木したもの。[*5] 人は惑い悩み学びながら「自分を意識して世界と繋がる」。

からだを媒介に、様々な言語や文化の環境世界と繋がり、こころは意味をコラージュするように服を纏う。国・民族・人種・宗教・職業、ときには性別などの境界を越えて、異なるものが融合し調和する時代。重なったり、解けたり、破れたり、ばらばらになりそうなからだを、こころの糸を紡いで、縫い合わせたら、刺繍を施したり、リボンで結んだり。豊かさを求め、過ぎると、苦しみが生じる。美しい衣装に身を包む心地よい体験。もはや動物には戻られない。

自分を意識して世界と繋がる。こころとからだは、服を着る。いま、ここ、一回一回、選びつつ、断たれる。刹那でも、表現行為のなかに、匂いが立ち上り、空気が彩られ、〈わたし〉の輪郭がぼんやり現れる。好きなものは移ろいやすい。疲れたら、人を脱ぐべく、森に入り鳥の歌に耳を澄まそう。智慧とは、自由への道。清浄なるものを、志向しながら。服を着るのは、からだとこころ。こころは服を着るからだ。

注

＊1　太田久紀『「唯識」の読み方』大法輪閣、二〇〇一年。初版第一刷は一九八五年に発行、本章中の仏教に関することばはすべて本書より引用。

＊2　メールアート……郵便を利用した芸術作品、あるいは郵便物そのものが作品となる。長距離間で送る人と送られる人がいて成立する、郵便システムを通して行う実験的パフォーマンスとなる芸術の手法である。一九六二年に、フルクサスのレイ・ジョンソン（一九二七─九五）が「メールアート宣言」をしている。日本では「具体」の作家嶋本昭三（一九二八─二〇一三）がメール・アーティストの代表的存在であり、「メールアートは現代美術の混迷から抜け出せる最先のランナーである」「美術界に汚染されていない子供や農夫には簡単に〝ワカル〟世界でもある」と述べている。

＊3　ロラン・バルト『モードの体系』佐藤信夫訳、みすず書房、一九七二年［一九六七年］。

＊4　宮崎裕助「脱構築はいかにして生政治を開始するか」『現代思想　特集人間／動物の境界線』vol.37-38、二〇〇九年、一四二頁。

＊5　岡潔『春宵十話』光文社文庫、二〇〇六年、一二頁。

我着る、ゆえに我あり

二〇〇七年夏、神戸で「詩と服の展覧会——あなたNOなまえ」という展示を企画した。緑に囲まれたギャラリー空間に cell dress 108と名付けた作品を展示した。ひとつのボディに一〇八枚の服を着せるというインスタレーションで、通称「煩悩服」と呼びながら制作していたが、日に日に大きく重くなっていき、途中で倒れかかってきたりするととても危険で、取り扱いに注意を要する物体になっていった。服をたくさん着付けるだけでも至難の技だったが、それを最終的にはひとつの衣装スタイルに仕立てあげることを目標にしていた。一九世紀末のヴィクトリア時代の女性のドレスをイメージしていた。ジェンダーが明確に分かれ、女性の衣装が華美になって、身体の造形にもメリハリがあった時代。西洋ファッション史のなかでも読解すべき面白い問題を孕んでいて、個人的にもその時代の衣装スタイルを好んでいた。

衣服と言語のアナロジーを軸に研究を続けてきて、一五年間分の論文を纏めて『闘う衣服』を上梓したのが二〇一一年春、念校のあたりでは東日本大震災が起こって、関西在住であっても運命が変わった者の一人である。本書は、前著を出した後に執筆した論文がほとんどを占めている。前回のタイミングに合わないと判断した論文も大幅に加筆修正して本書に収録したのが、文学作品あるいは文学者のことばを通して読むことのできる、日本の洋装の受容について扱った第二章の詩人北園克衛と第三章の小説家林芙美子である。

「人を着る」というテーマがいつどんな風にして現れたのかはわからない。大震災の後、人生の価値観が大き

く変わり、また長らく研究対象にしてきた現代ファッションだけでは何かが足りないような、また所属する学術界も西洋中心主義からなかなか逃れられないようなもどかしさのなか（自省の念もこめて）、衣服を研究していく上で虚無感のようなものを憶えるようになっていた頃だとおもう。

結論のようなものを書きはじめて、十年以上前に作ったじぶんの作品を思い出したわけだが、「人を着る」ということは、煩悩からなかなか解脱できない人間がこの地球上でいとなむ生活行為そのものを指し示していると言ってもいい。煩悩を着ている、と単純に表現してもいいのかもしれない。それは、簡単に脱げない、という点で「人」なのである。

あるいは、人が裸で外を歩いてはいけない規則が作られるようになった時代や環境のなかにいて、意味を着る、社会を着る、つまり、情報や制度を着ている、という捉え方でもいいかも知れない。序論で展開した問いをおもいだす。パジャマを脱ぎたくないのは子どもだけではないのだ。わたしたちは窮屈な衣服を着ているのかもしれないが、それはわたしたちが作った衣服でありルールである。

項対立的な言語とそのシステムをつかって、物事を認識して世界を作ってきた。前著では「人間は衣服を着る動物である」という結論に辿り着いたが、それは「人間だけが」という意味合いが強く、刊行後段々に、その特権的とも捉えられる人間観、動物観のようなものを乗り越えていかなければならない、と新しい問題意識を抱くようになっていった。方法は違えども動物もからだを保護するし装飾するに違いないが、動物も恥じらうということを実際に目の当たりに体験したことも大きい。

動物好きの家に生まれ、とりわけ常に小動物と一緒に暮らしてきた。類は友を呼ぶのか、気がつくとまわりも同じく動物好きの人が多くなり、共通の話題は自然に動物の話になり、動物も恥じらうという予感は気のせいでないことが確かになっていった。「我思う、ゆえに我あり」には飛躍し過ぎかもしれないがそれに連なる「人間だけが羞恥心（自意識）をもつ」という、衣服の根源的理由に掲げられる一要因がぐらつきはじめた。その頃は、イギリスのロンドンにしばらく暮らしていて、ジャック・デリダの動物論に触れることになった。前著の大きな

柱でもあったロラン・バルトのモード論もそうだったが、欧州に滞在している時にフランス人の思想家の書物を英語で読むという習慣を続けてきた。デリダの著作は、美術館の中の本屋で偶然出会ったような記憶がある。その頃執筆したのが**第一章第一節**で、まわりにいた欧州の作家の作品を分析することで「人を着る」を展開してみたかった。動物と人間を分かつところを探ろうとすることは、結局のところ「人間とは何か」という深い森のような問いに入ることだった。わたしの場合、着る行為にその手掛かりがあると信じ求めてきたのだろう。

『闘う衣服』の序論と結論がそれぞれ二つの大学の入試問題で引用された。名誉なことだが設問に向かえどもよい回答が思いつかない。高校の現代文の教科書にも採用されることになった。「人はなぜ服を着るのか」──いったんまとめて結んだはずが、研究者としてもう一歩先をいかねばならない。その途上で、所属する日本記号学会の年次大会の実行委員長の仕事がまわってきた。二〇一三年春に神戸ファッション美術館で「着る、纏う、装う／脱ぐ」と題して開催したが、企画したメインのセッションでは、人間が衣服を着なければならないこととそのものに迫ってみたい、と考え、僧侶、音楽家、フランス思想研究者に登壇してもらい、なるべく自由に語ってもらった。その内容のまとめは**第一章第二節**に本書のために改稿して収録した。我＝〈わたし〉の身体は拡張して、都市や自然という環境に融合していく。身体はひとつの楽器のように鳴り、音という波は漂い流れていく。袈裟は宗教服であ個人から集団へ、そして他生物と共存しているヒトである〈わたしたち〉が立ち現れてくる。袈裟は宗教服であるが、道元禅師の着ることへの根源的な探求に接して、衣服の可能性をふたたび見出すことのできる瞬間があった。人（＝意味や社会や煩悩）を着る〈わたし〉は、それらを脱していくこともできるはずなのだ。袈裟の存在は仏法の継承のあらわれであった。生きとし生けるものを尊び、二項対立を超えていく清浄なるいのちの世界。ばらばらな心身は衣服の存在によって一つになっていくような、生きる行為そのもの。人の手で一針一針こころをこめて縫いあげる布。からだに仏を着る。**第五章**と Chapter IV で論じている。

人を着ることとは、いくつもの自己を構成する要素＝アイデンティティを社会において脱ぎ着する、あるいは服によってそのアイデンティティを形成していく、ということでもある。前著でも扱ったこの衣服とアイデンティ

図1 昭和2（1927）年『婦人グラフ』6月号

ティの問題はやはり今回も避けることはできないし、衣服を叩けば自然に問題として浮上してくる。

一枚の写真と一つの詩を紹介しよう（図1）。昭和二（一九二七）年の『婦人グラフ』六月号では、エリーナ・テルノスカヤという名のロシア大使館秘書の女性がキモノを身に着けている。断髪のモダンガールの時代だから、洋風のヘアスタイルとの組み合わせに違和感はなくても、胸元が開いてやや乱れた感じは正統な和装には遠い印象を思わせる。しかし、そのまま看過することはできない。写真の下には、「東照子」という筆名で日本語の詩を書いている。「松島と氷島」というタイトルで、黒い島と碧い海、白い島と白い海、氷の島と松の島、日本に居てロシアを望郷するも「私はどちらも愛します」と最後は宣言している。内に抱える葛藤を日本語で韻を踏みながら詩情として表現する。詩を読んだ後に、ふたたび彼女の着物姿を見てみると、愛おしいような気持が沸き起こっていることに気づく。「日本」を懸命に着こなそうとしているのだ。

イギリスを中心に欧州のキモノ文化の受容につ

いて、第四章とChapter Ⅲで論じている。

存・継承されることを願う一方、世界で様々な外国人が、その美しさや豊かさに触れて実際に異文化を身に着ければ、新しく楽しい体験として広がっていくことも望む。経済主導のグローバリズムは、文化波及の側面からみれば、衣服に関しては可能性も感じる。衣装が海を渡るとき、価値観や世界認識の方法も共に渡る。そしてその影響は相互的であり躍動的であれば、衣服も文化として変化・発展していくに違いない。Chapter Ⅰは、日本の現代ファッションであるゴシック・ロリータが国外でも流行する兆しが見え始めた頃、講演として話した原稿が下敷きになっている。西洋服飾文化の伝統的形式を取り入れるこの日本のストリート・スタイルは、欧州においても新しい現代ファッションの形として、また近隣アジア諸国でも受容されている。

本書の原稿を担当編集者に出し終えた日、久しぶりに近所を散歩していた。少し足をのばせば観光地にあたる神戸の北野坂でまばゆいロリータ少女たちと出くわした。入稿できたことの興奮もあって、話しかけると秋の日らの観光客であった。「奇跡島」*1という名のロリータファッションのブランドのデザイナーとその顧客が秋の日本を訪れていた。礼儀正しく、また取材に協力的で、写真撮影を許された。一枚紹介してみよう（図2）。向かって右から赤い衣装は花さん、室内スリッパのような履物を恥ずかしがっていたが、かえって可愛らしさが際立っていた。眼鏡姿も愛らしい紺の衣装は海月森さんで、ロリータ必須アイテムの日傘もきちんと携えていた。全身ピンク色の爛童画さんは色白で目が大きく、ロリータのモデルのようだった。写真の中には入らなかったデザイナーの恵さんは、流暢な日本語を話して通訳も担当してくれた。ご本人もロリータファッションを身に着けており、ファッションを通して日本に大きな興味を持ち日本語も勉強しはじめたという。日本という国そのものがファッション化している。Chapter Ⅱはイギリス・ロンドンの芸術大学で日本のファッションの受容を紹介しながら、いまあらためてファッションとは何か、ファッショナブルな日本のイメージについて考えた公開講座の原稿がベースになっている。時空を隔てれば隔てるほど、イメージというものは結晶化していく。

着物に話を戻すと、本書の刊行予定時期と重なるが、二〇二〇年二月二九日から、ヴィクトリア＆アルバート

図2
ロリータファッションを愛する中国人観光客
筆者撮影（2019）

博物館で、Kimono: Kyoto to Catwalk と題して、国外で最大と言われるキモノの展覧会が開催されることになっている。　担当学芸員のアナ・ジャクソン氏に二〇一七年にインタビューをした際、キモノおよび帯などの生地を含むコレクションは現在充実しているが、キモノの展示方法がどのようになるのか、困難でもあり挑戦でもあ

る、と話していた。トータルな衣装として見せるのか、その場合はボディに着付けることが必要となるから、収蔵品の耐久性が心配事となるわけだ。同館は裂裳の収集にも近年積極的になっている。西洋が東洋を理解し、その認識の形を表現するという意味で、楽しみな展覧会になるはずである。

「花が咲くということは、花が咲くという心、つまり情緒が形となって現れるということです。その花の情緒に蝶が舞い、蝶の心に花が笑む」――大小遠近彼此の別がないわかりあいの世界を、数学者の岡潔は「情緒」と呼んだ。[*2]「こころは服を着るからだ」は、「からだは服を着るこころ」でもいい。こころとからだ、言葉では分かれていても実際には切り離すことはできない。世界そのものが重層的な〈わたし〉のこころの表現であることは、もう何度も本文で書いたので繰り返さないでおこう。自然と乖離して〈わたしたち〉になれない〈わたし〉はバラバラなコラージュのようなびつな身体イメージとともに在る。

第六章で扱ったコラージュ作品は、現代に生きる者の切実な叫びの表現のようであり、第三章においては洋装を必死で生活のなかに受容していく日本の女性たちの体験にも連なる。すくわれるのは、第二章のなかの詩において、トルソーが時代の風に軽やかに舞うように響くことである。禁止や抑圧を言葉の遊びに替えて新しい美や認識の表現を作りあげることで難局を乗り切ろうとしている。

上下が閉じて開いて円柱のようなからだは多少の違いはあれどもわたしたち動物が共通して持っているかたちだそうだ。[*3] 人という衣装を着ている人間、人という衣装を脱げない人間、裸になればヒトになって他動物と仲間入りができるのだろうか。人間社会においてそれは簡単なことではない。裸体は描かれればヒトになって他動物と仲間入りができるのだろうか。人間社会においてそれは簡単なことではない。裸体は描かれればヌードという審美的価値に晒される対象となるし、パジャマでさえ許されないのに裸のままで外へ走って行ったら過剰な意味を放つ奇怪な行動に晒され罪に問われる（少なくとも大人は）。原稿を執筆している最中の二〇一九年秋に鑑賞した京都国立近代美術館での「ドレスコード？――着る人たちのゲーム」展は、衣服にまつわる様々なルールを見つけ出してそれらを遊ぶ、ファッションの可能性を感じられる興味深い内容だった。服そのものの存在感におぼえたり、デザインする人のアイデアや技術に圧倒されたり、ファッションを楽しむ着る人＝わたしたちにも目が

向いたり。すべては人が作った不自由ともいえるルールという制限があってこそ創造できる自由のなかの表現なのだ。

ファッションに希望を見出せるような明るい気分に少しはなるのだが、それは安全なシステムのなかの閉じた世界の気晴らしの時空間のようにも見えてしまう。美術館を出たあと平安神宮を抜け鴨川沿いを歩きながら、また「人を着ているとは言えないだろうか」という問いの中に入っていく。キモノについて研究をするようになって、心身の奥深く見えないところが懐かしがっているのか、研究対象に向うとき妙な安定感があり、袈裟までたどりつくと、着ることの意味に少しずつ接近している感触を持つことができ、静かな諦念のような心地よい境地になる。

いつのまにか近年手が伸び読んでいたのは、物理学や生物学の本だった。難解で得意とは言えない分野だから、やがて物理学者や生物学者の人となりにも触れられる随筆を読むようになった。すべて日本人で、すぐれた日本語で書かれた文章によるもの。不思議なことに、わたしが選んだ科学者の中にも道元の曹洞禅の影響を発見する。

ファッション研究者とはどうあるべきか。この問いも繰り返してきた。服とは何かを考えることは、人とは何かを考えることと、わたしの場合は同じになっていった。そして現在は日本語について考えている。一神教の高みから神の視点で見下ろすために〈わたし〉*4 が必要になるのであり、厳しくも豊かな自然と共存して生きる環境では虫の視点から物事をとらえている。日本語は主語のない言語。日本人は、洋服や英語から「〈わたし〉であれ」と無理難題を強いられてきたのかもしれない。

Chapter V で、コミック批評家のポール・グラヴェット氏が予告していたが、二〇一九年夏に大英博物館でのマンガ展が実現した。国外では最大規模の日本のマンガの展覧会で、会場はイギリス最大の国営の博物館である。鳥獣戯画から葛飾北斎、少女マンガからガロまで歴史的に遡り、マンガから見るジェンダー・セクシャリティ・少数民族などの問題、作画の手法や版元などメディアの仕組みにも迫り、分類方法も充実しており、若者を中心に多くの観客動員数を得た。日本のキモノも美術館で展示されることが増えてきたが、このマンガのように自由

自在に世界を旅して愛される存在となるだろうか。

結論のようなもの、のままに本書を閉じることにしよう。未来の読者からのご意見やご教示を楽しみに待ちながら、そしてまた今日も問うことになる。人を着ているとは言えないだろうか。その根源的な問いは、現代のわたしたちを悩ませる「わたしとは誰か」「本当のじぶん探し」という難問に連なる。一日のはじまり、わたしたちは「選び」「決める」という「智慧」をつかう。何を着るべきか、分類して選び、服を決定することができる。その服はわたしを見つめる他者を内在している〈わたし〉であり、その服を通して辛うじて〈わたし〉が存在するのかもしれない。言い換えれば、服が〈わたし〉であり、服を通してしか脱ぐことのできない体験＝衣装そのものなのだ。着るということすなわち人なり。

人を着ているということ。その問いを生きていく。答えは、いつか風雲にのって、稲妻のように、落ちてくるかもしれない。円柱のなかは空。有機的に共に在る〈わたしたち〉の仲間＝動物植物鉱物昆虫微生物に連なって行かれれば。そのとき人を脱ぐことができてヒトになるのかもしれない。しかしそれは、人を着るということを

＊　＊　＊

新しい年が明けて、本書の校正の締切に追われていると、一葉の希望が舞い込んできた。二十歳を迎える儀式に臨む、はにかんだ着物姿。帽子とブーツとハカマのキモノ。帯のリボンはオートクチュールのソワレのよう。写真に撮られたくないと言う。少女のようにも、外国人のようにも、ミュージシャンのようにも見える。ひとりの日本人の肖像（図3）。

人を着るということは、ファッションを楽しむこと。あるのかないのか、あいまいな輪郭の〈わたし〉は、美しく力強くそして自由な〈表現〉となり、いま・ここに〈存在〉している。

「表現は、生れ落ちた途端に自己から離れて、獨立する」[5]

注

＊1　https://shop24528631.m.taobao.com/（二〇一九年一二月二三日最終確認）
＊2　森田真生編『数学する人生』新潮社、二〇一九年、四三頁。
＊3　本川達雄『生きものとは何か』筑摩書房、二〇一九年、一一七―一九〇頁。
＊4　金谷武洋『日本語と西欧語』講談社文庫、二〇一九年、二五―一一五頁。
＊5　原口統三『二十歳のエチュード』書肆ユリイカ、一九四八年、七三頁。

二十歳の青年
撮影：hair design cero（2020）

あとがき

本書の重要な位置を占める、袈裟についての研究は神戸妙香寺での幣道紀老師による曹洞禅についての長年のご指導がなければ実現しなかった。袈裟の制作および資料収集にあたっては、フランス禅堂尼苑での袈裟のワークショップ、岡山洞松寺でお袈裟摂心に参加させて頂いたこと、二つの寺院での外国人僧侶らとの情報交換は、禅文化受容の研究の途上で貴重な体験となった。仏教の勉強は、日本の袈裟の伝承に興味を持っていることもあり、京都大学こころの未来研究センター「日本仏教セミナー」に参加させてもらっている。色んなご縁やご教示に感謝をいたします。英語部分の謝辞でもできるだけ多くの方のお名前をローマ字で書かせて頂きました。

二〇一一年以降のわたしの研究生活は、とりわけ家族の協力がなければ、このような一冊の書物に生まれることはできなかった。愛書家の父小野原道雄には日頃から研究資料の入手や校正作業で助けてもらっている。指導教官が他界した後方向性に迷いつつも適確な助言をくれたのが母小野原榮子だった。こころの視力にすぐれた妹神田明子とも折に触れて問題意識を掘り下げる意義深い議論を交わすことができた。また、これまで色んなインスピレーションをくれて遊んでもらった動物たち。一人一人名前は挙げ切れないが感性豊かで知性溢れるわたしの友人たちにも。こころから、ありがとう。

最後に、本書ができあがるまで遅筆な著者を辛抱強く導いてくださった、ファッションにも造詣が深い晃洋書房の担当編集者阪口幸祐氏にお礼を申し上げる。そして、のんびりな研究者の十年分のしごとを、敬愛するブックデザイナー、ミルキィ・イソベさんによる衣装でお披露目ができることになった、有り難うございました。

二〇二〇年　春節　神戸にて

小野原教子

真夏の星座

黒いヴィクトリアンジュエリーが
花と虫の夜のように蛇行している
枯れたレースはギリギリ張りつめて
冷たく固い体の上を滑っては止まる

リップスティック・アッケラカン
もれなく、いかにも、とってつけた
睫に一本く、一粒く〉が浮遊し
髪に透明な雲のかたまりが割れて

黄色い退屈を解決しようと外に出た
塗りこめたのがますます気になり
気になり出すと厚くなっていく退屈の色
風よ吹け雨よ降れ雷よ轟け夏の嵐

ウソとホントの数をかぞえながら
星の花はナイフのように尖っている
物質の特性を磨いて息を吸って吐いて
重曹を撒いたその摩擦で闇の光沢を希む

MIDSUMMER CONSTELLATION

black Victorian jewelry
slithers like a night of flowers and insects
withered lace stretches fully
sliding and coming to a stop above a cold, tight body

in the hair a cluster of transparent clouds breaks
in eyelashes, one by one, grain by grain drift
not leaking, absolutely, took and applied
Lipstick Offhanded

I step outside aiming to solve the yellow boredom
what was sealed up worries me more and more
when worrying the color of boredom thickens
wind, blow ! rain, fall ! thunder, rumble ! Summer storm

counting the number of lies and truths
the star's flower pierces like a knife
polishing the distinguishing features of substance, breathing in and out
strewed baking soda, with that massacre, desired the luster of darkness

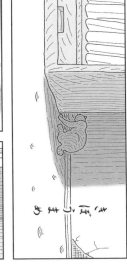

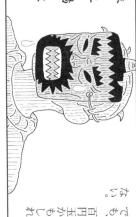

森元畼之

2-1 **Les haricots porte-bonheur**
2-2 Il a trouvé quelque chose.
2-3 Encore un insecte mort ?
2-4 Où ça pourrait être une pièce de 100 Yens ?
Nobuyuki Morimoto

*

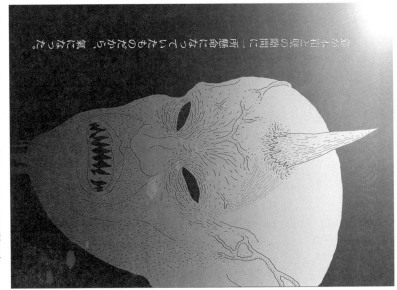

1 J'ai remarqué que le chat grattait entre le mur et l'étagère.

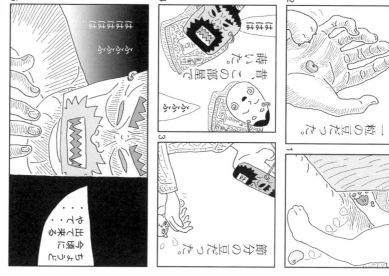

*Setsubun est une fête nationale japonaise qui célèbre l'arrivée du printemps. Encore aujourd'hui, la pratique associée consiste à lancer des graines de haricots grillées par la fenêtre des maisons en criant alternativement « Oni wa soto ! Fuku wa uchi ! » (« Dehors les démons ! Dedans le bonheur ! »), afin d'attirer la bonne fortune dans le foyer.]

4-2   C'était un haricot.

4-3   Un haricot de Setsubun. *

4-4   Il y a longtemps, je dispersais les haricots dans cette pièce.
Hahaha ! Huhuhu

4-5   Pourquoi a-t-il ressurgi à ce moment précis ?
Hahaha ! Huhuhu

3-3   **Frr Frr**
Eh, oh, je suis prêt de mon côté.

3-5   Qu'est-ce que c'est que ça ?
Miaou ?

4

6-1 Écoute, je ne pense pas que ce soit une bonne idée de me jeter les haricots dessus... C'est juste un jeu, et tu me balances les haricots trop fort ! Arrête de dire des bêtises ! Je ne peux pas m'arrêter comme ça, imbécile !

6-2 Dehors les démons !
Ouille ! Aïe !

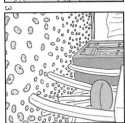

6

*

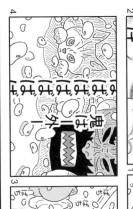

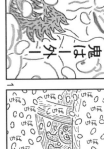

5-1 Dedans le bonheur ! **Tac tac tac tac tac tac**
5-2 Dehors les démons ! **Bam bam bam bam !**
5-3 Dedans le bonheur ! **Tac tac tac**
5-4 Dehors les démons ! **Bam bam bam !**
5-5 Dehors les ...
Stop, attends ! Attends !

5

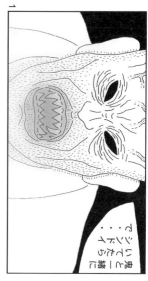

8-1 Moi je dis que tu vas en avoir marre d'être avec un démon...

8-2 Ok, eh bien dehors les démons !

8-3 Ho, arrête ! Arrête ! Aïe ! C'est toi le démon !
Non ! J'apporte le bonheur ! Dedans le bonheur !

8

*

*[Au Japon, lorsqu'un évoque ce qui peut se passer l'année prochaine, on se moque de lui.]

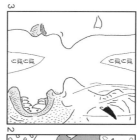

7-1 Bon sang, quel chantier, j'ai éparpillé deux paquets de haricots.
On va en avoir, de la chance !

7-2 Mange le même nombre de haricots que ton âge.

7-3 Eh, ça veut dire que je ne vais pouvoir en manger que 18 ?

7-4 Scrounch !-Scrounch !
Je sais que tu raconteras la même chose l'an prochain.
Tu crois que ça plairait au démon que je parle de l'an prochain ? *

7-5 Ok, je te raconterai la même chose l'an prochain, moi aussi.
Huhu !

7

10-1　Toc toc toc !
Attends ! Ne bouge pas.
Salut, je suis là ! J'ai rapporté du ragoût, mangeons !
10-2　Sois patient.
Toc toc toc !
Hého, mangeons du ragoût ! Tu dors ? Debout ! Y'a du ragoût !
10-3　Aïe ! Arrête de te débattre.
Toc toc toc !
Dînons ensemble.
Dînons ensemble.
Ensemble...

*

9-1　Dehors les démons ! Hahaha !
9-3　Bien, je vais disperser beaucoup de haricots, cette année.
9-4　Enfile ce masque !
9-5　Je sais que tu n'aimes pas ça mais sois patient, juste un petit moment.
Toc toc toc toc !

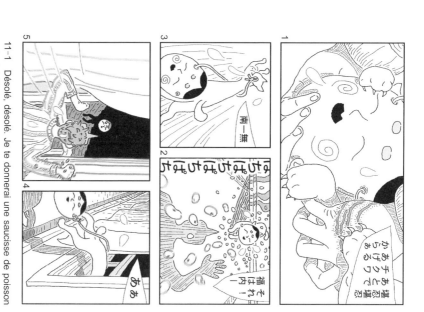

11–1　Désolé, désolé. Je te donnerai une saucisse de poisson tout à l'heure.

11–2　Hé, bonne chance ! **Tac tac tac tac**

11–3　Miséricorde !

11–4　Ah....

14-1　Dehors les démons, dehors les démons, dehors les démons, dehors les démons

14-2　**Shhhhh ! Shhhhh ! Shhhhh !**

14-3　Dehors les démons, dehors les démons, dehors les démons, dehors les démons, dehors les démons, dehors les démons

14

*

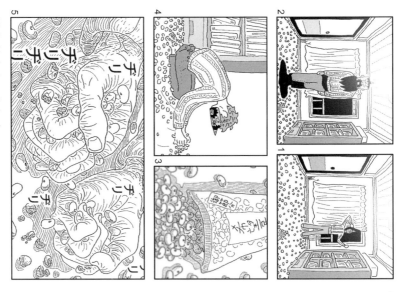

13-3　Haricots porte-bonheur

13-5　**Scrich scrich !**

13

ほなほあ痛
なにゃあ痛
・・

1

3

4

2

おまえは
やほなにあほ

5

6

あほ
あほ
あほ
あほ

16-1 Ça fait mal... Quel idiot! Qu'est-ce que j'ai fait?
16-5 Quel idiot, vraiment.
16-6 Quel idiot! Quel idiot!

＊

鬼は外
鬼は
鬼は
鬼は外
鬼は

1

鬼は
鬼は

2

目に
痛
痛
痛！

3

15-1 Dehors les démons! Dehors les démons! Dehors les
démons!
15-2 Les démons! Les démons!
15-3 J'ai mal! J'ai mal! Mes yeux...

18-1　Une voix que je pensais entendre d'une maison voisine …
　　　Dedans le bonheur, dehors les démons !
18-2　…continue à résonner dans ma tête.
18-3　Dehors les démons !
18-4　Dedans le bonheur !
18-5　Seul le démon est resté…

*

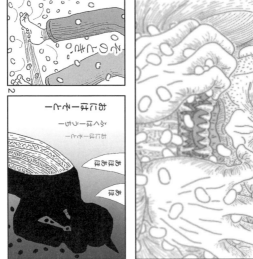

17-1　Quel idiot ! Idiot !
17-2　Idiot… Dehors les démons, dedans le bonheur, dehors les démons !
17-3　Alors…

小野原 教子 (おのはら のりこ)

大阪市生れ．兵庫県立大学国際商経学部准教授．文化記号論，ファッション研究．京都大学大学院人間・環境学研究科修了，博士（人間・環境学）．旭化成繊維マーケティング部，旭化成テキスタイル販促コーディネーター，ロンドン大学ユニヴァーシティ・カレッジ・ロンドン人類学研究科名誉研究員，ヴィクトリア＆アルバート博物館，パリ市モード博物館（ガリエラ宮）客員研究員を経て現職．著書に『闘う衣服』（水声社），訳書に『四コマ 幸福番外地』（幻堂出版），共著に『映画でわかるイギリス文化入門』（松柏社）など，詩集に『表面張力』（思潮社），『耳から菫』（highmoonoon），『刺繍の呼吸』（深夜叢書社）．

Noriko Onohara

Ph.D (Human and Environmental Studies, Kyoto University), Associate Professor at University of Hyogo (Cultural Semiotics, Fashion Studies). Born in Osaka, she studied in Kobe, Osaka, Kyoto and London. She was formerly an Honourary Research Fellow at Anthropology Department at UCL, University of London, and a Visiting Research Fellow at Victoria and Albert Museum, UK and at Palais Galliera, Musee de la mode de la ville de Paris. Author of *Fighting Fashion* (Suiseisha) and three poetry books: *Surface Tension* (Shichosha), *From ears, violets* (highmoonoon) and *Embroidery Breath* (Shinyasosho). Instagram: inorikout

人を着るということ
Mind That Clothes the Body
2020年3月30日 初版第1刷発行

著 者　小野原教子©

発行者　植田　実

印刷者　江戸孝典

装 幀　ミルキィ・イソベ（Studio Parabolica）

発行所　株式会社 晃洋書房
　　　　京都市右京区西院北矢掛町7番地
　　　　電話　075 (312) 0788代
　　　　振替口座　01040-6-32280

印刷・製本　共同印刷工業㈱
ISBN978-4-7710-3345-0

[JCOPY] 〈(社)出版者著作権管理機構 委託出版物〉

本書の無断複写は著作権法上での例外を除き禁じられています．複写される場合は，そのつど事前に，(社)出版者著作権管理機構（電話03-5244-5088，FAX 03-5244-5089, e-mail: info@jcopy.or.jp）の許諾を得てください．

Mind That
Clothes
the Body

Noriko Onohara

KOYOSHOBO

Front (Japanese) Cover: Michiko Nomura 'Summer Dress for a Poetess' (2012)
Back (English) Cover: Paul Ashley Brown 'Kimonologue' (2013)
Poetry: Noriko Onohara 'Constellation of Midsummer' (English Translation: John Solt)
(*gui 85*, 2008/2009)
Manga: Nobuyuki Morimoto 'Les haricots porte-bonheur' (French Translation: Benjamin
Hariot) (*AX vol. 33*, Seirin Kougeisha, 2003/2019)

Contents

Preface for English Part

In recent years, there have been discourses on Japan's soft policy of exporting Japanese culture to the world (the 'Cool Japan' movement) and its pros and cons. The author tries to do this here in the form of a research paper in English. Kimono as a traditional culture, Gothic Lolita and Manga as popular culture, and Zen Buddhism overseas—they have continued to change whilst being mutually influenced, across countries and times. With their decline and development, different cultures are mixed and may produce novel innovations. Some of them make loud noises, others are silent but still move dynamically. This part of the book consists of published research papers in English, including a newly translated one for this book from an international perspective. You can read the five chapters independently from the back cover, like the B-side of 7" vinyl singles; there is no strict set order.

In my first solo book *Tatakau Ifuku* (Fighting Fashion) (Suiseisha, 2011), whilst analysing specific examples of fashion and clothes, I considered the fundamental question 'Why do we wear clothes?' and discussed 'Human is an animal that wears clothes.' For readers who can read Japanese, I will examine in the Japanese part of this book the idea: '(Human is an animal that) wears 'humans''. I also slowly work over the theme: Children wanting to go out in pyjamas, Japanese coming to wear western clothes after a long history of Japanese Kimono, How the Buddha Robe is the Buddha Dharma itself, Mind and Body, and Human beings as a living creature and its relation with clothing. The author has treated these themes like cultural conflicts to be harmonised.

Below is the information of each chapter, based on their original related lecture and presentation. All have been greatly revised for this book.

I. Whom Do You Dress up for ? : Gothic Lolita Fashion in Japan

Key-note lecture 'Japanese Fashion Today: Gothic and/or Lolita ?' at Pop Culture Workshop 3 at Chukyo University in Nagoya, 8 July, 2006. Gosurori: A Globally and Totally Japanese-born Fashion. Presentation in 'Japan Cool' Round Table, 10th International Congress of Semiotics, University of Coruna, Spain, 23 September, 2009. Onohara, Noriko (2008) Whom do you dress up for ? Japanese Gothic Lolita Fashion, *Image of Japan in Europe* (pp. 215–239), Vytautas Magnus University.

II. Japan as Fashion: Contemporary Reflections on Being Fashionable

Open lecture 'Japan as fashion: Contemporary reflections on being fashionable' at TrAIN Research Centre, University of Arts London, 19 May,

2010. Onohara, Noriko (2012) Japan as Fashion: Contemporary Reflections on 'Being Fashionable,' *Acta Orientalia Vilnensia,* vol. 12(1): 29-41.

III. Costume and Trauma: Reception of Japanese Fashion in Britain Through Five Exhibitions in London

Presentation 'Costume and Trauma: Reception of Japanese Fashion in Britain through Five Exhibitions in London' (in Japanese), Trans-disciplinary Study of Organizing Traumatic Experiences and Memory, The Institute for Research in Humanities, Kyoto University, 25 March, 2013. Onohara, Noriko (2012) Costume and Trauma: Reception of Japanese Fashion in Britain through Five Exhibitions in London, *Reception of Japanese and Korean Popular Culture in Europe 2* (pp. 97-126), Vytautaus Magnus University.

IV. Design of Silence: Transmission of Kesa in Soto Zen

Presentation 'Kasaya and Fashion', International Symposium: Human Consumption of Cloth and Human Bodies Wrapped in Cloth, National Museum of Ethnology, Osaka, 23 Feburary, 2013. Onohara, Noriko (2018) Design of Silence: Transmission of Kesa in Soto Zen, *Transnational Popular Culture* (pp. 145-161), Nakanishiya Publishing (in Japanese).

V. You Are Everything and Nothing: To What Extent Does Japanese Manga, Comics and Fashion Culture Influence the Current Contemporary U. K. Comic Scene ?

Poster session with Dr. Kyoko Koma 'Comparative Studies on Reception of Japanese Manga in England and France: Reflection around Kawaii, Modernism and Traumatism', The International Conference on Design History and Design Studies ICDHS 2016, National Taiwan University of Science and Technology, Taipei. 26-28, October, 2016.

I would be happy as an author if any one of the papers interest you, and arouse your intellectual curiosity. Last but importantly, all the pictures as shown in this book are simultaneously used for academic purpose, and to appreciate each style.

Noriko Onohara, Kobe, January 2020.

I

Whom Do You Dress up for?: Gothic Lolita Fashion in Japan

Introduction

Western sociologists and anthropologists have increasingly brought up the topic of Japanese fashion when talking about modern Japanese culture. Within societies that have achieved a high degree of economic development (i.e. the post-capitalist world) Japanese fashion has attracted a lot of attention as being a unique phenomenon. Up until now, when talking of Japanese fashion, it has been the Japanese designers who are active abroad and present their designs in fashion shows called Collection that are well known, and they have been analysed in research, scholarly and otherwise. However, it is especially the fashion that is born on the street, that is, the fashion led by the wearer that has recently attracted much interested observation. I would like to consider an example of these distinctive street styles, in particular Gothic Lolita Fashion, which has gained a fanatical popularity amongst certain young Japanese girls of late (**Fig. 1**).

Gothic Lolita goes by the popular name *Gosurori* and refers to a fashion style. In recent years, rather than being confined to these shores, it has also been discussed as a topic of research in other countries[1]. Originally I used to study the English designer Vivienne Westwood, well known as a Punk Goddess, which gave me the opportunity to think about this Japanese new fashion style Gothic Lolita. This is not merely because the youth wearing such seemingly chaotic style also greatly respect Vivienne Westwood, but also for the analyses of fashion victim or identity crisis; if this sort of question should be worth the hassle with a wearer or a fashion researcher, might be remarkably the very phenomenon.

To put it simply, it is attracting a lot of attention anyway beyond the country to outsides in the world: as for the reason why, I consider that we can propose the following. To explain in more detail, in contrast to wearer-lead (i.e. street fashion) that has popular and casual elements to its style, the fashion of the

---

1 Introducing Gothic Lolita girls with photos of their gatherings at Harajuku, Tokyo ('Japan: All the shades of Black' in *Casa Vogue*, 638, Italy, 2003).

Figure 1
Gothic Lolita magazines for this research

previously mentioned international Japanese designers, notably Rei Kawakubo, Yohji Yamamoto, Issey Miyake and so on, is called Mode or High fashion. It is here that core meaning of the word fashion really lies. I have discussed the definition of fashion in more detail elsewhere[2] and have to pass over it here, but the Gothic Lolita style that I introduce in this chapter shows elements of both types of fashion, or alternatively you could perhaps say that it is neither one nor the other.

It is needless to say that the following modernisation in the Meiji period and after having been through two World Wars, clothing in Japan has become almost completely westernised[3]. The present-day Japanese fashion therefore displays qualities such as newness and growth, both as a social and cultural phenomenon and as fashion. It seems that these potentials of current Japanese fashion have given rise to the present situation where it is being debated as a research topic around the world.

1. The Term 'Gosurori'

The term ゴスロリ Gosurori (**Fig. 2**) was coined in Japan, through joining the words Gothic or Goth and Lolita. When written in English-language publications, Gosurori becomes Goth-Loli or Gothloli, although being faithful to the Japanese term; perhaps we should spell it Gosurori. Incidentally, in Japanese there is basically no 'l' sound, so it is written down as 'r'. In practice, both spellings are acceptable these days.

First, I will explore the term Goth or Gothic. Originally Goth/Gothic referred

---

2   Onohara 2011.
3   See chapter 5 in Japanese.

Figure 2
'Gosurori' featured as a new fashion style
in the Japanese newspaper *Kobe Shimbun*,
in 22 May, 2004 (evening)
神戸新聞 2004年5月22日（夕刊）

to a sub-cultural style centrered around music that arose in Europe in the 1980s. Before that, it originated as a historical European artistic and literary style including Gothic architecture and Gothic romance.

For instance, it was defined in the following way in the special Goth edition of cult Japanese magazine *Yaso* (literally "nocturnal thoughts"[4]). The following is taken from the article by a writer called Luv Ishikawa.

He writes that the Gothic scene with its religious and historical original meanings became separated from the punk and new wave music movement at that time, and drawing on just its decadent fashion and spiritual elements was reborn as a new form of pop culture. He also writes that Japan has now become the most progressive Goth country in the world, having drawn on such developments as the musical movement in Europe centered around England and Germany in the late 70s and 80s (Goths' roots are after all in rock), the rise of music and bands known as Visual-*kei* "style" in Japan in the 90s and the distinctive American Goth style. The Gothic of Gothic Lolita is often misrecognised as simply a Japanese version of the popular Goths in Europe and America, but we could safely say that it has already developed into something of a different type of Goth.

I should like to concentrate on the clothing aspects of Gothic Lolita in this chapter, so while trying not to stray from the current state of the fashion, I also

4 *Yaso: Goths Special*, April 2003, Studio Parabolica.

attempt to clarify the terminology involved. Hence, let me introduce a definition of the term from Rococo, a Gothic Lolita fashion magazine[5]. This magazine, issued in 2004, traces the origin of Gosurori for its readers. We may also touch upon the explanation given before, in which it has become separated from its historical definition. The characteristics of Gosurori fashion are as follows;

> Gothic is originally an architectural term. Buildings in the Gothic style first appeared in the second half of the twelfth century France. Gothic fashion arose from images to be found in Gothic literature (mystery novels) such as 'Count Dracula.'

Gothic fashion involves wearing a black coat or cape and wrapping one's entire body in black. Accessories in the shape of Christ's cross and a face made up to look like that of a corpse are particular characteristic. It has its roots in the fashion of Goth musicians and their fans. With a taste for vampires and roses as motifs, it is not surprising that the distinctive colours that appear in this fashion are black or black and red combinations, but also purple and occasionally white. You could say that it is frightening, decadent, anti-social and full of images of death and evil.

Moving on to the Lolita part again drawing on material from the same magazine:

> This stems from the novel *Lolita* written by the Russian author Vladimir Nabokov. The phrase 'Lolita complex' comes from this novel, referring to men like the protagonist who have sexual inclinations towards young girls.

The Lolita Complex refers to the disposition of a grown man to be attracted to young girls (i.e. paedophilia) and is known in Japan by the abbreviated *Roricon*. In a similar manner to Gosurori being faithful to the Japanese 'r' sound, it is written down as Roricon, not Lolicon and is also used in this form abroad. It is needless to say that it has greatly influenced Japanese manga[6] and anime, and that it is an important concept when talking about Japanese pornography including child pornography. Furthermore, it is well known that Japanese mass culture is often analysed in terms of *Kawaii* (roughly translated as "cute"), but due to page restrictions let us leave such psychological issues aside.

The characteristics of the clothing, Lolita is not simply about wearing the clothes of a child, but indicates a fashion like that of a French doll, with features

---

5 *Gosurori and Punk Style: Rococo* vol. 1, Oct 2004.
6 See Chapter V.

such as pretty frills as in the dresses of Europe in the Middle Ages. In contrast to Gothic black, it was a fashion that was centered around white, but recently various other designs, such as pink and blue colour variations and patterns featuring small flowers, strawberries, cherries and so on, are increasing. In a few words, you could say that it is soft, sweet and brings to mind images of young girls and angels.

This fashion is however probably more akin to Lewis Carroll's Alice (**Fig. 3**) than to Nabokov's Lolita. *Alice's Adventures in Wonderland* is somewhat adored by girls dressing in Lolita fashion. This is the reason that trump card shapes, crowns and white rabbits often appear as motifs in designs. To digress, these girls, even though it may sound

Figure 3
Alice from John Tenniel's famous illustration in *Alice's Adventures in Wonderland* originally published in 1865

very similar in Japanese, often double the 'I' vowel sound in Lolita ロリイタ and write the word Lolita inserting an old Japanese character ロリヰタ. Their way of writing it perhaps expresses their refusal to be the subject of adoration of middle-aged men. What is so interesting here is that a phenomenon has arisen whereby the characteristics of the fashion as well as the ideas and ways of thinking behind it are expressed via language.

In concluding this part I would like to add one more thing, that Gosurori is a term that has been used by people who do not wear the fashion, in other words, outsiders or people who are at a distance from it. Actually, the girls who wear this particular fashion do not usually use the word Gosurori themselves. This is because it has a strongly derogatory nuance. In my seminar group I showed films and magazines related to these girls and we discussed them. On asking the male students 'what do you think about this fashion ?' and 'would you like your girlfriend to wear it ?' the reply that comes back is 'no way'. The female students said 'it would be OK if you were wearing it to an event' and 'I would never think of wearing it normally'. According to a girl that I interviewed who actually wore this kind of fashion, when walking down the street people often whisper such things as 'look it's a gosurori or weirdo', and she often feels treated as if she were a monster. It is clear that Lolita fashion is not by any means easy clothing in which to live your daily life.

Current mainstream street fashions are casual 'dressing down' styles such as sporty and layered fashions. Although Gosurori fashion arose from the street, it is of a very different nature. These girls 'dress up', as in the original sense of the word fashion (i.e. as the preserve of the upper classes). Indeed there

exists a rather conservative street-style called *Mote-kei,* which can be translated as a "lovable style" in English; it is now also popular amongst girls and women who behave feminine. In comparing with Gothic Lolita girls, they are not too feminine nor too girly, but cute and pretty enough to be loved by the other sex. As for Gothic Lolita style, at first glance, because of its distinctiveness, it may tend to be thought of as a minority fashion or fad. You could say it is too girly and far too romantic for ordinary boys. However, related magazines are published regularly and a Gosurori film has been broadcast on a terrestrial channel, so in that sense it could almost be called popular. We might call it a 'high fashion' style street fashion.

2. Gothic and/or Lolita ?

As we have seen so far, if you look at Goths and Lolitas separately, they are contrastive fashions that do not seem to go well together at all. From early 2000, boutiques which in the same way mixed two kinds of styles that seem very different increased in number, at first being centered around the Kansai area, but then spreading to Tokyo and throughout the country. Previous Gothic fashion was a maniac's style so to speak, linked to a music trend and affiliated with a smaller group. Also, it was a trend entirely copied from America and Europe.

Returning to the previously mentioned magazine *Rococo,* it further grounded the concept of Gosurori by defining it as 'the name of a new fashion arising in the 2000s'. That is, one could argue, it had been established as a popular fashion and came to be recognised as a particular style. Other major magazines that present Gothic Lolita fashion were in publication: *Kera ! Maniacs* and *Gothic Lolita Bible* published at quarterly intervals (hereafter 'Index Magazine') that were both born from *Kera !,* a magazine that originally engaged in fixed-point observations of street fashion; *Gosurori* which has a strong sewing technique element (Boutique co.); *Maison* (Gakken) which is similar to a manner book; *Clara Bow* (Bauhaus) and so on. Currently, even though we speak of the single phrase 'Gothic Lolita', it has been separated into detailed styles. Using mainly these magazines as sources, let us attempt to classify this fashion.

Looking at the process of how the style has become more specialised, I suppose we can broadly separate it into styles approaching either Gothic or Lolita. Around the Gothic end of the scale are: Gothic, *Gossupanku* (Goths and punk) (**Fig. 4**), *Eregosu* (an abbreviation of "elegant Goth"), Punks, Fetish (an erotic bondage fashion using corsets), Cyber (near future style, inorganic, electric fashion), Vivienne (for English designer Vivienne Westwood lovers), *Iryou-kei* (with medical motif such as nurse, blood and bandage), etc. (**Fig. 5**),

Figure 4

A *gosupank* girl (right). She said, 'My Favourite fashion brands are Sexy Dynamite London, because it is cool, and Vivienne Westwood'

Figure 5

Iryou-kei (medical style). Her clothes are from 'blablahospital' designed by a Japanese girl in London

Figure 6

An *amarori* girl. Her favourite boutiques are Shirley Temple and Emily Temple Cute

Figure 7

Wafu-rorita. She loves Takuya Angel (clothes of that day) and Angelic Pretty. Surprisingly she has wings on her back of the dress

Rock and so on. There are also categories such as *Shirogosu* "white Goths", who in contrast to symbolic Goth black emphasise their white colour, and *Bangyaru* referring to Goth girls who are fanatical followers of certain musicians.

Lolita style also contains detailed divisions. *Amarori* is an abbreviation of "sweet Lolita" and, as its name suggests, places a particular emphasis on

girliness, with heavy use of pastel colours and prints (**Fig. 6**). Getting even sweeter, it is called *Koterori*: *kote* comes from the Japanese *kotekote* roughly translated as "very thick/heavy". Classifying according to colour, there are such divisions as *Shirorori* "white Lolita", *Kurorori* "black Lolita", baby blue and pink, too. *Kurarori* is an abbreviation of "classic Lolita", who, compared to Amarori look more grown up, preferring to wear clothes that are more classically constructed. *Decora* (with heavy usage of colourful, pop, toy-like accessories) and *Panku rori-ta* is basically a fusion with punk fashion. In addition, *Wafu rori-ta* (**Fig. 7**) has recently come to attention, referring to girls who like to wear kimonos or things remade from fabrics with Japanese motifs. *Wa* is a pseudonym for "something Japanese".

From this, it is now perhaps apparent that there are so many finely divided categories that someone unfamiliar with Gothic Lolita would not be able to distinguish between them. The person who originally coined the term Gothic Lolita is said to be a cross-dressing musician called Mana (e.g. Malice Mizer) who is thought to have first used the phrase. His fashion and make-up is that of the Japanese rock band movement called *Visual kei.* It is fair to say that the unique fashion brand 'Moi-meme-moitie' that his produces has something of a seminal existence within the now diversified Lolita fashions. In fact, the original term 'Gothic Lolita' is now coming to be used to refer to just one particular Lolita style among many. If you were to sum up the characteristics of Gothic Lolita, perhaps it would be a fashion that whilst being girly is run through with a decadent beauty aesthetic. Talking in images, perhaps it would be a fallen angel: a curious thing whereby even though the form of the clothing is cute, the colours are dark. We could say that seemingly disagreeing components were combined to become 'Gothic Lolita', the 'Gothic' and 'Lolita' elements were then emphasised respectively, transformed little by little and have now become various fragmented styles.

What exactly is the background to all of this ? To help illustrate, there is a type of song that Japanese children sing called *Douyou,* or a nursery rhyme. This kind of children's song always has a shadowy aspect that does not appear on the surface, and that there are hidden meanings full of fear and hate. Sometimes, the adult world and modern society are depicted through these stories created for the world of children. These elements can be seen in similar examples outside of Japan, such as in Grimm's fairytales and the Mother Goose allegories. Similarly, the cute, sweet little bears and rabbits that have become Gothic Lolita motifs, are depicted as ferocious animals, having facial expressions of narrow glaring eyes, blood dripping from their head and bandages wrapped around, have painful-looking scars and so on. You could say that they are using their bodies, through the medium of fashion, to express this dual sided

nature of things: that is light and dark. This comes across to me as a desperate resistance on behalf of these girls to the increasing commodification of their bodies in the day-to-day transience of the post-capitalist society.

Finally, let us return to the magazine *Yaso* that I mentioned in the last chapter in order to conclude this part. Quoting once more from there:

> Japanese girls, through a highly Japanese equation combined with historical, geographical, temporal and other miscellaneous conditions were the first in the world to release 'Goth' from the inquisition.

This 'highly Japanese equation' that Luv Ishikawa writes of is not elaborated upon. What exactly could this scheme be ? At this point, we shall leave it at: Gothic (that is *kowasa* "fearfulness") plus Lolita (that is *amasa* "sweetness") =gosurori (adding up to *kowa-ama* "fearful sweetness").

3. Fashion and/or Lifestyle ?

Since its first issue in October 2003, the *Gothic and Lolita Bible,* published regularly, has, exactly as the magazine's name indicates, held a bible-like existence for the individuals engaged in the fashion. At first, the magazine was presenting the fashion as centered around 'Gothic Lolita' fashion, that is Gothic-style Lolita, or Lolita style Goth clothes. However, as we have seen in the previous chapter, currently this style has diversified and it could be said that now all the fashions surrounding Gothic and Lolita in their abundant variations are represented on the magazine's pages.

Within *mixi,* the first internet Social Networking Service in Japan (started in 2004), there was an online community to discuss the definition of Gosurori where the members (2138 people in July, 2006) talk about the diversification of the style. For example: 'It is not Gosurori, rather Kura-rori' 'don't call me Gosurori just because I am wearing only black' and so on. Interestingly, the community was called 'it is not Gosurori', which seems to be named after the parodied title of painting 'Ceci n'est pas une pipe' by René Magritte.

Giving rise to the diversification, alternatively specialisation of the style is the fact that Gothic Lolita fashion itself is still developing as it is becoming popular. Gothic Lolita itself has also been called a subculture. The reasoning is that it is a counter culture opposed to high culture; it is also different from popular culture, but has its own culture and ideas centered around fashion. In fact, it is not only the clothes that are covered by magazines, but also tea party events are introduced, and suggestions are made as to music, films, novels and so on that will nurture the Gothic Lolita spirit. In that respect perhaps you

could think of it as a culture or way of thought.

Clothes by their very nature resemble words that carry strong meanings. Amongst the pages of the magazine is a special feature that teaches one the proper use of polite language. Through current Gothic Lolita fashion, we have the opportunity to once again re-examine the question of what fashion is.

In the past, there is no doubt that fashion existed as a social sign that expressed the wearer's sex, nationality, social status and occupation. However, now that it has become a word that indicates a phenomenon 'in vogue' with the added value of 'newness', that symbol itself has been played around with and has become somewhat distorted as a medium that carries meaning. That is, rather than being a means to attach and remove identity, the wearing itself has become the main objective.

Amongst a subcategory that we have not touched upon yet, is a style known as *Ouji* "prince". This is someone who imitates the ideal male image to be walking alongside girls dressed in Gothic Lolita fashion, although they are usually thought to belong to the miscellaneous style category. You could say it was a fashion similar to that of a Rococo or Middle Ages prince, but that would be a stereotype of the look. Although like princes, the standard items worn are black and white bordered socks or tights, characteristic of Gothic Lolita's leg fashion, more reminiscent of a prison uniform. The character Mana introduced previously is a man that dresses up so perfectly that he cannot be simply categorised as a cross-dresser or as androgynous.

This section is titled 'fashion and/or lifestyle' and in connection I would now like to consider cosplay for a moment. Cosplay is an abbreviation of costume-play, and as its name suggests, refers to playing, carried out via clothes in which you may become anyone. Originally it was an act in which uniforms, such as nurses or flight attendants work clothes, were worn in a context that was separated from their original purpose. That is, you could say it was a phenomenon whereby clothes that were once social signs became free from those meanings, and in which those signs turned into playing. At first it was a word that had sexual nuances and its purpose in role-playing games in the sex industry was emphasised.

Today it has become more mainstream, and is just another type of popular phenomena It is a sort of fashion game, strongly affected by *Otaku* "nerd" culture and their love of Japanese anime whereby you may become a character from an anime or manga by wearing their outfits. Cosplayers do not only buy ready-made costumes, but you also often hear of them making their own. Returning to our Gothic Lolita story, the girls who are fond of the Middle Ages, Rococo and Victorian periods and wear fashions that are like costume revivals of those times, in effect become ladies from those gorgeous Western periods of the

good old days. In other words, isn't it also fair to call those clothes cosplay? Since Gothic Lolita fashion attained a degree of recognition, there has also been an actual Gothic Lolita cosplay style. However, Gothic Lolitas hate their clothes being referred to as cosplay.

Perhaps, according to these girls, this is because it is not just a fashion, but there are ideas and cultures behind the clothes, and they are proud that they are keeping that aesthetic style alive. If cosplayers remove their costumes, they probably return to their 'original self'. Of course, we will have to argue the philosophical question of whether there is such a thing as the 'self' further at some opportunity, but we can think of these girls who wear Gothic Lolita fashions as being able to become themselves through wearing these clothes. Actually, the phrase 'true self' appears quite frequently in magazines. Perhaps we should think of that spirit residing in the places that you cannot see from outside your clothes. Furthermore, another important feature of cosplay is having your photo taken. This is surely another clear point of difference from these girls.

At this point I would like to explain the most important key concept for Gothic Lolita fashion. I believe that these girls' assertion that it is neither mere cosplay nor just a fashion lies in the underwear that they are so insistent about. To introduce the distinctive underwear items that appear among Gosurori, on the top half you find: corsets (underwear with no sleeves that holds in the chest to waist area), camisoles (sleeveless undergarment often known as a corset cover), bustiers (undergarment also called the strapless bra) and so on. For the lower half of the body there are such items as crinoline (a garment used to puff-up skirts), drawers (or mini-bloomers) and paniers (underskirt). The majority are not everyday garments in modern fashion, but are classical fashions used mainly in the Victorian era. There are also accessories such as garters, which are belts decorated with things such as lace that connect stockings to corsets.

In magazines there are many supplements with attached patterns, intended for making by people themselves, especially of these underwear items which cannot be easily got hold of ready-made and are therefore often made. I have discussed this in another paper[7], but the following phrase 生パン撲滅運動 Namapan-bokumetsu-undou roughly translated as 'the campaign to abolish visible panties' is something of a slogan amongst the Gothic Lolitas. It was born from the intention to avoid showing their underwear from below their short, puffy, airy skirts. Through not wearing their panties as they are, but instead wearing underwear like drawers or panniers on top of them, they are demonstrating both the appropriate shyness of protecting one's body by oneself such that

---

7 Onohara 2017.

Figure 8
With headdress, ribbons, frills, lace, platform shoes, and perhaps drawers, she is fully dressed up at a tea party in Osaka

even if someone was peeping, they would not be visible, and are also presenting the stylish way of wearing the garments such that the lace attached to the end of these underwear items is shown. These items are, so to speak, underwear that it's OK to show and are thus linked to the public trend whereby inners are turning into outer garments.

Shouichi Inoue, a historian of social customs, in reference to the Meiji period modernisation, wrote:

In that time of rapid growth, a dynamic of excessive adaptation that aimed at a level of Westernisation above that of its original countries was mobilised[8].

Although Japan today is not in the kind of period of growth that Inoue describes but rather in decline, it is still difficult to think of the girls living in this historical Meiji period using panniers, drawers and the like as a medium for aiming at globalisation or Westernisation. However, if you regard Westernisation to be the same as modernisation, then these girls have skipped over modern times and are going back in time to the Middle Ages, Classicism, the age of Rococo, Victorian and Edwardian time and so on, and through their fashion are embracing a feeling of longing or nostalgia for those times despite having no real reason to do so.

From modern Japanese society (the here and now) it is spreading throughout the world but also at the same time inclined towards past European societies —we could say that this is a surprising phenomenon for a modern fashion to have brought about. In actual fact, Japanese Visual-kei rock has been introduced to America and Europe and has something of the following, and now you can purchase Gothic Lolita fashion there without going to boutiques but instead by buying it through online sellers and so on.

Whilst they are not underwear, other characteristic items of this fashion

---

8   Inoue 2002.

include such things as headdresses (small cloth hats almost like a ribbon), and one cannot ignore the boots and shoes with soles that are so excessively thick it would be no surprise to fall over in them (**Fig. 8**). Platform shoes always unsettle one's balance when walking. The strings of the corset are there to make a sexually flattering shape and should not be loosened. These girls continue to dress up, resigned to subjecting their body to pain in order to keep to the dress code perfectly and create the required forms. Gothic Lolita fashion has surpassed present-day fashion, and has after much effort has arrived at an image from the European past (**Fig. 9**).

Figure 9
'Lady's Visiting Toilette' from *Victorian Fashions & Costumes from Harper's Bazar: 1867-1898*

In conclusion

The reason why Gosurori, as a Japanese style that is expressing Western images, is attracting attention from Westerners is, of course, partly because it is a unique phenomenon. However, if they themselves were to try out the fashion, there is a big risk that it would go no further than being nostalgic, self-Occidentalism, or that it would end up looking like theatre costumes or indeed cosplay, hence perhaps it is also because the fashion's significance is brought out in the fact that it is Japanese girls who are wearing it.

As we have come to realise, Gothic Lolitas like frills, lace, ribbon and so on. These accessories (whether they are there or do not have any relationship to the function of clothing) can be seen as signs of the ornamental or excessive nature of these girls' fashion. Does such extremely decorated underwear represent the progress in fashion? This fashion that is carefully considered not just on the surface but also in the places the eye cannot see is a yet unknown and excessive fashion, so it is ironic that it is actually a copy of a classical European fashion. That is although it is new it has just ended up being old again. But what is certain is that the bodily sensations involving special underwear, shoes and so on represent a new experience for these girls and an emotional attachment to a past of which, as Japanese girls, they have no actual experience!

Furthermore, the fact that a situation has arisen whereby Westerners are experiencing European nostalgia through a modern Japanese fashion such as this is surely also a very interesting social phenomenon (**Fig. 10**). It is rather a paradoxical representation, but couldn't it be argued that Gothic Lolitas have

18

Figure 10
An Australian Gosurori girl in Japan

taken the restrained dress code that applied to the original fashion and uninhibitedly applied it to their own bodies ? The act of trying to escape fashionisation is to 'create' a new fashion, which eventually ends up back at the roots of fashion.

Originally the word fashion was an English word describing the manners that upper class ladies should adhere to. That sense of not being restricted to clothes survives even now as in the word fashion meaning 'form' or 'way'. It is said that previously a woman's fashion expressed the society, status and so on to which she belonged. Size and breadth were particular characteristics of women's dress, and this is said to have borne the function of keeping men other than their fathers and husbands at a distance.

For girls living in the present times, the experience of the physical sensation of clothes is surely more important than their function as a social sign. An expansive skirt will billow and swing when walking, and wearing platform-soled boots sometimes as high as twenty centimeters must change one's line of vision and hence one's way of seeing things. It is perhaps in order to avoid the friction of cloth directly touching skin that these girls layer on their underwear and pay so much importance to the volume under their skirts. Or it may just be a form of social communication.

The last point I would like to raise is that this fashion appears to be some kind of resistance to the restrictions inherent in a society that has become too liberal and force wearer to seek themselves or make sure of their identity. The term Gosurori, a new name in fashion, all in all seems to be becoming part of the vocabulary of the 'Fashion System'[9] that must keep on developing for the future with constant help of the past, large varieties in stock. Whom do you dress up for ? Apparently we are living in more a liberal society than before, but the liberty, what or whom is it for ? I shall close this chapter with these questions left to think it upon further through the following chapters.

References
Barthes, R., 1967, *Système de la mode,* Seuil.
Blum, S., 1974, *Victorian Fashions & Costumes From Harper's Bazar: 1867-1898,* Dover Publications.
Brydon, A. and S. Niessen, 1998, *Consuming Fashion Adorning the Transnational Body,* Berg.

9　Barthes 1967.

Craik, J., 1994, *The Face of Fashion: Cultural Studies in Fashion*, Routledge.

Darcy, D., 2003, *Meat Cake Complilation*, fantagraphics books.

Gernsheim, A., 1981 [1963], *Victorian and Edwardian Fashion: A Photographics Survey*, Thames and Hudson.

Inoue, S., 2002, *Visible Panties: Modern History of Shame*, Asahi Shimbun Company.

Kondo, D. K., 1990, *Crafting Selves: Power, Gender, and Discourses of Identity in a Japanese Workplace*, University of Chicago Press.

Laver, J., 1969, *A Concise History of Costume*, Thames & Hudson.

Lise, S. and B. Moeran, ed., 1995, *Women, Media and Consumption in Japan*, University of Hawaii Press.

McVeigh, B., 2000, *Wearing Ideology: State Schooling and Self-presentation in Japan*, Berg.

Muggleton, D., 2000, *Inside Subculture: The Postmodern Meaning of Style*, Berg.

Onohara, N., 2011, Introduction: Humans, Animals Clothes Themselves, *Tatakau Ifuku (Fighting Fashion)*, Suiseisha.

——, 2017, Why Fuwafuwa-floating: Gothic Lolita Fashion, *Shinpansuru Shintai: Fetishism Studies, 3*, Kyoto University Press.

Page, C., 1981, *Foundations of Fashion: The Symington Collection Corsetry from 1856 to the Present Day*, Leicestershire Museum.

Reger, R. and B. Parker, 2003, *Emily's Book of Strange*, Chronicle Books.

Takahara, E., 2004, *Gothic Heart*, Kodansha.

Newspapers (articles)

Asahi Shimbun, an article about Japanese fashion at 'opinion: news project', reported by an associate professor Kawamura, Yuniya (FIT, New York), 8 April, 2006.

Kobe Shimbun, an article about 'Gosurori' at 'real time', reported by Hiramatsu, Masako, 22 May, 2004.

Magazines

Casa Vogue, 638, Italy, October 2003.

Clara Bow, DMNT, 2005.

Gothic and Lolita Bible, 2003- (vol. 1 Bauhaus, vol. 2-3 Nouvel Gu, vol. 4-Index Magazines).

Gosurori, Boutique co., 2004.

Gosurori and Punk Style: Rococo, Tatsumi Shuppan, Oct 2004.

Kera! Maniacs, Index Magazines, 2003.

Maison, Gakken, 2004.

Yaso: Goths Special, Studio Parabolica, April 2003.

Films

Kubrick, Stanley (director), *Lolita* (original script from the novel written by Vladmir Nabokov), 1962.

Nakashima, Tetsuya (director), *Shimotsuma Monogatari* (original script from the novel written by Nobara Takemoto), 2004.

Boutiques

Ahiruya Apartment (Jane Marple), Kobe.

Alice Auaa, Osaka.

Algonquins, Osaka.

Baby, the stars shine bright, Osaka.

Black Peace Now, Osaka.

Emily Temple Cute, Osaka.

Heart E, Osaka.

h. Naoto, Osaka.

Innocent World, Osaka.

Kera Shop, Osaka.

Miho Matsuda, Osaka.

Na+H, Kobe.

Sexy Dynamite London, Osaka.

Takuya Angel, Osaka.

Territory, Osaka.

Cafes

Sweet Maiden, Osaka.

Otsukimi Nekoousama no Fushigina Meichakan (a wonder tea-house of a cat king looking up
to the moon), Kobe.

II

Japan as Fashion: Contemporary Reflections on Being Fashionable

Introduction

I used to be a researcher in London and living in Britain[1]. For many of the British I met there, the Japanese were 'fashionable people'. This trend is however not limited to the Japanese and suggests a new, modern, contemporary way of looking at Asia.

The Hollywood movie *Sayuri,* which opened parallel to the London film festival during my first stay in London, features as the heroine a geisha played by the popular Chinese actress Zhang Ziyi[2], at Spitalfields Market[3], famous as a starting point for many emerging young designers and where several Korean fashion designers have opened their stalls. Furthermore, the Beijing Olympics in 2008 provided many occasions to update the image of the Chinese —or what Chinese is— as modern, contemporary and fashionable. The exhibition *Avantgarde China*[4] held at the National Museum of International Art in Osaka is an example of this.

The same can be said of the food culture. At present, Japanese cuisine is booming all over the world as a healthy lifestyle. But whether it is a Korean chef who creates sushi in a Japanese-style restaurant or an Indian chef who creates pan-Asian dishes at the popular restaurant called Wagamama, Japan is often equivalent to a more generic Asian style. Whether Japanese, Chinese or Korean, in everyday life there is often no pressing need to make a distinction between these national identities. But when I asked a young Irish scholar of English literature whether he could distinguish between Chinese, Koreans and Japanese people, he answered that the Japanese stood out immediately because of the clothes they were wearing. In his generation, the stereotypical image of

---

1 My research stay as an academic visitor in London: 2005-2006 as an honourary research fellow at UCL, 2009-10 as a visiting research fellow at the V&A.

2 *Memoirs of a Geisha* (dir. Rob Marshal, 2005). The film was nominated and won three awards at the 78th Academy Awards. It is a movie about Japan, but the main actress was not Japanese, which was also a controversial topic in the USA.

3 This is one of the most popular markets in East London, well known as a fashion market that can give young and anonymous designers the opportunity to contribute.

4 The exhibition covers Modern Chinese arts for these twenty years since the Cultural Revolution.

Japan as a land of geishas and samurais has been replaced by a notion of 'Cool Japan' inspired by computer games and Manga.

In this chapter I would like to not so much look at whether the Japanese can be recognised by their sense of fashion, but to reflect upon the statement 'the Japanese are fashionable' as ideology. At the same time, I would like to investigate the double meaning of fashion in the present and what it means to be fashionable.

Fashion contact zone

But who is described as fashionable, and by whom? Who uses these labels and whose power of definition do they relate to? When Japanese fashion is spoken of in Western circles as quirky, innovative and often 'mad', what is referred to is in most cases the iconic street fashion photography in such magazine as *FRUiTS* and *Tune*[5] that are available in specialist bookstores in London for example. This means that the photographers of these magazines become arbiters of taste; in other words, what counts as fashionable depends heavily on their sensibilities.

While such sensibilities are very difficult to describe and explain, it is perhaps helpful to grasp the specificities of these magazines. Both *FRUiTS* and *Tune* emerged from a magazine called *Street*. *Street* is their predecessor and is published and edited by the same group of people, so an understanding of *Street* will help us to understand its other incarnations. *Street* started out as magazine dedicated to high fashion. By high fashion I refer to the Collections that are shown at the biannual fashion weeks in places like Paris and Milan, both as haute couture and prêt-a-porter. Images of these professional fashion events dominated the contents. Special issues documenting Tokyo street fashion and individual Japanese style would also appear. These were assembled by the publisher and photographer Aoki Shoichi. It is very important to understand the specificity of what came to be known as Japanese or Tokyo street fashion, what counts as fashionable in this context of a sensibility that emerged from taking pictures of European haute couture and prêt-a-porter.

Some photographers of street fashion, for example the famous Mamy[6], started out as people who were photographed for these special street fashion editions. When she first appeared on the pages of *Street,* she was a student at

---

5   *FRUiTS* was first published in 1997 and *Tune,* in 2004. This chapter is based on research of the magazines till 2012.

6   Shitourei and Mamy are well known as 'hunters'.

7   Keet 2007.

8   *Street* was first published in the mid 1980s (irregularly, by Aoki Shoichi: Street Henshushitsu).

a fashion college[78]. She subsequently became one of the 'hunters', as those photographers roaming the streets looking for interesting people to photograph are called. So Aoki, who from his own background in European fashion thought that she was fashionable, helped her to start her career in a new magazine, thus perpetuating the sensibility of the fashionable. It is often forgotten that the eye for originality and creativity that the success of the 'hunters' is based upon in the backstreets of Harajuku is derived from the influence of the high fashion produced traditionally by the European fashion industry. Hence we need to understand Harajuku as a contact zone rather than a fountainhead of fashion.

Is 'photogenic' the same as 'fashionable'?

Before we move the argument further, let us dwell on the kinds of social contact that are made between those who wield cameras and those who become their objects in the area known as Harajuku. It is contact between those who see and those who are seen, between the semi-professional photographers and the tourists, and the girls who wear Lolita fashion. That they wear such ostentatious fashion to go out does not mean that their priority is to be photographed, but it nevertheless is a good opportunity to leave an impression. This means that in this context, to be fashionable means to be photogenic.

To illustrate this, let me quote from the novel *Emily*[9] by Takemoto Nobara, an author known as a charismatic gothic Lolita. In this novel, set in the streets of Harajuku, girls who wear Lolita fashion do appear, but the equation of photogenic and fashionable cannot be held up. The heroine is a girl who likes Lolita fashion and who on the way home from school kills time in front of LaForet Harajuku, a fashion building. One day, while she watches the passing crowds from her usual spot, a photographer of a magazine shows interest in her. She reluctantly has her picture taken, but with the publication of these photos, the bullying she is experiencing at school escalates. As the photographer asks her for a name to be published with the pictures, she answers with 'Emily' because the brand she is wearing at that time is called 'Emily Temple Cute'. This name does not provide her proof of being fashionable but is subsequently used by her classmates as a derogatory nickname. The girls wearing Gothic Lolita fashion I interviewed were also reluctant to have their picture taken and emphasised that they did not simply wear this kind of fashion to be photographed

---

9   Most of the scenes in this novel are set at Harajuku. Takemoto frequently writes about main characters who are fond of Lolita fashion. Also see the categories of Gothic Lolita fashion in the last chapter I.

in[10], something that distinguishes them from those engaging in cosplay, short for costume play. For them, to change from their school uniform into their Gothic Lolita gear means to become their 'true self', it is not for them a mere costume change with the intention of being photographed. In many cases, young people in Harajuku do not like to be photographed, and the kind of friction depicted in the novel does also belong to Harajuku as a contact zone.

The home of fashion

But what do we mean when we speak of Harajuku? Harajuku does not simply refer to a geographical place in Tokyo. For fashion, Harajuku is a place of imagination, a space that acts as something like the spiritual heartland of fashion[11]. It is not simply a place to buy clothes, but also a place to exchange information and to create more than simple customer/shopkeeper relations with those working there who double as models of what it means to be fashionable. If we treat these shops as dots on a map and connect the movement of the fashionable between them, we create a map that overlaps with the territory known as Harajuku. Harajuku is like a house that allows a relaxed and agreeable experience of fashion while shopping, wearing clothes, conversing, and also eating and drinking.

In *FRUiTS* issued in 2012 around, you find a page on which pictures of readers are published. Made without much ado with a digital camera or a mobile phone, the readers have submitted their own pictures. In most of these shots, it is clear that the person depicted is taking the picture him/herself. The heading of this page is 'Fashionable snaps you took yourself', and it is clear from this that the readers are invited to express their own ideas of what it means to be fashionable. Perhaps in order to publish as many pictures as possible, each snap is very small. But to be published in this place is a positive acknowledgement of one's own status within the hierarchy of fashion and the performance that underlines this. Furthermore, it is interesting to note that in almost all snapshots a mirror is present. Some are taken in their own rooms; some are taken in the

---

10 I had been interviewing a Japanese girl in Gothic Lolita fashion since 2005 (the same girl I interviewed in Chapter I). She seems to be very sensitive about being seen and photographed by someone, not only because she dislikes being photographed, but also because she had sad experiences of being called a 'weirdo' in the street, being pointed at, or being photographed secretly by pedophilic *Kameko* "amateur photographers".

11 It could be said that Harajuku also exists in Shibuya. Some of the shops in Shibuya have Harajuku fashion taste and actually share the same customers. Since 2000, many shops have been opened along Meiji-*dori* "street"; you can automatically get to Shibuya by walking along the street while visiting the shops. There is no strict boundary between Shibuya and Harajuku. See Watanabe 2005.

bathroom; most of the pictures depict part of what it is to be at home. For those people, this is a chance to have their own ideas of what it means to be fashionable validated, even if they go to Harajuku and walk the length of Meijidori without being validated or acknowledged by the photographers who are present. Presently most mobile phones are equipped with a camera. This is a simple tool to create contact with the symbolic space that is Harajuku. The boundaries of Harajuku can thus be stretched endlessly. This page with snapshots was not present when the magazine was established in 1997. Harajuku as a contact zone does change and evolve ceaselessly. The technique that transforms the symbolic contact into a physical thing is the mobile phone camera.

I want to go to Japan to buy shoes !

Let us go back to London. A friend who was born and raised in London and with whom I was sharing a flat had her room decorated in Thai and Indian textiles and had perfumed the space with oriental incenses. She went to China to study Chinese medicine and she said she was interested in Japan as a country of fashion. In short, she was a Western woman with Eastern tastes.

One day she said to me, 'Some day I want to go to Japan. Where do they sell these shoes ? Please tell me !' What she pointed at was a page from *FRUiTS*. Those thicksoled boots to me as a Japanese seemed to belong to the items of punk fashion that were after all invented in England and that she, an English woman, would think that they were somehow Japanese deeply puzzled me.

The magazine *Street* was the focus of my research in the 1990s[12][13], but then the sister publication *FRUiTS* became a worldwide phenomenon. It became increasingly available in continental Europe and in London as well[14]. That Harajuku, rather than being a part of Tokyo, was increasingly being known as a city of fashion, I learned in London. But let us go back to the flatmate already mentioned. She also collected the American-made Blythe dolls. These were quite difficult to get hold of in Britain. In spite of the fact that the doll was an American product, she wanted to go to Japan to buy it. Apparently these are called 'NeoBlythe'[15] and are manufactured under license in Japan, in special

---

12   Onohara 1999.

13   Clothes are analogous to language; when you express yourself by the medium of dress, it is like writing poetry to express yourself with your own words and breaking grammar rules sometimes for a new perception of the world or creating beauty.

14   Miura and Narumi discuss the magazine as follows: 'We can find *FRUiTS* easily at any popular bookshops in Paris' and 'Western people were attracted by Japanese fashion through the magazine *FRUiTS*'.

Japanese versions in order to appeal to Japanese consumers. These have countless variations in dress and there is even the possibility for the consumers to design their own clothes for the doll and have them manufactured for the market. The pricing is also lower than the American original and therefore more affordable. Indeed, for my flatmate, Blythe has become a Japanese doll and therefore fashionable.

For a European with oriental tastes, Japan is a country of and in fashion. Perhaps it is not even necessary to say 'oriental' taste. Whoever likes new fashion will like what emerges from Japan. It seems that the Japanese and the fashionable have become overlapping categories.

Not Orientalism but Japonisme

We shall investigate when the popularity of Japanese fashion started in the West and precisely what kind of clothes they were. Exports of Japanese goods began in earnest after the long period of isolation up to the 19th century in Yokohama. The occasion for this was the world exhibitions in the West that were held in Philadelphia, Vienna, Paris, etc.

Since the French city of Lyon, India and China had each already established their markets for silk, the rise of the Japanese silk trade in the West was only possible through tactical production. It was the use of the shape of the kimono to create what would come to be known as a 'tea gown' that the Japanese silk trade broke into the market for indoor wear[16]. This was a garment that used the cut of the kimono to create a more floating silhouette. Thin, light and yet warm, this high quality gown was meant to be worn while enjoying one's domestic space and to provide a sense of luxury and fashion. An advertisement in the Liberty's (British department store) catalogue of 1892 is of great interest here; I quote: 'Japanese silk embroidery dressing gown'. Liberty's had this produced especially in Japan and it contained delicate, beautiful hand-made embroidery. This kind of sleeping wear provided a sufficiently dressedup feel to be worn around the house and not only in the bedroom and was the first item of Japanese fashion that was imported to the West. Hence Japanese fashion was not initially known as public clothing, but as private lounge wear and as clothes to sleep in.

---

15 Blythe dolls were originally produced by the company Kenner in 1972 and were designed by an American woman called Allison Katsman. The original Blythe dolls are well known as Vintage Blythe and can fetch an impressive price today. The Japanese toy company Takara (Takara-Tomy at present) got a license in 2000 to reproduce Blythe dolls called 'Neo Blythe'. Interestingly, Takara used the same body of their famous product, Rika-chan *ningyo* "doll", for the American Blythe doll's body at the beginning.

16 Suoh 2001.

The word fashion itself had a very different meaning then; it denoted a classbased sense of cultural accomplishment and enjoyment only available to the limited numbers of the upper classes.

As Japanese fashion that has truly influenced Western couture, we have to make special mention of Issey Miyake, who started out in Paris in the 1970s, then Rei Kawakubo, who participated in the Paris Collection from the 1980s on, and Yoji Yamamoto, all of whom have produced fashion rich in individuality. At that time. Comme des Garçons (Kawakubo) and Yohji Yamamoto became brands that exemplified the traditional Japanese aesthetics of simplicity and constraint (*wabi* and *sabi*) without actually being kimonos. This influence was often referred to as the 'Japan Shock'[17] and has its offspring in the young avant-garde designers based in Antwerp, Belgium. Many actors and artists became passionate fans of this new Japanese wave and helped to raise the profile of these brands remarkably[18]. Their creations were treated as objects of art and purchased by museums and exhibited side by side with Western designers. The work of Issey Miyake is very well known in U. K. for his unique creative ideas and techniques, and he has been awarded an honourary doctorate from the Royal College of Fashion in London. We can say that this class of high fashion belongs more to the realm of art than to the realm of fashion as such. While these designers have opened flagship stores in the Aoyama and Omotesando districts of Tokyo (in close vicinity to Harajuku), their fashion remains somewhat limited to the upper echelon of taste, and while the shops are open to the public, they retain a high-class, almost intimate boutique atmosphere.

These designers have established themselves in the world of fashion as influential and lasting presences. The traditional folk garment of the Japanese is no longer representative of Japanese fashion. These modern creations are now seen as representations of Japanese culture and objects of art in their own right that have earned the respect of the Western fashion world.

From cuties to *kawaii*

There can be no doubt that the significant keyword for fashionable Japan is *kawaii* "the cute". This notion of cute is intimately linked to the street fashion and subculture and is very popular now. This new craze for kawaii, however, has a different quality from the reception of Japanese fashion so far. The style

---

17 Kawamura 2004.
18 The German film director Wim Wenders documented Yohji Yamamoto in the film entitled *Notebook on Cities and Clothes* (1998). He was initially motivated by Yamamoto's clothes through an actress in his film who was a great fan of the designer.

in cute fashion that started in Japan in the 1980s is exemplified by white, pink and pastel colours, by blouses with puffy sleeves and frills, fancy dresses with ribbons, and all kinds of paraphernalia decorated with cute characters and slogans from cartoons[19]. In fact, the magazine *CUTiE* (Takarajima-sha, 1989-2015) —the name says it all— was established in the 1980s and bears the subtitle 'For Independent Girls'. It becomes clear from the alignment of 'cute' and 'independent' here that in the context of the 1980s this was part of the counter-culture or subcultural independent movement that emerged with the so-called band boom and the increasing number of self-producing indie bands. We can safely say that this indie style is connected to what is now known as Otaku culture. They are not content to just wear prepubescent female clothing, but they form small groups and in these underground communities they swap information and enjoy their individual taste.

The most extreme example of this highly decorated girly fashion is the contemporary trend of Lolita fashion in Japan. When I did my research in London, I also met a journalist from Eastern Europe who had made a documentary on the Japanese Gothic Lolita. He had been living in London for a long time, and when I asked him whether cuteness was also sought after in Europe, he replied, 'Cuteness is not regarded as a positive value because it is associated with immature, childish traits'. It seems that Western girls want to be adults as fast as possible and place emphasis on being sexy rather than being cute. When I showed pictures of Lolita fashion to another researcher who specialised in Indian recycling fashion, she said, 'There can be no doubt that they do this strategically to appeal to the other sex' and strongly questioned this link with what is known in Japan as the Lolita complex, the preference of men for childlike women. It seems that it is difficult for Western people to understand Lolita fashion, which partially adapts baroque Western dress, as part of the same form of Japanese cute fashion.

Through the worldwide popularity of Japanese Manga and Anime, the concept of cute that has only very weak roots in the West has been established and received as part of 'Cool Japan'. Dressing up in character costumes and purchasing the copious merchandise inspired by Manga characters is popular not only among children, but among adults of both sexes. Japanese high-tech exports have changed from cars and large electronic appliances to the Tamagochi and the Playstation, inexpensive game machines[20]. Further proof of this is that the Japanese word kawaii is increasingly used worldwide in its alphabetical

---

19 Kinsella 1995.

20 Yomota 2006 states that Japanese *chijimi* "shrink" culture is significant in describing Japanese *kawaii,* which is closely linked with its one of the factors, smallness.

spelling. This culture of kawaii has become a globalised mass culture, popular not only in the countries of the West, America and Europe, but also in the Asian nations[21]. Even if Japanese industrial production and its high-tech sector have been overtaken, its cultural production and sensibilities cannot easily be imitated. As a new image of Japan as the desirable and exotic Far East, the notion of kawaii has been very successful.

The imagination of the Other through the Other[22]

Here I would like to draw attention to the second contact zone, which the anthropologist Tanaka Masakazu described in his 2007 publication. This second contact zone emerges when we think of the contemporary globalised world as infected by European influence and modernity. Any field the anthropologist may choose is no longer a first contact zone. Wherever he goes, the effects of globalisation are already palpable. He is, in short, always already in a second contact zone. This is a useful way of rethinking some of the political implications of the exercise of anthropology as such.

Applied to fashion research, we can rethink this idea through the notion of the kimono. Kimono in Japanese simply means 'thing to wear' but of course refers to the traditional dress worn in pre-modern Japan. The same phenomenon that happened with the word Kawaii is also happening here: kimono, spelled with the letters of the alphabet, has become a fashion phenomenon in its own right[23]. When I wanted to talk with the aforementioned anthropologist investigating Indian recycle fashion about the kimonos that were stored and exhibited in museums as part of collections of traditional attire, what came up first in the conversation was that a young Japanese girl was making accessories such as purses from old kimonos to go with Western clothes. When the conversation about kimonos got stuck, she showed interest when I mentioned that young Japanese girls would wear miniskirts made from old *yukata* "summer cotton kimono". I had the impression that rather than to talk about the traditional kimono, she was interested in the way the kimono was appropriated in modern fashion. So this notion of kimono is increasingly accepted as part of Cool Japan.

The focal point of Tokyo street fashion, Harajuku has become a tourist spot for visiting foreigners like Akihabara. Historically, Western culture was adopted in these places faster than in others. When we talk of Harajuku as a contact zone, we are talking about the second kind of contact zone. Different styles

---

21   Zheng 2005.

22   The phrase is originally from Tanaka 2007.

23   Onohara 2007.

come into contact in this imaginary space that unfolds along Meiji-dori, a space in which a strict hierarchy of being fashionable is enacted with European haute couture at the top of the hierarchy. Harajuku is constituted by the contact of different styles, not only in a harmonising style but also often with friction and communication, as a dynamic phenomenon.

In London, for the English, Harajuku, mediated through the magazine *FRUiTS,* has become an experience and a symbol of all that is fashionable. Set between Shibuya, the centre of subculture, and Aoyama, the centre of high culture, it is a paradise for pedestrians, a breathing underground for the independent movement, a place teeming with visitors and teenagers alike, a place whose gravitational pull does not only extend to the homelands of Western fashion, but also to the surrounding Asian countries. When my former flatmate for example thus takes pictures of herself and her Blythe dolls in cute attire and sends these to a magazine, we can then say that she is within the frame of 'Harajuku'. And this in turn may feed back into Japan and has an influence on the real streets of Harajuku.

On being fashionable

Fashion is a holistic system in which looks and styles change according to the times but are also reborn regularly with small modifications. To be fashionable thus is different depending on the period of time and where you are; there can be no absolute notion of being fashionable. Change is the only constant and a value in itself, as each look embodies and materialises a certain moment in time.

At present, Japan is fashionable and the Japanese are thought of as fashionable people. That means this thesis itself is fashionable. To be interested in Japan, to read *FRUiTS,* to be aware of Japanese fashion, to collect small items and to combine them into a style informed by Japanese aesthetics is fashionable. It is no longer necessary to wear high fashion by Japanese designers or a traditional kimono to participate in this. Eating sushi, reading *FRUiTS,* talking about kawaii, all these actions denote that Harajuku has been globalised and has become a new contact zone, a new anchor for the system of fashion, with a dynamic interplay of harmony and friction. It seems that the ever-evolving Western fashion is deeply implicated in the politics of friction and is looking for an Archimedean point to anchor itself.

Is Japanese fashion therefore becoming something anyone can wear? Indeed it seems that everyone independent of nationality can do so. Like a character in a fantastical story of the near future, you can become Japanese by wearing Japanese style. There is no longer a need to be in Japan physically. Through the instantaneous media that connect people, Harajuku becomes part of a

Figure 1
Blablahospital: A Tokyo fashion bland designed
by a Japanese girl originally started in London

dynamic virtual space.

Fashion has come a long way from being simply a cover of the genitalia, a means to appeal to the other sex, a way of decorating the body. Changing clothes without any necessary reasons is something that makes us profoundly different from animals. Furthermore, through the quick pace of change in modern fashion, the semiotic function of fashion to differentiate between genders, between ethnicities, between classes and between different trades has somewhat eroded. One could maintain that fashion has become a mere game. We want to be similar to other people, but also to be different. Fashion is born where these two at first sight contradictory desires clash. There is also the contrary notion that only those who can pull off a style naturally and do not seek the attention of the cameras are truly fashionable. When too much is staked on being fashionable, then fashionable can become a parody of itself.

Transcending individuals and places, even overcoming time, as if denying that time exists, merely existing through the material one puts on one's body, this is an age of the fetish of fashion. Or maybe it is a return to the basic function of fashion of decorating the body? It is necessary to think about the intimate relationship fashion has to the individual body, not simply as a functional garment, but in terms of the remaking of the self, some through the infliction of wounds

to the body (**Fig. 1**).

Conclusion

When a fashion researcher Philomena Keet interviewed the photographer Aoki Shoichi, she asked him, 'What is the meaning of fashion?' He answered, 'It seems that human beings are looking for revolutions, for violence, for erotic thrills. This is the deep meaning hidden behind Western fashion. But the young people in these magazines, they simply play with clothes'. This interesting comment could bring us the opportunity to discuss. Are these young people really just playing, or are they using their body as a medium to express something, to question something? Are the people depicted in *FRUiTS* and *Tune* merely looking for that elusive goal of being fashionable? It could be said that they exist as the modern European body, straggling through the political impact, the hidden violence, and the complexities and contradictions of the age expressed in Western fashion.

The old image that equalled Japan with the kimono as traditional value has been well received in the West. The 'Japan Shock' that Japanese high fashion created in the Western world emancipated Japan from the image of the kimono-clad woman and earned Japan's citizenship in the world of fashion. Finally the sub-cultural, the popular and modern notion of kawaii, the cute, has freed itself from the confines of nationality and has become a truly encompassing international value. It is not classical or traditional, not like the earlier imagery of the Far East, mysterious or oriental, and has recently also been taken up by the European world of high fashion.

A place named Harajuku does not exist. It is in fact not the name of a place, but merely the name of a train station. The addresses around the station are in fact 'Jingumae', meaning 'In front of the shrine', referring to the Meiji-Shrine, this symbol of modernity that is the true core of this space. It is a place in which one can become the object of a photographer's lens and be transformed into a fashionable body, where one can participate and compete in the hierarchy of fashion. It is a place where foreign tourists and locals can mingle, and on New Year many people dressed in kimonos can be seen, a place where all these streets intersect. In the teeming traffic, one can see the fashion industry professionals with their branded bags and the Lolitas who wear classical Western clothes that are made in Japan; all these different persons cross their ways walking towards Omotesando.

Thus when the Japanese are spoken of as fashionable, the image of ethnic specificity has waned. This does not mean to deny one's own history and values but means that the style and the rules of Western fashion have been thoroughly

digested. That again does not mean that there is in Asia the existence of a symbolic 'West', nor a 'Non-West'. What emerges cannot be grasped by these binary notions but is a truly new notion of Japan as fashion. The worldview in which everything is referred to with the adjective kawaii, cute. Identity as play. Such a kawaii wearer no longer aims to be self-consciously fashionable, no longer who to be or where to be or when to be, but simply enjoys the performance of watching oneself in the mirror or through the lens.

Take an item from the mountain of old clothes, fallen out of 'fashion time', and create something new by customising it. Anything can be put together. If you cannot find it, put it together from something already there. Do not think about how to wear it, the adornment of the body is a goal in itself. Already we have moved closer to the original raison d'etre of clothing. The models in *FRUiTS*, the costume players, the Lolita girls, they all like to make things by hand. Originality, or customise! Fashionable Japan and European modernity are fighting or playing over one's body while 'I' dress and undress.

Contact, friction, struggle, exchange, harmony: from these experiences the experience of being fashionable is born, whether fresh or nostalgic or creating a pleasant frisson. Style is born and disseminated and finally accepted. Japan as fashion thus means new, means no one is rejected, independent of culture or ethnicity, old or new. It does not mean that all these various 'others' are transgressed, but that we should enjoy wearing them over each other, in a new style perhaps best described as 'overlapping'.

References

Barthes, R., 1967, *System de la mode,* Seuil.

Furuya, Y., 2001, *Hybrid Modernities and Anthropology: from Latin America Contact Zones,* Jinbun Shoin.

Kawamura, Y., 2004, *Japanese Revolution in Paris Fashion,* Oxford, Berg.

Keet, P., 2007, *The Tokyo Look Book: The Stylish to Spectacular,* Tokyo, Kodansha International.

Kinsella, S., 1995, 'Cuties in Japan', in *Women Media and Consumption in Japan,* ed. Lise Skov, Brian Moeran, University of Hawaii Press.

Matsuura, M., 2007, *Sekai to Watashi to Lolita Fashion,* Seikyu-sha.

Mears, P., 2008, 'Exhibiting Asia: Global Impact of Japanese Fashion in Museums and Galleries', *Fashion Theory: The Journal of Dress, Body and Culture,* 12, 1.

Miura, A., 2006, *Jiyu na Jidai no Fuan na Jibun,* Shobun-sha.

Onohara, N., 1999, 'A Semiotic Study of Rhetoric of Clothes: A Brand-new Dress Is Born Where There Is a Will to Self-expression', *Hyogen Kenkyu,* 69.

——, 2000, 'Anglomania and Anglophilia: We Love Vivienne Westwood', in *The Sex Pistols File,* ed. 'Rock Jet', Shinko Music.

――, 2007, 'Fashion: to Dress and to Undress', in *Chi no Literacy: Bunka,* ed. Haguchi, Hideko, Manabu Kawada and Sacko Oussouby, Nakanishiya-shuppan.

Suoh, T., 2001, 'Imported Dressing Gown in the Early Meiji Period: A Case of Shiino Masabei's Store', *Dresstudy: A Bulletin of Fashion Study,* 40.

Takemoto, N., 2002, *Emily,* Shuei-sha.

Tanaka, M., 2007, 'To Contact Zone of Anthropology', *Contact Zone,* 1.

Urry, J., 1995, *Consuming Places,* International Library of Sociology, Routledge.

Watanabe, A., 2005, *Street Fashion no Jidai,* Meigensha.

Yomota, I., 2006, *Kawaii Ron,* Chikuma-shobo.

Zheng, Xiu-Juan, 2005, 'Suppin no Tokyo ni Deau―Nihon Boom no Atosaki', in *Tokyo Studies,* ed. Yoshimi, Toshiya and Mikio Wakabayashi, Kinokuniya Shoten.

III

Costume and Trauma: Reception of Japanese Fashion in Britain Through Five Exhibitions in London

Introduction

I would like to think about Japanese fashion and how it has been accepted in Britain, including Kimono, Japanese traditional dress, and look at our national costume globally in a modern way. Also, I shall try considering Japanese fashion as art, which has been influencing the western world for a long while, as well as through more than a few exhibitions held in London, focusing on Japanese fashion and art. My interest in such Japanese culture and art, spotlighted at exhibitions in Britain, started in 2005. This paper, consisting of three chapters, could aim to ultimately argue that the mystic image of Japan is being produced by both uniqueness and modernity in her culture and art; discussed with the key themes of 'tradition', 'trauma', 'technology' and 'trend'. I shall examine some exhibitions in London that featured Japanese fashion, and consider how the Japanese image is described in presenting Japanese fashion through Japanese costume.

Fashioning Kimono

The exhibit, called *Fashioning Kimono: Dress in early 20th century Japan* (from the Montgomery collection), at the Victoria and Albert Museum in 2005-2006 (13 Oct-2 May), was a significant project at the Toshiba Gallery, which offered British people the opportunity to understand the knowledge of the costume from historical meanings of design and pattern, to modern technical aspects of weaving and dying, all influenced each other in an interesting fashion.

Although Kimono is so to speak a uniquely Japanese national costume, Japan had to import a purple dye technique that a British dyer named Perkins invented for her kimono industry in the late nineteenth century. The purple dyes especially, had been expensive and hard to obtain, but new chemical based dyes were already created in Europe in the latter half of the nineteenth century. It is considered that these revolutionised the world's dye industry at that time[1].

1　Assche 2005: 19-20.

Figure 1
Art nouveau styled kimono
©Victoria and Albert Museum

Figure 2
Young boy's kimono of Japan images
©Victoria and Albert Museum

As for the design, some of the Kimonos were found as Art Deco style, for example, its special Scottish pink art nouveau designs dynamically set off with orange and dark red (**Fig. 1**). Not only colour but the Japanese patterns (motifs) and curving (lines) influenced European artists in the early twentieth century. European artists who were stuck in the traditions mentioned that Japanese art style, from asymmetric inspirations to dynamic forms, had 'set us free and made us bold'[2].

Today, we can understand Kimono as a fashion which was also influenced by European designs and technique, and also being an important motif for European fashion, not only as ethnic traditional images of Japan, but also playing an important role as a modern style in Western fashion. When the culture is adapted newly, we cannot avoid mutual influential phenomena occurring. These dynamics could make the culture richer; this process occurs naturally, not just in the fashion and design world.

Furthermore, in this exhibit, I may state that the way they selected and exhibited was remarkably unique when I regarded their exhibits of men's kimono and boy's kimono. As national costume is to be designed to improve people's morale, kimono seemed to be utilised and worn in such a way. Illustrating here a piece of *juban* "under-kimono" in the Meiji period, you can find an obvious reference to the war between Japan and Russia in 1905–1906, through the images of Yokohama port and two men in Japanese military uniform.

Juban is a mostly made of cotton, easily washable and worn directly to the skin, which is physically and symbolically closer to the wearer's body so that he can feel Japan's military campaign more intimately and raise his nationalism

2 Assche 2005: 31–33.

unconsciously. In the example of the young boy's kimono (**Fig. 2**), the design is playful and friendly, but air force, military force, the national flag and the Mt. Fuji-they are all that could grow Japanese nationalist spirit for his developing mind.

It is notable that the catalogue (related to the exhibit) included images which demonstrated the idea of women's liberty, aesthetics, of Japanese beauty, and the futuristic image of kimono that are stylised by younger girls today in a modern way. The look of the younger Japanese women wearing kimono reminds me easily of the western girls in kimono. When the traditional costume becomes fashionable today, it has to travel across culture boundaries as well as the oceans. It is true that kimono is still a formal national costume mainly worn only on special occasions, but younger girls wear kimono more casually and freely without the fear and anxiety that afflicts western wearers of the costume.

Future Beauty

Looking at the exhibition, entitled *Future Beauty: 30 years of Japanese Fashion* at Barbican Arts Centre in 2010-11 (15 Oct-6 Feb) we might realise how Japanese fashion designers stand out uniquely in the world of global fashion (**Fig. 3**[3]). The Paris Collection designers such as Yohji Yamamoto, Rei Kawakubo and Issey Miyake are mainly spotlighted in the exhibition. However, they are displayed alongside rather younger independent designers like Undercover and Matoh.

This type of exhibition focusing on Japanese fashion designers has presented a quite new approach to British art scene. I could suggest that Japanese avant-garde fashion designers represented by Yohji Yamamoto and Rei Kawakubo that both started their collection shows in early 1980s in Paris, tended to be introduced to Britain through French media and the French fashion business. Amongst them, Issey Miyake appears to be more accessible and admired in the British fashion scene. My research indicates that Issey's style is commonly talked about in relation to his unique idea in connection with technology and design. One of his representative works called 'Pleats Please' was created in 1993 and since then it has been remarkably successful all over the world. It is a kind of an innovative design technique of pleats but based on the concept of Japanese tradition found in the way of kimono. It looks like a simple functional compact pleated cloth but becomes variable according to those who wear it,

---

3 'Barbican' is written as 'バービカン'. It shows awareness of Japanese letters Katakana, which is said to be originally made for loan words from the West.

38

Figure 3

Flyer of the exhibition of *Future Beauty*

which means the dress is totally open and free to everyone regardless of the age, ethnicity, gender, and size; it is flexibly changeable and adjustable to the wearer. His concept 'East meets West', adopted later for the title of his first book published in 1972, attracted respect for Japanese tradition and technology and could transcend the boundary between the West and the East. He achieved this by coming back to the original idea of 'A Piece of Cloth' (to wrap your body) as the world standard design which also later inspired his next idea called 'A-Poc', which was also displayed in this exhibition. Interestingly, he was born in Hiroshima during the war time and his first encounter with design was in his home town where there were two bridges named 'to live' and 'to die' which were located near the site of the A-bomb strike (Miyake Design Studio 2009-12).

Akiko Fukai, previous chief curator of The Kyoto Costume Institute that has constantly presented Japanese fashion globally as interesting exhibitions, looks back in the catalogue for this exhibition, at the history of thirty years of Japanese fashion. When Kawakubo and Yamamoto figures debuted in Paris in 1981, following after Kenzo Takada, Hanae Mori and Miyake, who already appeared on the international fashion scene in the 1970s, their clothes were shocking to the western fashion world. With their dark colours, shabbiness, asymmetry and dragging oversized style, this was far from the proportional elegant look that had been long successful in European fashion. The dominant western fashion world could not accept them properly at first.

There was an interesting comment in the catalogue on Kawakubo's dress: 'Her apocalyptic clothing is proceed with holes, tattered and torn, almost like clothing worn by nuclear holocaust survivors'. For Yamamoto's dress, 'clothes for the end of the world that look as if they have been bombed to shreds'. Both are quotes from fashion critics in the high end French popular fashion journals, *Jours de mode* and *Le Figaro*[4].

I contend that, even considering the new perspective and experimental creative value to the western fashion world that we Japanese have brought to the west, our works were considered as nothing more than what comes from the far east, and are interpreted merely as 'The Other' with oriental value. A traumatic approach for the defeated nation, as highlighted by Miyake's and

---

4   Fukai, Vinken, Frankel & Kurino 2010: 13-16.

Kawakubo's concepts, enabled the western mind to access and understand the new and unusual fashion ideas from the East. Such a process may be required to be acceptable to the Western aesthetic value. My thought might sound negative and pessimistic, however I will discuss this issue a little more and positively with a dress designed by Kawakubo. This dress was initially featured as the cover image of this exhibition, shown as the front cover of the pamphlet and conspicuously, the motif of this dress is the Japanese flag 'rising sun' ('Hinomaru' in Japanese).

Significantly, an essay in 2010, by one of the most famous Japanese architects, Kenya Hara, is cited in this catalogue, displayed next to the page of the Hinomaru dress. In his essay, Hara discusses the possibility and receptiveness of the design of the Japanese flag; 'the simple and abstract quality of a red circle on a white background is so equivocal, it can be filled with various images. Therefore, even if our flag inevitably reflects a sad history, it can still hold every possible meaning if we place our will and hope in it. The Japanese flag fulfils its function silently while embracing the contradictory notions of sadness, disgrace, hope and peace'. He even introduces a painful interpretation: the countless soldiers and the killed and the dead, who placed the flag on their foreheads, but he holds onto the hope contained within the iconic image[5].

Concluding my comment on the exhibition, I would like to consider how the modern Japanese image was projected today at this contemporary gallery. In the final part of the exhibition, I found 'Japan' to be a little strange and even awkward, when I saw lots of comics and Hello Kitty merchandising. It was obviously different from all the high fashion styles we had seen just before reaching the last section. What Japanese contemporary designers have done so far; is to deconstruct the static western fashion value, to develop the power of clothes into artistic form. However, introducing cool, popular Japanese culture to the exhibition was surprising to the contemporary gallery visitors.

But we may think about it in rather a different view, who will be the target audience, and what is the purpose of the exhibition. Now Japan is fashion itself as I discuss in Chapter II, Japanese fashion like Tokyo street style is leading the fashion world internationally. Weird x weird = cool, as my German friend used to say to me describing Japanese fashion. It seems to have taken a long time for fashion to be considered as art and allowed to join the high culture. But, by collaborating strategically with the trendy pop image of Japanese manga or animation, such artistic designers from the privileged high fashion world become more familiar to the western audience. We could recall those examples of Japanese pop art being exhibited at national museums around the world, and

---

5 Fukai, Vinken, Frankel & Kurino 2010: 108-109.

the subsequent elevated values when sold at what would be considered, high culture auction houses and galleries.

Aware

I am going to take fashion as art, looking at the exemplified works to show how Japanese art has influenced modern western art and fashion. At another recent significant fashion exhibition in London, *Aware: Art Fashion Identity* at the Royal Academy of Arts from 2010–11 (2 Dec–31 Jan), we can go though Japanese fashion and arts vividly represented by collaboration with contemporary foreign artists in the world.

Interestingly, at this exhibition, Japanese traditional art was represented by a London based Turkish fashion designer, Hussein Chalayan. He introduced a new dress design in his installation, inspired by the three hundred year-old Japanese ancient art of puppet theatre called Bunraku. The project, called 'Son of Sonzai Suru' (*Sonzai Suru* means "exist"), illustrated the invisible in the visible, or vice versa, very much like the Ninja or Islamic subjects that animate the clothes as he suggested. He stated 'Both dress codes define a territory where the individual can become invisible and anonymous[6]'. The project questioning the meaning of 'identity' was inspired by the method, in Japanese performing arts, of hiding one's existence while functioning at the same time. This was done with live models clad in totally black clothes, being absorbed into the darkness like the *kuroko* in Japanese theatre that move invisibly in support of the main actors.

Also exhibited was the French artist named Marie-Ange Guillemniot. The historical photographs of war victims' clothing had moved her creative desire during her stay in Hiroshima. Her art/fashion installation entitled 'Kimono Memories of Hiroshima' (**Fig. 4**), is inspired by the memories that a second hand Kimono could convey. Her Kimono were displayed together with a bag which could remind us Japanese instantly of some protective equipment distributed at war time. According to the catalogue of the exhibition, her works are described as follows; tradition, living (as opposed to nostalgic) memory, healing and the intensely personal are all imbued in the work of Guillemniot[7]. So, it was not only Japanese aesthetics but also her understanding of the traumatic impact of war on the country which may have caused her to confront her European sense of reality.

At the exhibition, you could watch the short film of Yoko Ono's well known

---

6   Coppard 2011: 74–77.
7   Coppard 2011: 94–101.

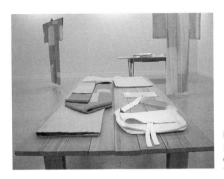

Figure 4
Kimono Memories of Hiroshima
© Marie-Ange Guillemniot.

'Cut Piece' (1964). 'Cut Piece' is to be categorised as an art performance or art action if necessary. It was interactive, with the audience given the scissors and allowed to participate in her work by cutting her clothes wherever they liked. She was becoming almost naked and exposed in her vulnerability. The work examines the tension between our recognition of art performance and our sense of shame in front of a show such as striptease, and in this way it tested and challenged our potentially masochistic eyes.

It seems that past and present, traditional and modern images of Japan have repeated themselves to establish a recognisable existence so that the country's international image may be stronger and more authentic in the world of art. We could say that, in this exhibition, fashion is expressed as one of the art forms. However, it appears that the traumatic approach, extracting the wartime images, cannot be the ignored when Japanese fashion and art are exhibited in Britain. Then I wonder if the strength of our country's authenticity in the fashion world could dwell mainly in the powerful economy growth after we had overcome the devastation of atomic bombing at the end of the World War II. Needless to say it may be a question of whether the image of the country as the defeated power has been manipulated by Europeans.

Yohji Yamamoto

Once again, I will introduce the exhibition at the Victoria and Albert museum. One Japanese modern designer Yohji Yamamoto was featured in the special exhibition in 2011 (12 March–10 July). Although he often states that he hates his exhibition to be held because he is still alive and active in designing clothes. However, not only Britain, but the other European countries like France and Italy were eager to exhibit his archive works in a retrospective way. Referring to the outstanding method in displaying his clothes at the gorgeous palace in Italy together with the historical masterpieces and elaborated furniture, the exhibition (installation) at the V&A was rather orthodox, but we were also given

the pleasure to find some of his works placed naturally, slipped away like secrecy in the labyrinth of the great gallery. During the months of the exhibition, there was also an interesting event outside the museum showing his white silk wedding dress with huge crinoline made of bamboo in the name of 'Yohji's Women' at Wapping Project.

His works are also well known for the beautiful collaboration with the film directors Wim Wenders and Takeshi Kitano. On the film *Dolls* (2002) directed by Kitano, Yohji designed all the costumes but the oversized kimono the main character wears was very impressive in its colour and style, and played an important role in the story.

Besides the theatrical costume design, he adores Japanese craftsmanship so much that he often adopts kimono motifs into his modern clothes: ancient colour coordination, pattern and dyeing, and above all, characteristic textiles and fabric. In the conversation with the curator in the catalogue, he confessed special regard for Japanese craftsmanship; 'Maybe I'll be the last designer who cares strongly about 'Made in Japan'. If I stop, maybe young designers cannot afford to do business 'Made in Japan', because it costs a lot, because a Japanese man's hand has become the most expensive in the world. So it's my duty, not duty, it's my desire to protect these small Japanese traditional techniques[8]'.

This was the first Yohji's exhibition in Britain. Recalling his style, I find it surprising that he had been impressed by the British punk movement and had visited Vivienne Westwood's World's End shop before going to Paris in 1970s. However, it is not that surprising, if we could remember the fact that he worked with some great British artists including photographer Nick Night and graphic designer Peter Savile in his early creations. 'The British artists opened my world ten times wider', he states in the same catalogue. 'Every time with them, I had a surprise, because an English artist has very strong focus, so when they touch my clothing, the finishing of a magazine or catalogue is totally far from me. It begins with their creation, but in that creation I have found my new Yamamoto[9]'. A new discovery of oneself. It seems to be the happiest collaboration between the artists across the oceans.

I had not found any traumatism in his design, until a Japanese anthropologist told me about it. He talked simply about Yohji's cutting, for the anthropologist the cutting is weird, but I need to remember that international Japanese avant-garde designers including Yohji, Kawakubo and Miyake used to be called 'Post Hiroshima' merely in the western context for understanding unusual works from

---

8   Salazar 2011: 73.
9   Salazar 2011: 94.

Asia. As Dorine Kondo discussed the concept of 'Japaneseness' in analyzing modern Japanese fashion, so the Japanese fashion phenomena tends to be interpreted as the establishment of a new sophisticated nation or the image of trans-nationality[10]. I found this confirmed in Yohji's confession of his height complex and traumatisation in the interview reported in the exhibition catalogue; 'I was born in a very bad moment in Japan. There was no food to feed babies, so my generation of people are very small. So naturally I am angry about my size, so I design big sizes[11]'.

Through the exhibition, visitors could experience his special affection towards the fabric and textile in his clothes. He said, 'Fabric is everything. Often I tell my pattern makers, "Just listen to the material. What is it going to say? Just wait. Probably the material will teach you something"'[12]. He says that his ideal clothes are firm army styles and vintage clothing, because his primary aim in his designing dress is to protect the human body. To support this aim, his designs should be bearable to be worn for a long time. I suggest that the significant key word for his aesthetics and creativity is 'air'. He talks about Ma which means "space" in Japanese, and it is an important factor in traditional Japanese art. He explains; 'We have to find a new vocabulary. I understand why European people take my creation as very Japanese: it is probably because, if you see a creation as whole, as 100 percent, I will always try to finish before arriving at 100. This five, seven or 10 percent-in Japanese we call it 'empty' or 'in-between' or 'uncompleted'...We need this space, so I design space...The space of expression is even more important than the visual or written'[13]. Would it not be possible to believe that he talks about 'air'? Meaningful emptiness for the air to go through; the space between body and dress?

Lastly in Yohji's exhibition and his works, I would like to discuss the image of women in his dress and the male image in his men's collections. He says his collection is his literature, particularly a story about women that he loves. Furthermore, he presented a challenging menswear collection for the autumn/ winter in 1998, whose models were all women including actress Charlotte Rampling and Vivienne Westwood. The silhouette of menswear through the female body might be received upon your eyes dramatically and even sensually. At the same time he 'fights with fashion history', as he often says. I could assert that he has been questioning the convention and the ideology of gender and sexuality, inside a fashion business still mainly led by white male dominated

---

10　Kondo 1997: 55-99.
11　Salazar 2011: 85.
12　Salazar 2011: 14.
13　Salazar 2011: 78.
14　Onohara 2011: 103-23.

companies and institutions[14].

Art activity is often interpreted as a kind of recovery over the artist's traumatic experience, as Judith Herman writes in her work 'The first principle of recovery is the empowerment of the survivor. She must be the author and arbiter of her own recovery'[15]. This idea, might be too simple, but let us confirm here the statement that Japan is the defeated country of the Great war and, since those traumatic events, has recovered as the world model of economic success. I propose that Japan's expression through its unique art and fashion has played a large part in that recovery and success; along with the work of skilled artisans and modern technology, and by continuous industrious efforts, whilst still keeping her beautiful tradition and culture. I find that, when taken in the context of the western-centric world of high fashion, the passionate Japanese avant-garde designers have continually expressed Japan's role as the traumatised nation in their work.

Yohji shows his admiration for women and their natural strength in talking about female designers from Chanel, Vionnet and Schiappeli to Kawakubo, Westwood and Stella McCartney. He says he has been fighting with them but cannot beat them. To approach his complex feeling, I could also refer again that his aim in designing clothes is to protect human body. Actually in his speaking of 'human body' he seems to focus on 'women's bodies', to hide their adorable sexuality. In order to overcome his complex, he might need to write his own literature on the fashion stage, as opposed to tracing western fashion history. He could make his unique writing understood to the western fashion world with the use of variable female characters and his oft-quoted sadness, romanticism, craziness and madness. It is not only because of his traumatic experience, but also for the sake of female vulnerability, as he describes himself 'I am a designer like an ancient shell found in the mud, who loves woman'[16].

A Night Of Constraint

Here I would like to think about Kimono again as well as Tokyo street fashion by introducing Miss Akimbo, an English gay male performer based in London with a fascination with oriental culture, especially Japanese. His alter ego Miss Akimbo explores modern and traditional imagery surrounding oriental figures such as Geishas and concubines through a combination of costume and performance art. He is also inspired by Kabuki, a Japanese traditional play where all characters are actors/men. Most of his performance is dedicated to

---

15   Herman 1997 [1992] : 134.
16   Salazar 2011 : 82–85.

Figure 5
Hurricane Akimbo performance

the Geisha, female entertainer who performs Japanese traditional arts such as music and dance usually in front of the male guests at extravagant dinner and drink parties. It would be easier to see how he is through his videos, but in this chapter, I will introduce his performance by illustrating some images.

The Japanese national costume Kimono is a crucial property for his theater performance. Hurricane Akimbo was a piece about Celine Dion talking from her dressing room in Ceaser's Palace in Las Vegas about the disaster left in the wake of Hurricane Katrina (**Fig. 5**). Akimbo loosely wears a white wedding kimono then later changes into a red juban towards the end of the number as she is reborn in the form of the spirit of the Hurricane. He purchased kimonos from the shop called Ichigoya in Osaka, they are amazingly well made and beautifully adjust to western people, who are bigger and taller than the original Japanese wearers, to be enjoyable to wear, even for men. In the proper, traditional way of wearing kimonos, we need lots of strings and we tie them tightly around the body with a special complicated technique. But the modern Kimono is easy to wear like western dress. Belts are normally attached already to the customised kimono of Ichigoya, and the strings are also fixed to the dress to be easy to form the proper style. With these modern styles there is no need to worry about the length of the sleeves, and nor adhere to the strict rules of combination between special patterns and colours. You can see most of the Ichigoya customers are living abroad who could gain access to the kimonos on line easily at its well-organised website. To adopt the gorgeous and decorative, rather oriental look, you do not have to struggle with difficulty any longer to master how to wear. Just enjoy.

They might not be real Kimonos, but what is Kimono? If the Japanese unique traditional style is to survive in the future for a longer period, it has to become more accessible to anyone who is interested in this ancient costume and appreciative of our art and culture. For this Japanese tradition to acquire popularity, the style ought to be changeable to the wearer's needs. In his performance of Camouflage Akimbo wears a kimono with surplus patterns with

Figure 6
Camouflage Akimbo performance

the army helmet (**Fig. 6**). Camouflage is Military Akimbo and the act is called 'We Need a War'. It was a political piece about the Iraq war. The kimono was the first kimono he made for himself. He liked the clash of images between soldier and peaceful geisha. It is an exciting fusion of manly casual street style and feminine classic kimono look.

Thinking about the domestic fashion situation, younger girls in Japan dress in kimono as street fashion, an easier kimono called *Yukata* "summer kimono made of cotton" in particular. Unsurprisingly, some of them have the skills to remake it attractively, cutting its length shorter and attaching frills and ribbons to the hem. Far from the authentic Japanese tradition in the past, but we could say they appreciate kimono culture, at least they enjoy putting the dress on, even if it is in their own style and taste.

In 2010 (12 August), I organised a Japanese art performance event in London with Miss Akimbo and our mutual friend who is a Swiss anthropologist on contemporary Japan and has been learning a martial art Aikido for many years. The event is entitled 'A Night of Constraint', funded as a research project by the academic institution called Japanese Association for Semiotic Studies. We hoped to present Japanese contemporary art and culture in a different way from the ordinary Japanese events that had been held in Britain. The key concept of our show was 'constraint'.

Constraints are all around us: in the way we dress appropriately, in the way we behave towards others and in the way our surroundings constrain our actions. Most of those constraints we inflict upon ourselves in the name of normality and most often we are not aware that we are doing this. However, an encounter with a contrasting culture and its rituals can provide us with a new perspective on things we are already deeply familiar with. Contrary to the Western idea of a struggle between constraint and freedom, we think Japanese culture has embraced constraint as a means of development of the self. We also think our

show 'A Night of Constraint' allows our guests to explore this concept in an intimate dinner party context. Through a series of performances inspired by various Japanese arts we wanted to make tangible what is normally invisible. We felt that nourishment of the body has to be complemented with nourishment of the mind and that the original musical format of a 'soiree' is ideally suited to present a theme with such variations. The evening, held at a dim sum restaurant's private upper floor, progressed through a four course dinner interspersed with poetic performance, live flower arrangement, Japanese rope bondage, Butoh dance, martial arts, short films and performance art accompanied by traditional *Shamisen* "Japanese three-stringed instrument". At the bar, a series of sake and plum wine based drinks was served. We are

Figure 7
Kimono Dressing performance at *A Night of Constraint*

not Geishas but we would prefer the Geisha spirit to entertain the customers, and the audience to be intoxicated with performance and fine food.

In the show, I tried Geisha Dressing for Akimbo while he read a *Maiko* "the daughter stage before becoming a Geisha" poem. My challenge was to express 'constraint' and 'release' in dressing him and de-constructing the Kimono (**Fig. 7**). The audience might enjoy the process of dressing, but dressing him was also like undressing him in the performance. Dressing down kimono is a sort of new experiments we are challenging the orthodoxy for this Japanese costume which is originally designed for dress-you-up. I know lots of Japanese events could astonish the western people at the perfect way of dressing up with kimono, but my performance was of a different type, and I did try expressing fashion as art with a traditional national costume motif. Not only deconstruction, reconstruction of the beauty. It also meant that I needed to wrestle with the totally customised kimono in clothing the western man, regardless of my knowledge of proper Japanese kimono dressing. I needed to try to forget what my body remembered unconsciously.

Besides this performance, I was also in charge of another poetry performance, it was a flower arrangement, without any flowers but with my poem. I read my

Figure 8
Birdcage Performance

works sitting in Zazen style after making tea to create silence with tuning folks and a singing bowl. Collaborating with an English florist, Francis Rushby's *Ikebana* "Japanese traditional flower arrangement", I already gave him a constraint in advance; he was to use the colours only from green to brown gradation *ha* "leaf"-*mono* "one" and *eda* "branch"-mono. Also in our night of constraint, French dancer Thierry Alexandre, gave us a performance of his art. In his dance we could see the spirit of Ohno Kazuo (this legendary pioneer Butoh dancer passed away just before the show, on 1st June, 2010), in the beauty and freedom of his dark underground conceptual dance with use of the rope. His expression was very charming and strongly presented Japanese stoicism or minimalism, in his interpretation of 'constraint'. Lastly on stage, Nawashi (means 'rope artist') Murakawa and his model Miyo (also appeared as a front-act Shamisen player) performed a *Kimbaku/Shibari* "bind tightly with rope" show in which they observed careful respect for each other, retaining the equality between the roper and the model to be bound. Kimbaku seemed to be a solemn ceremony itself that brought the silence totally back into the venue because every audience member stopped eating and drinking to take his/her own breath.

It is true that I, a Japanese, was impressed by the way of wearing and attitude towards Kimono of a male British wearer. At least he dresses our national costume more frequently than I do. His look and his performance are weird but original with good respect for Japanese tradition. To de-construct the Geisha dressing that I tried for him is a challenge to release the constraint of the heaviness within clothes carrying long history and old tradition, and to express the existence of my country and her enduring culture and costume.

I must note here that Miss Akimbo is also conscious of the cool aspect of Japan's Harajuku style street fashion. Looking at his leg fashion, he often puts on stripe tights Gothic Lolita girls are said to be fond of, sometimes he combined them with his kimono. At his birdcage performance, he tried expressing another Japaneseness, — that of twisted cuteness/kawaii wondering who/what I am,

with the birdcage covering his head, and bondage garment laced on his body.
The Bird cage performance (**Fig. 8**) is entitled 'Le Terrible Enfant Oiseur'
which means 'The Terrible Bird Child' in French. The figure has a beak and a
cage is worn over the head. The look was inspired by certain art works he saw
in Australia. The act explores ideas about freedom and becomes increasingly
poignant when performed to the song 'Green Finch and Linnet Bird' from Sweeney
Todd. His performance aims to reveal to us the hell of our latest capitalist
society of ceaseless seduction and obsessive consumption. I would like to
suggest here that western acceptance of this Japanese ethnic dress is not only
historical, but to Miss Akimbo is also seen as a solution of identity crisis through
dressing in it as fashion. Kabuki actors often are said to be more feminine than
women, and in Miss Akimbo's charming performances we may find hope.

Conclusion

Whilst I was about to start writing this paper, I received good news from a
fashion editor in Tokyo; Issey Miyake just took the prize from the Design
Museum of London. The New York Times on-line reports as follows, 'Among
the extraordinary inventions and progressive ideas are the winning outfits from
Mr. Miyake's studio that seem to encompass different kinds of modernity:
clothes that fold flat, opening with 3D dimensions and made from recycled
polyester. Just looking at the mathematically calculated designs, creating prisms
of unfolding shapes, is to realise that the Pleats Please invention from Mr.
Miyake, which started nearly 25 years ago in 1988, was only the beginning of
a series of futuristic ideas'[17]. This award celebrates the great success of one
Japanese designer leading the fashion world with high technology and new
trends, but it is far from the image of a traumatised nation, traditionally presented
by our designers.

   This divergence from the traditional trend of presenting Japan as the
traumatised nation was apparent by the appearance of two separate articles in
English newspapers on January 23rd 2012[18]. One newspaper discussed the
possibility of a re-explosion at one of the nuclear power plants in Fukushima,
evoking the trauma theme; whilst the Evening Standard newspaper introduced
a Japanese pop girl singer Kyary Pamyu Pamyu in the article of 'Trends' by
Emma McCarthy. Japan's image makers seem to be working hard to progress
our new popular appeal. Anyway, Pamyu Pamyu is not an absolutely proper
name used for a human, it sounds like the name for pets, or is made just to

---

17 Menkes 2012.
18 McCarthy 2012: 27-28.

50

enjoy the sound or rhythm as onomatope; we Japanese have the special liking for this, one of our most characteristic usages of language[19]. Pamyu Pamyu appeared on the media scene all of a sudden, with her wholly sweet and girly image but even more friendly and nostalgic than the Lolita girls.

According to McCatrthy's article, 'It's not just Japan's latest music export, J-Pop, that is taking London's teen scene by storm, so is it's street fashion'. Kyary Pamyu Pamyu is the trend itself but her public existence seems likely to be replaced very easily by an alternative idol. Fashion and music go together strategically in commercialism by aiding each other to make the image powerful accompanied with each other's popular aspects. The journalist added that Japanese music was playing an important role at night club scenes in London at present and introduced Ayumi Hamasaki as the Empress of J-Pop with her great contribution to London based brands of Rimmel and Aquascutum. I should also note from the article that Miu Miu recently presented a fashion line that reflected the doll-like styling favoured by Japanese Lolitas, at her Spring/Summer 2012 collection.

French thinker Guy Debord, well known as a Situationist, revealed what the world was like after the great economic crash of 1929. Introducing his original use of the word 'spectacle', he states 'In societies where modern conditions of production prevail, all of life presents itself as an immense accumulation of spectacles. Everything that was directly lived has moved away into a representation'[20]. Everything is presented as image in our modern capitalist society to be consumed one after another and split up with reality. Debord says 'spectacle' doesn't mean 'a collection of images' but he warns it is a 'social relation among, mediated by images'.

We can quote the Japanese fashion designer, Yohji, again here, 'I was not very sure that I would become a so-called fashion designer. It sounded very light...When I think about the image of a fashion designer, I have to think about trend. I have to think about what's new, what's next, what kind of feeling consumers want. It's too busy for me. So, from the beginning I wanted to protect the clothing itself from fashion'[21]. He dreams of the dress that can 'live forever'. So he struggles on. Debord described the age of 'spectacle' in the following way; 'The first phase of the domination of the economy over social life brought into the definition of all human realisation the obvious degradation of being into having. The present phase of total occupation of social life by the accumulated results of the economy, leads to a generalised sliding of having

19 Onohara 2011: 295-324.
20 Debord 1970/1983 [1967]: I-1.
21 Salazar 2011: 78.
22 Debord 1970/1983 [1967]: I-17.

into appearing, from which all actual "having" must draw its immediate prestige and its ultimate function...'[22]. Could this statement also be relevant to the work of his Japanese contemporary, Yohji Yamamoto? For Yohji's fight, is for the 'being' of dress. It is against fashion, the desire of 'having' and consumption of 'appearing', which seems to be a non-stop race or information war, to be the faster and the cheaper.

Historically, the holes in the Japanese dress were nothing less than revolutionary to the perfection of design in the context of the western fashion world. Invisible air traverses body and dark colour swirls in the broaden cloth. Dress realises; the person exists. And we may observe that traumatised Japan today, continues to push the boundaries of contemporary trends.

References

Assche, A. V., 2005, *Fashioning Kimono: Dress and Modernity in Early Twentieth Century Japan,* 5 Continents.

Coppard, A. ed., 2011, *Aware: Art Fashion Identity,* Daimiani.

Debord, G., 1970/1983 [1967], *Spectacle of the Society* (English Translation by Fredy Perlman and friends), Black & Red.

Fukai, A., Vinken, B., Frankel, S. and H. Kurino, 2010, *Future Beauty 30 Years of Japanese Fashion,* Merrell.

Herman, J. M. D., 1997 [1992], *Trauma and Recovery,* Basic Books.

Kondo, D., 1997, *About Face: Performning Race in Fashion and Theater,* Routledge.

McCarthy, E., 2012 (23rd, Janurary), *The Evening Standard.*

Menkes, S., 2012, *The New York Times* (on line), http://www.nytimes.com/2012/04/26/fashion/26iht-faward25.html?_r=1.

Miyake Design Studio (2009-2012), *Issey Miyake Official Site,* http://mds.isseymiyake.com/im/en/work/.

Onohara, N., 2011, *Fighting Fashion,* Suiseisha-Rose de vents.

Salazar, L. ed., 2011, *Yohji Yamamoto,* V&A publishing.

IV

Design of Silence: Transmission of Kesa in Soto Zen

Introduction

This chapter examines the garment worn by Buddhist monks and nuns, especially the Kesa[1], symbolic Buddhist robe, from the perspective of transmission. Dating back to the time of Gautama Siddhartha, this religious garment has a long history of more than two thousand five hundred years. The Kesa was introduced to the Japanese archipelago from the Korean peninsula via China, originally from India. Just as a disciple takes over the Buddha Dharma from his/her master at individual level, so were Sutras that teach Buddha Dharma transferred across the oceans, over the mountains, beyond linguistic differences amongst ethnic groups and countries. This process appears as a dynamic history, passing through colourful networks of cultures and societies over many eras: the Kesa is part of this adventure.

The term 'Silence', the title of this paper expresses the posture of the body when Shakyamuni came to enlightenment (i.e. the posture of Zazen, Za means "sitting"). As the subtitle shows, I would like to consider the case of Soto-shu, a school of Zen Buddhism, based on Zazen practice. Born in Japan and then studying Buddhism at Tendai and Rinzai schools, Dogen travelled to China (Song period) to study Zen Buddhism further, after which he founded the Soto-shu in Japan. He placed a special emphasis on the Kesa in his teachings. The essence of his teaching can be found in the two volumes of 'Den'e' and 'Kesa Kudoku' in his greatest book entitled Shobogenzo, which was written during his lifetime.

I will discuss: what the Kesa is for Soto Zen and Master Dogen, the transnational aspect of this religious costume, the development of the Kesa in Japan and with Zen Masters, the transmission of the Kesa in Europe and in contemporary Japan, and the possibility of considering the Kesa as an aspect

---

1　A Buddhist robe. Worn on top, it is a patchwork-like cloth obtained by joining square pieces of cloth. In ancient India, Ittan "a bolt of cloth" had an exchange value just like money, and the value is eliminated by cutting it into pieces. The design of the Kesa originated from the landscape of the beautiful countryside in India, and closely related to rice culture in Asia. Another name for the Kesa is Fukuden'e (fuku means "happiness", den means "rice and fields", e means "robe").

of Zen culture. From my point of view as a fashion researcher, this study will be an attempt to consider the Kesa as a cultural feature that has been passed down from generation to generation and has travelled the world with the wearer.

Butsue Buppou (Buddha Robe, Buddha Dharma)

Shobogenzo[2], written by the founder of the Japanese Soto school, Master Dogen[3], consists of ninty five volumes. In two volumes of 'Kesa Kudoku' and 'Den'e', he described Buddhist robes as Buddhist teachings. I have written about the basic understanding of the Kesa in Chapter 5 in Japanese. The purpose of this chapter is to focus on the transmission of the Kesa, and in this part, I would like to summarise what this religious costume means to Zen Master Dogen.

The Kesa is Dharma to be transmitted. It must be worn correctly (*takkesa*) and must be sewn correctly. There are many words that describe this religious garment in the volume 'Kesa Kudoku,' originally written around 1240. Every expression brings respect for this prestigious robe that is meant to be always cherished. Buddhist terminology is included, and is expressed in various ways.

Amongst Buddhists, the Kesa is Dharma that can be traced back to ancient India, and represents the correct inheritance of the Buddha Dharma that was, preached by the Buddha himself. Thus, Buddhists should appreciate and respect the extent and depth of its merits. It is said to be that it is a symbol that Buddhists should recognise as belief, goal and practice itself.

Bodhidharma[4] who was part of the twenty-eighth generation after Shakyamuni, traveled from India to China and introduced Buddhism, becoming the first Chinese Buddhist ancestor. Five generations later, Daikan Eno Zenji, known as the sixth ancestor of Soto school[5] was part of the thirty third generation who passed down the Dharma and supposedly the robe of Daruma Daishi (Bodhidharma).

---

2 In this book, I refer to the Iwanami Bunko version of *Shobogenzo,* especially 'Den'e' from the second volume of the collection (notes: Yaoko Mizuno, 1990). This volume, like 'Kesa Kudoku', was written at Kosho-ji temple in 1240, but it is said that Dogen added some additional parts based on 'Den'e' to 'Kesa Kudoku' to be published after he moved to Eiheiji temple (Mizuno 2007: 6-7).

3 Dogen is the son of Michichika Kuga, *Naidaijin* "Inner Minister" and his mother is a daughter of Motofusa Fujiwara. He started his Buddhist monk career with the Tendai School at Mount Hiei at the age of 13 and studied under Myozen, disciple of Yousai at Ken'ninji temple of Rinzai Soto school (*Zengaku Daijiten,* p. 917).

4 He lived during the 5th century or the 6th century. He travelled China to preach Zen Buddhism from India. The first ancestor of Chinese Zen Buddhism (*Zengaku Daijiten,* p. 831).

5 Every school of Zen Buddhism, including Rinzai and Soto schools flourished in Japan and China, has been developed from the root of Dharma of Daikan Enou (*Zengaku Daijiten,* p. 103).

At that time, in China, Buddhism had a strong bond with the emperor as a national religion, and successive kings worshiped the robes and kept them for their magical powers. Dogen Zenji, who lived in the Kamakura period in Japan, encountered Nyojo Zenji during the Southern Song dynasty in China. While Dogen was studying in China, he learned the daily customs of a Buddhist monk (such as how to eat and how to dress), and brought these teachings back to Japan where they are still practiced today. The Kesa is called *Geddapuku,* which means "enlightenment clothes" and in Soto Zen (defined *Shikantaza,* nothing but just sitting), it is to concentrate on Zazen in the Kesa.

Dogen Zenji studied various sutras that had been transmitted since the time of Shakyamuni. He explained the designs of the Kesa (*tai, shiki, ryou-*each means "materials", "colours", "measurements"[6]) and illustrated the method of sewing a Kesa in detail. This method was a strict one based on the precepts of Buddhism, but also included his proposals and ideas that were to be adapted to the times and the environment, which showed the scholarly Buddhist understanding of Master Dogen. The fact that *Ehou* (Kesa) equals *Buppou* (Dharma) was transmitted to Japan, would not have been possible without his previous experience in mainland China. He also tried to interpret the texts in more a practical fashion. For instance, criticism arose against the change of method and attitudes towards the Kesa, such as the text written by Dousen Zenji, however, Dogen pointed out that the exact same materials used in the original for Funzoue[7] could not be found in Japan today[8].

The Kesa and transnationality

Dogen Zenji's *Shobogenzo* also describes how to make the Kesa with methods taking into consideration materials (*tai*), colours (*shiki*) and measurements (*ryou*). Since the prototype is a costume of a subtropical South Asian country in 2500 BC, its design inevitably adapts as the period and the country change. However, it is said that the spirit of the Buddha robe has been safeguarded without any change, and the Buddha Dharma has been transmitted without

---

6 See chapter 5 in Japanese. *Tai* "materials", *Shiki* "colours", *Ryo* "measurements". Basically, the material was a plant-derived (hemp, cotton, etc.), the colour is muddy, mixed colours called Kasaya (the original Sanskrit term Kesa), and the measurements comes from the disciple Dharmagupta-vinaya "covering the three wheels", which is about the size of an amount of cloth that hides the three points of both knees and navel. Measure using human bodies like elbows and arms.

7 Funzoue, the most prestigious and ideal Kesa, which is made of abandoned wasted cloths gathered, wasted and the used as material (*Zengaku Daijiten,* p. 1103).

8 Dousen (the first ancestor of Nanzan Risshu, lived during the 7th to the 8th century) (*Zengaku Daijiten,* p. 932). He prohibited the use of silk thread made of cocoon because it involved animal killing (*Shobogenzo,* p. 269).

any alteration. In this section, I will discuss the transition and universality of the Kesa over the oceans and over the times.

The Kesa is a cloth-like costume wrapped all over the clothes of a Japanese Buddhist monk, but in India, a hot country, people wear this piece of cloth directly around their body in everyday life. As stated, in Japan, it was transmitted through continental China, where the cold weather was severe during the winter. In the process, the religious meaning was being emphasised even though the shape remained unchanged, and the Kesa became more symbolic than functional. Unlike India, where a single piece of cloth might be enough, in China, the number of clothes one has to wear in order to survive the coldest weather is significantly higher. In Japan, which has a relatively warm and rich four seasons, the priests are allowed to own three types of Buddha robes and one bowl according to the precepts[9]. This has resulted in the wearing of the Kesa on top of a Japanese kimono style clothing. I would like to introduce the costumes taking as an example the case of one Soto Buddhist monk.

Hei Douki *Roshi* "old master" at Myokouji temple in Kobe, when he studies and works in the garden, seems to wear the clothes that are not very different from ours. However, he always wears the Kesa on the top of his kimono during the Zazen *kai* "meeting" (Zazen workshop he organizes regularly at temple). When I interviewed him in October, he wore a light grey kimono with a white *juban* "undergarment of kimono", over the kimonos[10] putting on another black Buddhist kimono called *Koromo*[11] (**Fig. 1**). The structure looks like a normal kimono at first glance, but the sleeves are longer just like *furisode* "girls kimono with long sleeves" or much longer than that. The Chinese original of Koromo was a two-part type pattern but this was merged into one piece in Japan[12]. The waist and abdomen part are belt-like, easy to move, stable in posture, functional, simple and beautiful design, and it can be considered the uniform of monks.

Tying a braid around the waist completes the dressing. The braid called

---

9   The Kesa has different names depending on the number of strips, and the larger the number, the more formal clothes. A strip is a rectangular cloth that is a combination of long and short pieces of cloth. *Andae* "five strips", *Uttaraso* "seven strips" and *Sogyari* "nine to twenty five strips", respectively, to mean underwear, casual wear, the ritual—*houmongi*.

10   Also called *Jikitotsu* (*Zengaku Daijiten*, p. 36).

11   According to the catalog of a Buddhist clothing store, the material is compatible with seasonal changes such as synthetic fibers of polyester, hemp and silk. There are a lot of diverse and calm colours (published by Nishikawa Houebutsugu-ten, pp. 79-90).

12   The Indian costume corresponds to *Sanne, Andae*. In China, the *Gojo-e* could be the garment of the upper body part of the underwear, and worn underneath something like pants. When entering Japan, it seems that the separated parts were united into one in order to be achieve the shape of the kimono (*Zengaku Daijiten*, p. 421).

Figure 1
Hei Roshi at Myoko-ji, Kobe（2017）

Shukin seems to be characteristic. The length is *ichi jou ni shaku*（about three meters, *ichi* "one", *jou* "3.0303m", *ni* "two", *shaku* "303.030mm"）, and it is not only used as a waist strap, but also as a string to tie up kimono sleeves while working or travelling, and sometimes plays a role in rolling up the long length of cloth in moving easily. The history of *himo* "strings" in Japan is very long and goes back to Jomon period[13]. *Himo* is one of the most important Japanese cultural aspects. Not a few influences of design from China were found, and ancient strings were discovered on the Korean peninsula. Strings can make decorative effects not only with the functionality of tying and binding things, but also with the way they are assembled and the colour combinations. The *jimi* "restrained" taste of Hei Roshi was reflected by the black garment, which can also be a sophisticated choice.

    Clothes play an important role in regulating body temperature and humidity in the cold or hot environments. As stated, in India, one would wear a large wide cloth wrapped around the body. In China, the Indian cloth became a symbol of Buddhist authority and was added on top of clothing. As politics and religion were closely linked in China, the function of the robe was separated from the convenience of everyday life. Hence, the religious and decorative elements could be strengthened, and then worshipped with devotion and comittment[14].

13　Domyou 1963: 21-37.

The Kesa that Hei Roshi wore looked very old. The fibers were thin and the seam gaps open. Given its extreme lightness, he seemed to have worn it for a long time. The colour was elegant orchid and he said it had been re-dyed recently. I would like to remind you once again that the name Kesa is derived from the name of the colour Kasaya, muddy mixed colour that represents distance from human attachment and greed. The colour of the orchid is a typical one, and has been transmitted and preserved until now.

Hei Roshi told me that the length of the sleeves clearly shows that the Buddhist monks do not work, but a thin string is attached onto each left and right side around both shoulders. With these strings, you can easily move both arms out by tucking up and rolling the cloth, for instance while doing *Samu*, cleaning and washing. It seems that decoration and functionality are well balanced by these simple small strings.

When I asked about the number of the Kesa in his possession, the answer was higher than I expected. In Soto Buddhism, *Rakusu*, which can be hung from the neck, is a mini Kesa, and maybe easily damaged due to the frequency of wearing. He has more opportunities to be presented the Rakusu as a gift at memorial services.

The Roshi wears about *go-ryo* "five robes" every summer and winter[15]. Because his Kesa is worn on top of other clothes, there is almost no need to wash it and it is air-dried by the wind. It seems that he does not like *hade* "glamorous" colours and patterns such as gold, so he mainly wears black, grass green or light blue coloured robes. However, at funerals, Hei Roshi can also wears a scarlet Kesa. This is called *Shogon'e* which means "dressing beautifully for other people". In honour of the dead who maybe became a Buddha and out of respect for the grief of the bereaved family, the Kesa turns out to be the language of a quiet prayer during funeral rituals. In addition, 'scarlet' and 'yellow' are the colours known as noble ones in China, that are also called *Shikakue,* showing the rank of monks[16]. The Kesa, originally a garment that one never took off in India, became a garment for displaying social meaning when traveling to China and Japan.

High ancestors who inherit Dogen

Dogen Zenji in his *Shobogenzo* stated that the Kesa, derived from Shakyamuni,

---

14 Matsumura (2017: 217) discussed gold brocade Kesa and Funzoe from the point of view of fetishism.

15 *Ryo* is a unit for counting Kesa in Japanese classical way.

16 In contrast to *Seishoku* colours (red, yellow, white, black, blue), obviously the Kesa is of *Fu-seishoku* colours.

has been adapted by later disciples, with the original spirit, shape and production method. In this section, I will discuss the Kesa, focusing on its implications under Master Kodo Sawaki (1880-1965[17]). He is well known for his devotion to the study of the ancient Kesa and transmitted its tradition to his disciples.

When Hei Roshi was studying at Komazawa University, where many Buddhist monks of Soto school were enrolled, he listened to Prof. Sawaki's lecture and participated in his research meeting *Genzokai* during which Sawaki Roshi gave his lectures on *Shobogenzo*. When Hei Roshi graduated from the university, Sawaki Roshi handed over a nun's hand-sewn Rakusu with its holder bag to Hei Roshi[18]. In the interview, Hei Roshi said 'Soto-shu' is also called 'Kesa-shu'[19].

Sawaki Roshi's life is described, in a few good books written by his disciple Sakai Tokugen Roshi based on the records of Sawaki Roshi's other disciple Uchiyama Kosho Roshi (1912-1998[20]). In the book, one can read his extraordinary hardships during childhood, his tough experience of war in the military, as much as his extremely industrious Buddhist practices. It is impressive to read Sawaki Kodo Roshi's words full of hope, optimism and longing only for the Kesa. Sawaki Roshi did not settle down during his lifetime, having no family, and devoted himself to Zazen[21].

His study of the Kesa started with the encounter with the robe worn by a nun of Shingon-shu, another Buddhist sect. He studied intensely in the *Houfuku Zugi* written by Jiun Sonja (1718-1805), who was a pioneer of research on the Buddha robe[22]. Working on exploration and investigation of real robes with the book *Houfuku Zugi* with the help of previous historical studies, he continued to encourage people to sew the Kesa for themselves.

Sawaki Roshi's apprentice, Kyuma Echu Roshi (1934-), continued his

---

17   Kodo Sawaki was born in Mie Prefecture. In 1896 (during the Meiji Era), he entered Eizenji temple in Echizen at the age of seventeen. In 1898, he ordinated under Master Sawada Kouhou at Shushinji temple in Amakusa, Kumamoto. In 1935, he became a professor at Komazawa University and the *Godo* (teacher) at Soujiji temple. He opened the 'Shikurin Sanzen Dojo' at Antai-ji, Kyoto (*Zengaku Daijiten*, p. 387).

18   Hei 2017: 54-55.

19   I was able to confirm the word 'Kesa-shu' by the real voice of Sawaki Roshi in the video 'Sunday visit' March 1965 broadcast, NHK, interviewed by Shunpei Kamiyama (voice only). https://www.youtube.com/watch ?v=7JJk2kV0ygl (lastly confirmed the link in Setptember, 2019).

20   After the passing of Sawaki Roshi, he became a resident of Antaiji. He was also well known as an Origami artist.

21   Sakai 1956: 120-127.

22   A priest of the Shingon school, he is said to have been practicing Zazen at the temple of the Soto school. Religious exchange beyond the Buddhist schools were frequent at that time.

master's research by writing a book that explains the production method and that has been published for more than fifty years despite its detailed explanation. Introducing various types of Buddha robes[23] along with many illustrations and other precious materials, the author seemingly received advice and instructions from his master Sawaki Roshi, who was sick in bed at that time.

Fukuden-kai, voluntary sewing groups where people gather to learn and to sew the Kesa, started in Tokyo, and continued to spread to other areas in Japan[24]. At the Fukuden-kai, people sew various Kesas, from the Rakusu to the Funzoue, and its principle is 'hand-sewing with all your heart,' and then presenting it as a gift when it is completed. Researchers on the Kesa must have an interest in these Fukuden-kai gatherings[25]. In closing this section, I would like to mention Uchiyama Roshi's words prefacing to Kyuma Roshi's study of the Kesa.

'Our great master, Kodo Sawaki Roshi always said, 'Wear the Kesa to Zazen, and that's it.' So 'that's it' means for Buddhist practitioners, both lay practitioners or monks, that the Kesa is above everything: it is the Buddha Dharma. There is no need to explain and say anything'[26].

Reception of Soto Zen and the Kesa in the West

The word 'Zen' seems to have been established as an independent concept in foreign languages, as the romanised notation from the original Japanese sounds Zen. However, to what extent do foreign people understand Zen Buddhism correctly — from different kinds of Zen schools to costume of Buddhist monks ? This question came to mind when I first studied the Kesa and the writings of Dogen Zenji about the robe and then began researching the theme of the transmission of the Kesa. In this section, I will consider the reception of Soto Zen and the Kesa in Europe, where Zen celebrated its fifty years anniversary in 2017.

Firstly, I would like to introduce the words of German monk Nerke Muho,

---

23   Kesa is also known as *Nyohou-e* (Kyuma 1967: 30-33).

24   Buddhism researcher Mizuno started a sewing group with two other women in May in 1941 after receiving the ordination from Hashimoto Ekou Roshi, who was also introduced to the Kesa study by Sawaki Kodo Roshi (Mizuno 1987: 8-13).

25   Matsumura (2006: 132-161) also referred to the activity of Fukuden-kai. In addition, Riggs (2004: 332-333) conducted field research on Ichinomiya Fukudenkai, and pointed out that the group is also supported by the existence of women who are not interested in participating in Buddhist retreats but are delighted to sew together.

26   Kyuma 1967: 1

who used to be resident at Antaiji, where Sawaki Roshi and Uchiyama Roshi also resided[27]. His book, I believe, could be the clue to understand Zen abroad.

A Japanese Buddhist scholar Suzuki Daisetsu traveled to the United States in 1920. He published a book introducing Zen Buddhism to English speaking audiences and that was the first time Westerners were acquainted with the term Zen. The book became very popular and Zen culture was brought under the spotlight in the U. S., Suzuki Daisetsu made a great contribution in spreading Zen as a doctrine and philosophy, but it seems that 'Zazen' did not become a practice there until much later. As Muho points out in his book, 'there was no mention of Dogen' and 'Chinese Zen and Hakuin were introduced' in the books written by Suzuki Daisetsu. 'Zen' automatically meant Rinzai school for a long time"[28].

Dogen was introduced when his *Shobogenzo* was first translated into Western languages in 1944 (in German), while the English translation had to wait until 1958, when the direct Romaji reading *Shohogenzo* was used as the title. English translation by Nishijima Kazuo Roshi[29] published in 1983, became a reference today. A research project team at Stanford University was founded in the 1990s in the United States, and is currently working on providing an enhanced English translation.

Deshimaru Taisen Roshi (1914-1982), who started teaching Zazen overseas in France fifty years ago and founded the European Zen Association, considered Suzuki Daisetsu as a 'teacher'. Deshimaru Roshi was sent alone to Europe by his master Sawaki Kodo Roshi, due to his former career as a business person, combined with his well-known eccentric personality. Deshimaru Roshi expressed his Zazen focus in many books written by himself and his French disciples who respected him and called him 'Sensei'. Certainly, Sawaki Roshi had a great influence upon him, and Deshimaru Roshi devoted himself to Zazen just as his predecessor had done, and as do his disciples today. 'Zen' was, in this case, Soto Zen. In other words, 'Wear the Kesa to Zazen. That's it'[30].

In Paris, the Zazen *Dojo* "training hall", started out in the underground warehouse of an Asian grocery store and continued to operate while moving to various places, to eventually become a dojo facility called 'Paris Zan Bukkokuji' located in the south part of Paris city. Later on, a spacious temple was also

---

27 Muho 2013: 54-59.

28 They say that two Suzukis contributed to the popularity of Zen in the United States. Within the Soto school, a monk called Shunryu Suzuki (1905-1971) traveled to the US in 1959 and became the chief priest of the San Francisco *dera* "temple".

29 He was also a Buddhist scholar who gave lectures and Zazen instruction in English to foreigners mainly in Tokyo.

Figure 2
Laurent Ama in the atelier of La Gendronnière (2017)

established, named La Gendronnière: 80 square acres in the forest near the Loire river. The main building was originally a castle with vast green yards, a proper dojo. Buddhist scholar Nara Yasuaki, Seido of Eiheiji, wrote about his experience at La Gendronnière in the Buddhist journal[31] after he participated in the ceremony of giving the precepts, *jukai,* held in the French temple in the summer of 2016. There, out of about one hundred fifty participants, half were monks and the other half were lay people. So is the ratio of men and women, which count roughly the same amount of practitioners. Nara was impressed by the fact that every participant was wearing a black robe[32]. The 'European Zen Association', now called 'International Zen Association', is based in Paris and half of the foreigners of the European Soto school are French[33].

I was able to interview a French nun Françoise Kosen Laurent who received ordination under Deshimaru Roshi. She is a teacher of the Rakusu and the Kesa during workshops at La Gendronnière (**Fig. 2**). During summer Retreat, so-called summer camp there[34], monks and lay devotees gather from all over Europe. For those who are to receive ordination, she instructs them on how to sew a Rakusu, and for those who are to become monks, how to sew a Kesa.

---

30   Brosse 1980: 111–113. He describes the ordination ceremony. When the monk receives Kesa, he is also given a Buddhist name of Japanese-Chinese—style by his master, which is written on the white silked back of the Rakusu.

31   Nara 2016.

32   There is a shop called Boutique Zen in front of Bukkoku Zenji, where you can purchase clothes, kimonos, zafu and books. All customers who are interested in Zen are welcome. The clothing is sewn by French people, and they also sell colourful kimonos imported from Japan. A French monk is keeping the store.

Laurent Ama was taught how to sew the Kesa by her Dharma sister (the same disciples of Master Deshimaru) while learning Zazen under Deshimaru Roshi. She told me that if a mistake was spotted by her Dharma sister, she needed to sew it again and continue sewing until approved. 'Eventually', she said, 'Sensei (Master Deshimaru) asked me to sew the Rakusu'. Since then, she has sewn the Kesa and the Rakusu for many priests[35]. Moreover, the way of sewing has not changed at all for forty years long, as she said.

However, since the number of people, who hopes to enter the Buddhist priesthood, began to increase, and Master Deshimaru passed away in 1982, the nuns decided to teach them how to sew the Rakusu and the Kesa for themselves. It seems almost established now. Laurent Ama says: 'Sensei did not directly explain the technique of sewing to me. However, there was a strong request upon me to make it correctly according to the authentic method inherited from Sawaki Kodo Roshi. I understand it is not technique, but the spirit of the Kesa, its spirituality. I learned that Zazen and the Kesa are inseparable'[36].

I interviewed a French monk who completed sewing the Kesa under Laurent Ama, which took over a year and a half (**Fig. 3**). I heard similar words from him: 'Sewing the Kesa was a big adventure for me, like Zazen, I concentrated on one stitch at a time, made a back stitch each time, and over and over again, it became a big long cloth before I knew it, it's a piece of the Buddha robe'[37]. The first time I saw him, he was not in a monk costume. Afterwards, he looked very different to me, in his own sewed Kesa. Along with his impressive words, I could imagine the scene that he was making small stitches

---

33 In his books and TV appearances, Deshimaru Roshi said, 'France is a country where Zen Buddhism is easy to spread. This is because many philosophers were born in this country.' For example, he picked up the names Montaigne and Descartes in the interview and pointed out the similarity with Dogen Zenji by introducing his crucial statement 'To learn the Buddhist path is to learn the self' and explaining that Zen explores the self. Sagesse Bouddhistes 1 Oct, 2017 http://www.youtube.com/watch?v=NYBNn7e7w_w (Documentaire de Michel Baulez) (lastly confirmed the link in September, 2019).

34 'Don't let your heart fall and let it scatter.' *Sesshin* "retreat" here is Zazen workshop during which specific Zazen participants gather for a certain period. They concentrate on practicing Zazen without any other things during the Sesshin (*Zengaku Daijiten,* p. 663).

35 It seems to be natural that monks can sew their own robes because there is no such Japanese shop specialised in Buddhist things abroad and they cannot easily purchase them. Also, a longing and respect for Zen from far east Japan could make monks seek for originals and authenticity all the more. The statelessness and excess of culture were discussed in my paper about the acceptance of *Kimono* in other countries (Onohara 2017). Hei Roshi said he has never experienced sewing the Kesa for himself but he was handed down the Rakusu, hand-sewn by nuns, from Sawaki Roshi. The special shops do not always use sewing machines, as Riggs's paper reports, the garment is carefully treated and manufactured even in production at the store (Riggs 2004: 351).

36 Her words are from email interviews during mid to late September 2017.

one by one very carefully with all his heart. The monk first got interested in Zazen from the experience of meditation. He began to go to the Zazen Dojo in Paris, it happened after the death of Master Deshimaru, so he seemed to have no opportunity to meet with his Old Master in Europe. Soon after he started Zazen, he started to sew the Rakusu and then sewed the Kesa under a French Master who was the disciple of Deshimaru Roshi and opened a temple in southern France.

Figure 3
A French monk's ordination at La Gendronnière (2012)

Master Deshimaru says in his book:

the Kesa and Zazen are not two separated things, but one[38].

In Europe, the Kesa, as the Buddha Dharma, has been transmitted correctly with the right method of sewing[39].

In conclusion: the possibility of Zen culture

The Kesa is made by cutting a big cloth (seen like cutting through attachment) and stitching the small pieces back together. By washing dirty old cloths or dyeing them in muddy colours, the unclean coloured Buddhist costume, as its name shows, has been transmitted with the Buddhist teachings, without changing the way it is worn. The other clothes, worn on the inside, have been changed and designed according to the environment (country and climate), but that which should be worn over the top is the Kesa, Buddha's robe. Strictly described by Shakyamuni, the Kesa has been made to be worn all year round, over the body, whether it is cold or hot.

---

37 His words are from an email interview during mid to late September 2017.

38 Deshimaru 1973: 176.

39 According to my last investigations, the San Francisco Zen Center in the United States encourages monks and nuns to sew their own Rakusu and Kesa. They have workshops for hand-stitching, but I am not certain of the technical aspects. On their website, Sawaki Roshi and Deshimaru Roshi's method are cited. In other words, it can be said that the knowledge was transmitted from Europe to North America. Master Deshimaru's technique is also published in French as part of a collection of his works under the title *Grands Classiques Zen series* (published by Daruma and Paris Zen Bukkokuji). The book is meant as complemetary to the direct guidance of an experienced teacher, and cannot in any case replace the participation in sewing workshops.

Both Hei Roshi and Laurent Ama wear Japanese traditional costume on the inside, which is also influenced by Chinese design. In order to conceal the *fujou* "unclean" left hand and reveal the right shoulder at the same time, the body is wrapped by the cloth, and the Indian costume is worn on the outsides. From the perspective of costume culture, it looks like a well-balanced style as a result of hybrid mixed cultures of the three countries. Laurent Ama said she started to sew her Funzoue, supposedly the purest form of the Kesa. This was the first time she tried *Sashiko,* quilted cloths of small stitches, to create the Funzoue, although she made a lot of the Kesa in her Buddhist life[40]. After the long interview, Hei Roshi folded his Kesa very silently. As if he was facing the cloth for the first time. Slowly and carefully. He said, 'Wearing the Kesa is uniting into one, with Buddha.'

In Japan, the word *Takumi,* from *Yamato Kotoba* ancient Japanese language signifies both hand work and pondering. *Ishou* means 'design' of the Chinese register appeared and then combined. Therefore 'design' has been applied to the word, which was translated from the West in the Meiji period, afterwards the word design in Katakana notation became popular.

I would like to conclude with the words of an art historian from the same Meiji period. While being caught in modern civilisation wave of the time, Oomura Seigai, continued to study the authority of Chinese art.

Now, *Rakuso* "thinking" is regarded as *In* "a cause" and *Ga* "the result" is of the performance, *Isho* "designing" is slightly *En* "the link" with its embodiment[41].
今落想ヲ因と見バ、其果ハ即實演ニシテ、意匠は僅に其縁ナリ。

References
Barthes, R., 1972 [1967], *Système de la Mode,* translated by Nobuo Sato, Misuzu Shobo.
Brosse, J., 1980, *SATORI Experience,* translated by Kazuo Morimoto, TBS Britannica.
Deshimaru, T., 1996 [1986], *Le Livre du Kesa* (Grands Classiques Zen series), Daruma.
――, 1973, *Diary of European Crazy Clouds*, Yomiuri Shimbun.
De Smet, M. ed., 1969, *Words of Zen,* translated by Shinichi Nakazawa, Kinokuniya.
Dogen (notes: Mizuno Yaoko), 1990, *Shobogenzo,* (2), Iwanami Shoten.

40 Originally *Funzoue* was made by washing and re-dyeing waste cloths into a single piece of patchwork-like cloth, but it is not easy to find such material nowadays. However, Japanese traditional *Sashiko* technique and a design to reinforce old cloth inspired by the layout of *Toyama* "faraway mountains" are the basic of the Funzoue. Since the Funzoue is still being sold at Buddhist shops today, probably the image of the purest Kesa made of dirty cloths detached from human luxury is still relevant to contemporary monks. In addition to hand-sewing, it goes without saying the Sashiko technique takes time and effort.

41 Higuchi 2016: 76.

Doumyo, S., 1963, *Himo* (*Strings*), Gakuseisha.

Hei, Douki., 2017, 'Learnings from Dogen Zenji Now', *Daihorin*, 84 (7), pp. 54-59.

Higuchi, T., 2016, 'The Meaning of *Isho* Discussed in Design Promotion during 1887-1896 period — Linguistic Conception as Design in Japan (7)', *Bulletin of Japanese Society for the Science of Design*, vol. 62 No. 6, pp. 69-78.

Kerouac, J., 1973, *Satori in Paris*, Quartet Books Limited.

Kyuma, E., 1967, *Study of Kesa*, Daihokaku.

——, 2003, *Kesa to Zazen*, Hozokan.

——, 2010, *Kesa Story*, Hozokan.

Matsumura, K., 2006, *Study of Funzoue*, Hozokan.

——, 2017, 'Fetishism Research on Cloths of Kesa: Kinran (gold brocade) Kesa and Funzoue', *Shinpansuru Shintai* (Invading Body), Kyoto University Press, pp. 221-247.

Mizuno, Y., 1987, *On Dogen's Kesa: Reading Kesa Kudoku of Shobogenzo*, Hakujusha.

——, 2007, *Reading Kesa Kudoku of Shobogenzo*, Daihorinkaku.

Muho, N., 2013, *Reimporting Dogen: Understanding Genjo Koan in English*, Sangha.

Nara, Y., 2016, 'Participation in the Ordination at La Gendronnière: Interest in Zen Buddhism in Europe', *Daihourin*, October issue.

Onohara, N., 2011, *Tatakau Ifuku* (Fighting Fashion), Suiseisha.

——, 2017, 'Reception of Kimono Culture in Contemporary British Fashion' *Design Studies*, 15.

Otani, T., 2000, *Eihei no Kaze*, Bungeisha.

Riggs, D. E., 2004, 'Fukudenkai: Sewing the Buddha's Robe in Contemporary Japanese Buddhist Practice', *Japanese Journal of Religious Studies*, 31/2, Nanzan Institute of Religion and Culture, pp. 311-356.

Sakai, T., 1956, *Sawaki Kodo: Living in Zen*, Seishin Shobo.

Uchiyama, K., 1973, *Approach to Zen: The Reality of Zazen / Modern Civilization and Zen*, Japan Publications, Inc.

——, 2013, *The Meaning of Zazen and Practice: Live Real Life*, Daihourinkaku.

Yamakawa, S., 2000, *High Priest and Samurai*, Kyoto National Museum.

Zengaku Daijiten Hensanjo., 1978, *Zengaku Daijiten*, Taishukan.

V

You Are Everything and Nothing: To What Extent Does Japanese Manga, Comics and Fashion Culture Influence the Current Contemporary U.K. Comic Scene?

Introduction

I shall introduce Manga, Japanese comics influence on UK comics scenes. My primary research was in London and developed through a number of connecting environments such as attending comic and zine fairs, exhibitions and talks by artists and makers, and the specialist Comic bookshops Gosh! and Orbital Comics as an ongoing place for a ready resource of material, particularly as both shops actively encouraged and promoted a number of works by the majority of creators. I would like to break down the elements of the potential influences on creators into specific components, namely: Technique and Style, Content (Approaches to Story and Narrative) and Culture (the influence of Fashion and Spirituality). Generally I would think of how the artists fit into those categories (**Fig. 1**). In this chapter, I will focus on five comic artists work, from Independent Alternative, to major creative professionals, and consider how their work has been influenced by Japanese culture, specifically Manga, Comics and Fashion, and in what ways. At the same time my purpose is to develop my fashion theory.

Figure 1
British Comics for this research

1. Technique and style

Cuteness (big eyes, soft and round lines)
Violence (blood colour, rough lines)

I will point out the influence of Manga in UK comics. Firstly, some can be found in facial expression of characters, the way eyes and mouths, sometimes noses and eyebrows are drawn. They tend to be rough, soft and round lines. Softness and roundness can easily express cuteness and immatureness in the characters, not only for the girls but for the boys sometimes. It is closely related to the component of Kawaii, one of the important features in Cool Japan movement. Roughness can be replaced by wildness, which obviously tends to be used in male characters to show violence. 'Violence' is a key word and theme in introducing contemporary Japanese subculture art forms, from games and animation to films, with ever increasing levels of violence and high speed. In scenes of large numbers of people being killed, or battle scenes, there is often an emphasis placed on the amount of blood in the battles or images of conflict, violence. *Battle Royale,* directed by Takashi Miike in 2000, is one of the most popular Japanese movies, and it is surprising to note that the respected BFI (British Film and Television Institute) in London chose it as one of the ten best Japanese films of the 21st century for their visitors to see. These influences seem to crossover various diverse mediums, and influence each other.

At Gosh! in Soho, the shop assistant Mike (he used to be in charge of exhibition at the shop) introduced to me books and zines, showing an influence of Japanese comics. In *Hell Chapter 4* (2015) by Jey Levang and C. Vinter, basketball players are fighting each other not only with a ball in the playground but with a knife in the filed. Team uniforms are sometimes depicted in blood so that the readers can be by the expression of their darkness and violent desires.

Round eyes should show cuteness, but in the comic of *Deadendia* (2015) by Hamish Steel, the dog of main character furiously changes into a violent monster. Readers might enjoy the gap or unbalance between Kawaii and *Kowai* "scared" (we have the word *Kowa Kawa* in explaining Japanese culture).

For comic artists and writers, there are a variety of book such as How-to-Draw-*Shojo* "girls", a series of the tutorial books by American comic writer Christopher Hart (*Manga for the Beginner Kawaii* (2012)), which seemed to be popular at Orbital Comics, another specialist comic book shop located in Soho. The assistant Camila introduced me to the books of this kind, and said they sold quite well, when I asked her who bought them, and how well sold.

Actually, 60-70% of the books sold at Oribital were Japanese comics with English translations. This suggests the influence of Manga cannot be underestimated or avoided, not only for the readers, but also of the writers who must be good readers of comics including Manga.

2. Content (approaches to story and narratives)

Battles and sports (violence)
Science fiction (neo-future city)
School life (innocence)

(These components may often overlap throughout a single story/narrative)

As I have previously stated, battles and sports are inevitable themes in comics with Japanese manga influence, and some of them mix each feature into one. It may be argued Science-fiction is one of the more important or popular themes here. I should note here that this may well be due to the influence of *Akira* (1982-90, Kodansha) is one of the most popular Sci-fi comics written and illustrated by Katsuhiro Otomo. The animated film version directed by Otomo himself in 1988 had a tremendous impact internationally, particularly with Western audiences, and was responsible for a sudden interest in Japanese manga and comics in the West, especially in America and Britain.

I saw the animated film with French subtitles in 2012 at Angoulême Festival in France, which is the biggest annual comic festival in Europe. Earnest fans gathered in the theatre, they seemed to come to see it amongst the many events and exhibitions of B. D. (short for comics in French language — *Bande Dessineé*) and international comics going on. Indeed Sci-fi often includes the battles of one brave fighter against the evil enemy, sometimes for the sake of the Earth. Often the images of violence and killing painted in blood red colour. *ODY-C* (2015) (**Fig. 2**) by Matt Fraction and Christian Ward, are a series of zines which, in the construction of the illustration and the story, one can easily see the influenced of Japanese Sci-fi.

Besides Sci-fi, Shojo-manga is also popular. The location of these stories are often a high school, where a shy girl falls in love with an elder boy in the same school, such as in 'untitled' by a Polish comic writer xuh (**Fig. 3**), as featured in *Gaijin Mangaka* (2016), and a Japanese word *Senpai* "senior" is well-known as a Japanese expression to the foreign comic fans. Usually, he is a popular and sporty student belonging to the tennis, football, basketball and volleyball clubs. Pure love relationships are emphasised as emotional expressions or character traits. The main character of *Scott PilGrim's Precious*

Figure 2
ODY-C

Figure 3
untitled by xuh

Little Life Volume1 by Bryan Lee O'Malley (2004) is a boy, but he is a shy high school student trying to make a special relationship with a girl at the same school.

3. Culture (1) (influence of fashion)

Fashion (cuteness-kawai, experimental creativity)
Food (bento, izakaya full of multi-mixed styles)

Yasmine Surovec writes essay-style Manga entitled *CAT vs HUMAN* (2011) and her drawing of cats are identical to the Hello Kitty character (interestingly Kitty was born in London in the original story) without particular facial expression because of their tiny little mouths. Yasmine likes fashion as girls do, the story is often related to her dress. Most of the clothes are not sexy-showing physical femininity, but they are cute girly styles. The main character in the story, a young girl, is troubled by the mischievous cat which damages her dresses. It is however, not very serious, as the dress looks more fashionable after the cat's touch-slashing and cutting.

As I mentioned earlier, there are books of tutorial type books available at the comic books shops. *How to Draw Shojo* covers posture, hair style, facial expression and to mostly Shojo costume, often featuring school uniform. In the zine entitled *What's the time Mrs. Woolf Pirates Summer 2014,* there are pages of DIY 'sewing sans pattern' to make a sailor collar to a shirt or a dress, by using a unique hand written description and drawn design. In chapter I, my

Figure 4
Memento Bento

Figure 5
断末魔 *Death Rattle*

research on Gothic Lolita and Cosplay, they are different fashion cliques, though they look similar at the first glance, and both share a similar DIY ethic, interested in making their own costumes and clothes.

Zarina Lieu (See 5 comic writers, **Fig. 8**) is a Chinese comic writer born in Britain, who has been working as a fashion illustrator. The characters in her works look very fashionable, even if the variation in the clothes seem few. That is because her drawn lines of ink made with a brush flow smoothly and expressionistic use of watercolours is atmospheric. It could remind you of traditional ethnic Japanese costume, especially the emphasis placed on the unique colour co-ordination and flowing silhouette of the Kimono. Her work could be a perfect example in seeing an influence in technique and style. Obviously influenced by Manga in the way she draws, particularly her brushwork which is something of prime importance in Japanese art, the reliance and influence of the brush in making pictures, rather than the pen, and of course, inherent in how the language itself is written/drawn. Her weekly web comic is entitled *Le Mime volume1* (2012) which is a series of 4 *koma* "panels" style. Readers can enjoy British humour in this Japanese traditional comic style. It is notable that she was awarded Second Place in the Manga Jiman run by the Japanese Embassy in London.

Pop styles of cool Japan can be found out not only in fashion influence but in food culture in Manga. Alessandra Criseo's *Memento Bento* (2015) (**Fig. 4**) is an essay comic, where she draws and writes her experience during her stay in Japan. She often introduces her favourite Kawaii fashion in Tokyo, too. It could be said that *Bento* "lunch box" is a kind of metaphor when you describe Japanese culture, mixed of different cultures from abroad, from historical to modern. *Izakaya* is a "Japanese friendly restaurant" you can pick up a variety of food from traditional Japanese to Chinese, Italian and French. In the zine entitled 断末魔 *Death Rattle* (2015) (**Fig. 5**) by Paul Arscott, *Izakaya* is depicted

in a scene in the comic, with includes Japanese dialogue. The writer asked his Japanese friend to help him to write it, to ensure an authenticity of language.

When we recall Japanese fashion, we should not forget about Japanese avant garde designers. In the zine called *Ono Land* (2011) by Paul Ashely Brown (See 5 comic writers; Paul, **Fig. 9**), we could see the approach of drawing influenced by the experimental Japanese designs. He makes a series of independent zines called *Browner Knowle* (2008-), where he creates narratives depicting ordinary and incidental moments of characters lives, or internal emotional existences, in an attempt to find the decadent or melancholic beauty in human lives. As stated at the end of the opening story in his zine; 'and the man is me, and the girl is you, and this is us all, this is the story of our lives'.

Paul says in the interview, such ordinariness of life and people would be in the work of filmmakers like Ozu, or Kurosawa's *Ikiru* (1952) —one of the most beautiful and moving pieces of cinema ever made which always reduces him to tears. And the concern with an ordinary man's life or story, and the possibility to find the extraordinary there, or the heroic, or especially the poetic, that is what he has in mind when making *Browner-Knowle.*

It is a pleasant surprise that in his interview, he mentions an interest and inspiration for his creativity in designers such as Yohji Yamamoto and Rei Kawakubo, more for an artistic and emotional ethic in their work, rather than the clothes themselves. The mood of his work often has a monotonous air of melancholy, which expresses his characters vulnerable human solitude and sadness. However they are not just that, because of very articulated lines and calculated subtleties of colour pencil drawing. His pretty Kimono drawing (back cover of this book) is what came from his emotional impulse, without any model or specific influence at the time, although one could perhaps see an indirect Ukiyo-e influence in the picture. Could we wear a dress freely in such a way?

Fundamentally, we humans have to wear clothes in our social lives. We are not allowed to be naked when we go out. We continue to choose what to wear as long as we live, thinking what to wear and how to wear must be a pleasant routine, but I sometimes wonder why we have to dress our body also for our tiredness and emptiness, like we cannot live instinctively always.

4. Culture (2) (influence of spirituality)

Zen (Buddhism (non/meaning of life)
Origami (paper art and Do it yourself)
Wabi-sabi (Minimal sense of value)

If the Orientalism works in comics world, the East must be a land of mystery

and wonder to the West. I will pick up the spiritual Japanese influence in UK comics here. Manga is one of the strong influential Japanese culture at present, it sometimes plays educational role for a child reader. The first influence is not always the direct effect from Japanese comics, however, it seems harder to recognise which originally comes from: because it is more religious and spiritual one.

Paul Gravett, a London based comics historian and curator, wrote an interesting introduction to the Baltic comics magazine *Gaijin Mangaka* published in Latvia. He is well-known and influential critic in Europe, but one who has a peculiar fondness for dark Japanese underground Manga and weird cult comics. He deliberately chose quotes from the comics writers who were greatly encouraged and influenced by Manga. Manga sometimes gave them 'freedom', 'the story of masters and disciples' thought, and 'unskillful works (heta-uma)' that often went beyond 'conventions of what is perceived'. Such an affinity with these works suggest that we cannot neglect such a discovery of archive independent Manga material in relation to the more mass commercial body of work. Both have had an impact and influence on Western comic artists and writers surely feel the change in artistic sense of value and way of life.

As an artist Mike Medaglia (recently successful in his book *One Year Wiser* (2015) a periodical graphic essay that regular appeared in *The Huffington Post UK*), Tezka Osamu was his number one influence in his comic making and artistic life. He had not been taught graphic or visual artistic technique but came across Tezka's work by chance during his travels abroad after graduating from University. Then he suddenly found what he wanted to do to be a Manga-ka. He was not able to tell me clearly because it is a total influence to his body and mind, both in his work and life which is not interwined not separate. Not only the attraction of the drawing technique, but also the world and story created, and Tezka's profound thoughts within it. However, he is interpreting Tezka's world in his way, for example, in his drawing 'Atomic Boy' (**Fig. 6**).

He edited *Wu Wei* (2013), a book collection of comics and drawings on the subject of Eastern Spirituality, meditation and mindfulness by a number of diverse and varied UK comic writers and artists, and within the collection, there are interesting works to be considered here. 'Origami Comic' (do it yourself type) by Andrew Poyiadgi (**Fig. 7**) uses physical convention of origami as readers have to tear along the lines of the page in order to fold it into a small but self-made comic. The artist drew a kimono wearing woman on it, dancing with a Japanese soldier, which seems to become a sad story which readers should imagine making it from the imaged bri-collages. Another participant, artist Lizz Lunney appears to be interested in Buddhism or Zen Buddhism in particular. Her contribution shows a simple illustration of a cat-like human lying

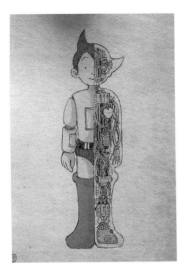

Figure 6

Atomic Boy

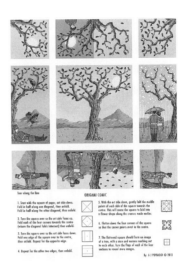

Figure 7

Origami Comic

down, simply saying 'I am everything and nothing', which is exactly the most difficult concept *Ku* 空 to understand in Buddhism. With her soft touch of humour and direct simple drawing style, her work has a gentle abundant warmth and good humour to it.

As discussed often, the category/name of Manga, Comics, and graphic novels are not very facile for you to differentiate. If you are into manga world, we do not have to care about it or have little chance to think about, as it is the case, comics, graphic novel be the same. I once enjoyed the argument amongst my comic writer friends after one of the biggest independent zine event named International Alternative Press Festival in London in 2012, though I mostly was listening to their discussion. If I can sum it up with my own words, recalling their talks, graphic novel is correspond to classical music, comics; popular hit songs, manga is J-pop. Graphic novel sounds noble and literature as an art form, and it is indeed some manga has the same sort of characters. Manga and comics sound consuming goods, but graphic novels are good to be kept in your bookshelf you can read repeatedly once in a while in the future.

Gareth Brookes (see 5 comics writers, **Fig. 10**) who won The Myriad First Book Award for his short story *The Black Project* (zine, 2011) (subsequently published by Myriad as a Graphic Novel to great critical acclaim) readily confesses his prejudice for Manga and Japanese comics. After he had the chance to read the writers and artists from Japanese underground magazine *GARO* (1964–2002, Seirindo), he felt he had artistically awoke. His abstract graphic

drawing style could suggest at times a creation of a visual language to describe an entire world, not dissimilar to the way Japanese writing characters describes the words equally in visual terms, a language of visual signs and meanings. This characteristic features of him seem to fit what *GARO* contributors were pursuing in its underground magazine for a long time. Breakdown Press in the UK has started to reissue and republish some of the independent Manga such as Hayashi Seiichi and Masahiko Matsumoto. The publisher also runs an annual zine and comic event called Safari Festival in London, which is open to international independent comic artists. I was able to meet up with long standing comic friends as well as new artists and writers from Germany, France, Eastern Europe and Scandinavian countries.

To return the topic of Japanese manga and particularly that of Manga of the past, a lot of the works of this period depicted the realities of Post-War Japan, a nation coming to terms with a sense of defeat and destruction after the Second World War, while also attempting to illustrate the small hopes or simple beauty of everyday life within a difficult, vulnerable landscape, scarred by war. Equally, some of the British artists and writers are concerned with an empathy towards ideas of landscape, not just physically but emotionally, and the underlying effect of landscapes and space on their inhabitants, or their stories. This may well be a universal value, a fundamental question we may ask ourselves, though we can easily forget, ignore or get rid of it. 'I'm not really interested in this, telling you stories...well, none you'd want to know', as the artist and narrator of *The Story of Our Lives,* Paul Ashley Brown, dismissively and duplicity states, before telling us that very thing, a story, which he suggests may well contain universal truths, if not individual personal ones, we may not 'want to know'.

When we talk about traditional Japanese culture that globally well known, there is the shortest form of poetry: Haiku. Once again our featured British artist Paul states he is influenced by Haiku for his writing and drawing, trying to reduce both elements to their 'essence', attempting to find a poetic language and landscape for his stories and observations. From the same city as Paul resides, Bristol, we have another wabi-sabi aesthetic understanding artist and writer Simon Moreton (see 5 comics writers, **Fig. 11**). He normally draws using simple Black and White lines and shapes, with equally minimal use of words. His work is very economical and uses abstract graphic elements. A characteristic of his work is the visual space of his pictures and pages. I wonder how the Western readers can feel and receive it ? This could be said haiku-like, too, in it's simple direct poetic visual language, or very wabi-sabi — I desire to consider their work as such, but the authors may not be very conscious of it. However, these two Bristol comic writers creating 'landscape' in their own views, in addition Simon is a geography researcher, possibly share an interest in compressing

material, trying to find the essence of a feeling memory or mood, suggested by the use of minimal visuals or language, trying to create a poetic visual space the reader can inhabit to share emotion and memory and narrative.

As I discussed already, *Ku* usually translates as "emptiness" into English, *Mu* is "nothingness" but Ku and Mu exist in nature inseparably. As Yohji Yamamoto once said, he always designed 'space' for his clothes. Space is not always 'nothing' or 'empty, could be 'everything' and independent beauty in itself. In this way, the model of the haiku, and Ku and Mu could be applied to explain their arts and methods, and be a good comparison to make.

Conclusion

The British Museum has been exhibiting Manga since 2015. The original gallery for the exhibit is called Asahi Shimbun Gallery, and located in a cosy space near the entrance to the museum. As Paul Gravett was happy to point out, the museum is also beginning to translate and start publishing a book of Manga, as well as in the near future printed material will also be exhibited in the main Japan gallery. The museum attracts visitors from all over the world, and for some, it will be in these auspicious surroundings they may discover Manga for the first time. As previously stated, London capital has specialised comic shops in central locations you can visit, and many independent comic events are happening the whole year round.

The independent self-publishing Zine culture has been a significant environment from which future creators can have emerged. For instance, co-founders of Alternative Press Fair, Dimitri Pieri and Peter Lally are both poets and comic book artists and zine makers. Zine events in Britain are very open to artist genres, such as graphic designers, photographers, illustrators, printmakers and musicians. They can turn up and meet their audience in person and discuss and sell their works, whether comic, zines, posters, prints, T-shirt designs and badges. In Gravett's introduction for *Gaijin Mangaka* (anthology of homage to Manga), an American participant Nou says Manga 'allowed me to expand my horizon and find new ways to communicate my thoughts...I have always liked writing poetry and songs, so I'm close to finding my happy medium.' Paul Gravett describes her work 'Heta moe' from *heta-uma+moe* "intriguing". You can now access comics from all over the world, and Manga influences are discovered not only in British creators works, but internationally, even globally. We cannot measure the extent to which Manga's influence has spread out today. Even the idea of 'Ku' might be changing meaningfully, when in the fans of the serious practitioners responsible for creating the Sci-fi comic zine *East of West* (2015) by Jonathan Hickman and Nick Dragotta, and the comic-strip Zazen.

In this chapter introducing authors and their works, the Japanese influences are widely scattered and diverse, even in one comic book where multiple factors exist combined as if they support each other to create one world. Lando (see 5 comics writers, **Fig. 12**) is also responsible for the ongoing comic series of zines, *Decadence*, his own self-publishing enterprise. Breakdown Press, a UK comic publisher, published a collected book of Lando's best strips from the *Decadence* zines in 2015, entitled *Gardens of Glass* (2014). I have known him since he attended Birmingham zine festival and the Alternative Press Zine events and fairs in 2010 around, turning up with a luggage bag 'full of Decadence'. In his interview, he pointed to some pages he knew of *Akira* that were a huge influence for him. But for me not only as a researcher but also as a fan of his work, the ordour of his book senses Japanese forgotten beauty, his unique quiet but passionate points and lines like post-impressionists used to try, his pen expresses the heaviness/existence of a flower of Japanese chrysanthe-mum. Chrysanthemus is a flower of 'end' in Japan, precisely it is the last flower to bloom at the end of a year. In Japanese *Kiku* 菊 originally comes from the verb *Kiwamaru* 窮まる meaning "terminate" "come to an end". In Lando's book *Gardens of Glass,* after the greatest battle, there appears an illusion in front of the characters, everything is gone but nothing seems to end, then the decadent landscape remains. In Lando's work the characters and the worlds they inhabit are in constant flux, ever-changing, transforming, decaying, renewing, both floating and disappearing worlds.

Comic artists do not write or draw merely to entertain readers. They have the will whole words in which to share stories. As Gareth Brookes, for the first time, challenged *Yotsume-toji,* "traditional Japanese book-binding", to make his drawings into a book. It is called *The Land of my Heart Chokes in Abundance* (2014). We have to go outsides by dressing ourselves only if we cannot stay inside and undress our body and mind. At last but not least, I shall finish this chapter with the words in Simon's zine *rain and other stories* (2016):

'Let's go for a naked walk' 'It was October...'

* * * *

Spotlighting five comic artists: interviewing about 'you as a comics creator and Japan/Manga influences' (by email in 2016)

Zarina Lieu (author of *Le Mime 1* (2012) and *The Art of Sleep* (2012))

Figure 8
Zarina Lieu, *Le Mime* 1 (2012)

'By chance, in the mid 90s, my older sister brought home a translated copy of Rumiko Takahashi's *Ranma* and left it on a coffee table at home. I picked it up—and I was hooked. I couldn't stop thinking about her wonderful characters, ingenious plot twists and the comic timing behind her panels—her artwork was also extremely lush. I didn't know comics could be so expressive and engaging. Takahashi is timeless and gender neutral in her storytelling—her stories are full of classic humour, great observations about people but paced with a good mix of action, fun and serious moments. I mean, *Maison Ikkoku* is emotional. But hilarious too! You smile when you read her work, and that is the feeling I would love people to have when they read mine.'

'I also fell in love with Yukito Kishiro's *Alita* (*Gunnm*) —even the reboot is mesmerising and involving. Here is a strong female character who stays true to herself, even as she transforms. Her physical and mental transformation is as complex as the artist's style transformation and as you grow with her, you grow with her world and all the characters around her. Kishiro is not lazy in nailing his characters and their dark moments. He demonstrated to me that you can be a soft artist and slowly build up your characters over time and not be afraid to, there are no big heroics, just humans and droids, trying to make life better.'

'I also love *Honey and Clover* by Chika Umino—it's an emotional ride but

beautifully paced. It's nostalgic—very nostalgic. I think about my youth a lot when I read it, the emotions you go through when you're unsure of yourself. Wondering about what will happen when you leave university, where they the best days of your life ? Umino illustrates this feeling expertly. Every time I walk in the fields (I live in the country) I pass a huge clover patch and I think of the scene when they are trying to find a four-leaf clover. It's so cute.'

Paul Ashley Brown (author of *Browner-Knowle* (2008-) and *Ono Land* (2011))

Figure 9

Paul Ashley Brown, *Browner-Knowle* (2008-)

'I have never really read Manga, or Japanese comics/Graphic Novels, but am more aware of Japanese animation, Imported US/Japanese cartoons like *Marine Boy, Battle of the Planets* when younger, then things like *Godzilla* movies, & *Akira,* and more recently the films of Miyazaki.'

'I don't think my work is influenced at all by Japanese comics, but there are other Japanese influences that have always been in one's mind & heart. The style & structure of Japanese haiku I find interesting, because of the emphasis of compressing poetry or a language to an essence that describes a mood, feeling or emotion, or atmosphere. It's an idea that I'm interested in when trying to combine words and pictures together within a space to create an interesting visual narrative, particularly in one-page pieces. In effect a condensed language or form.'

'As to the Japanese fashion designers, I was always intrigued by a certain

minimalist aesthetic in Japanese work and design, and in the Nineties I became oddly interested in certain fashion designers, like Yamamoto, and what Kawakubo was doing with COMME des GARÇONS. Also of course Junya Watanabe and Issey Miyake. I think what intrigued was considering clothing almost like sculpture to be worn, a crossover of aesthetic disciplines that was somewhat new, or at least on the cusp of those kind of considerations that became commonplace with advanced technology. All these things inspire and shift and move you, often I'm surprised at the kind of things that I am inspired by, but I think it is about allowing yourself to be moved by others voices and spirit and creativity.'

Gareth Brookes (author of *The Black Project* (2011) and *Land of my Heart Chokes on its Abundance* (2014))

Figure 10

Gareth Brookes, *Land of my Heart Chokes on its Abundance* (2014)

'I only read stuff like *Weather Woman* and that was before I started making comics. I had the wrong idea about Manga, I thought it was all *Sailor Moon* type stuff, but Lando lent me *A Drifting Life* by Tatsumi and after that I got more interested. Recently in the UK the excellent Breakdown Press has been reissuing rare alternative Manga stuff by Hayashi Seiichi and Masahiko Matsumoto and I've been hugely impressed by the work.'

'I'm sure there is some but it would be difficult to unpick. I'm predominantly a relief printmaker, and I don't think you can be one of those without absorbing some Japanese influences.'

'When I was at college we had a book binding day where one of the bindings we learned was Japanese binding. I was very impressed with the idea of being able to bind without glue or anything else other that twine. I thought it

a very elegant system and liked the idea that you can see how it's put together from the outside. I'm not sure why I used it for *LOMHCOIA*, it just felt right.'

Simon Moreton (author of *SMOO* (2007-) and *Rain and Other Stories* (2016))

Figure 11

Simon Moreton, *Rain and Other Stories* (2016)

'I haven't explored as much Japanese work as I would like, and I feel somewhat disappointed in myself for that! I have read a few titles, and seen things on the Internet. But wider elements of Japanese art, and zen art, I think are in my work. But I think it's more like I'm seeing similarities in what I do, but not direct influences. I think there is probably something very important I could learn from reading more about those approaches to making art, and I am hoping to start exploring those more.'

'I've never worked in colour. It's something I'd like to explore, but I'm not quite sure in what way yet. I'd be interested in colours as shapes and textures, not 'realistically' trying to make something look like a photo. As for how I draw, I also only work in pencil, and I like pencil because it shows the imperfections of process, and it shows that it is something that is 'drawn' — very often comics and drawings are about great skill in making something look 'perfect', like it isn't a drawing. I don't want people to think that because I want people to be inspired to pick up a pencil themselves.'

'Lots of my comics are based on drawings that I do very quickly because I also think drawing quickly captures moments, and feelings, and how transient they are. I think that drawing, for me, is a very meditative act. It helps me connect with and look at the world. I don't know too much about wabi sabi aesthetics, but from what I do know, I think it seems that there is a connection.'

Lando (author of *Decadence* (2003-) and *Gardens of Glass* (2014))

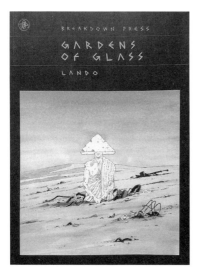

Figure 12
Lando, *Gardens of Glass* (2014)

'As a teenager I collected a Magazine of translated Manga that came out monthly called *Manga Mania*. The main story that ran in the magazine was Katsuhiro Otomo's *Akira,* but it also published a number of stories alongside it, such as Masume Shirow's *Tank Police* and *Appleseed*. I really enjoyed reading the 20-30 page instalments of *Akira* in the magazine when it came out, and loved the cheap pulpy off white paper it was printed on. I still like to try and print all my comics on the same kind of paper today.'

'Otomo and Shirows work really blew me away because of the level of detail and realism in the artwork and the dynamic narration, as well as the serious undertones to the Sci-fi stories. Some examples might be the use of transition panels to show the passing of time (example—'Last Drink' in *Gardens of Glass*), Dynamic cross cutting of camera angles to show action (example—'Olympic Games' in *Gardens of Glass*).'

'The use of limited screen tones which I had seen used in Japanese comics helped me find a way to add depth to my line drawings. I also liked the aesthetic and pacing of black and white Japanese comics because they were longer and more decompressed than western comics.'

Acknowledgements

I would like to express my gratitude to all—academicians, curators, Buddhist monks and nuns, artists, comic writers, poets, editors, my friends, my colleagues, my students and anonymous people in the photos: The late Professor Tadashi Matsushima, Professor Masakazu Tanaka, Professor Takashi Kitamura, Professor Makoto Kinoshita, Professor Teruo Sekimoto, Professor Masataka Noguchi, Professor Noriyuki Nozue, Professor Gen'ichirou Itakura, Professor Ryuta Koike, Dr. Kyoko Koma, Dr. Kentaro Matsumoto, Dr. Christien Guth, Dr. Wendy Wong, Dr. Yuko Kikuchi, Dr. Fabio Gygi, Dr. Philomena Keet, Dr. Mie Asakura, Dr. Sayaka Ogawa, Dr. Seiji Kumagai, Mr. Akinori Yasuda, Ms. Marika Joyce Hashimoto, Ms. Anna Jackson, Mr. Kunio Hamada, Ms. Naoko Jiroku, Ms. Megumi Hirabayashi, Mr. Makoto Ishizeki, Ms. Naoko Tsutsui, Mr. Takashi Yamada, Ms. Mizuki Tsuji, Old Master Douki Hei, Old Master Seido Suzuki, Old Master Douchi Nakano, Ms. Françoise Kosen Laurent, Mr. Brian Kodo Morgan, Mr. Damien Mokuzan Fayolle, Mr. Ulpiano Dias, Ms. Alina Turco, Ms. Nichola Orlick, The late Ms. Yoko Mitsui, Ms. Mieko Shiomi, Mr. So-si Suzuki, Ms. Milky Isobe (Studio Parabolica), Ms. Marie-Ange Guillemniot, Ms. Michiko Nomura, Ms. Luise Harrison, Ms. Sara Kläpp, Mr. David Richard, Ms. Aisha Franz, Mr. Hitoshi Kanazawa, Dr. John Solt, Mr. Kou Itoh, Ms. Mariko Nishitani, Ms. Masako Hiramatsu, Mr. Kousuke Sakaguchi (Koyo Shobo), Mr. James Mudd, Ms. Sonoe Sugawara, Ms. Akari Moffatt, Ms. Mari Toda, Mr. Mio Nozaki, Mr. Paul Ashley Brown, Mr. Benjamin Hariot, Mr. Peter Lally, Mr. Dimitri Pieri, Mr. Gareth Brooks, Ms. Zarina Lieu, Dr. Simon Moreton, Mr. Dave Lander, Mr. Mike Medaglia, Mr. Andrew Poyiadgi, Mr. Paul Gravett, Mr. Nobuyuki Morimoto, and you, possible readers.

Also thankfulness to my family: Michio Onohara, Eiko Onohara, Nana Onohara, Hiroyuki Kanda, Akiko Kanda and Paddy Kanda for their love and support.